T5-CUU-848

THE SMALL GARDEN BOOK

THE SMALL GARDEN BOOK

R. Milton Carleton

The Macmillan Company, New York, New York

Collier-Macmillan Limited, London

The Macmillan Company
866 Third Avenue, New York, N.Y. 10022
Collier-Macmillan Canada Ltd., Toronto, Ontario

Printed in the United States of America

CONTENTS

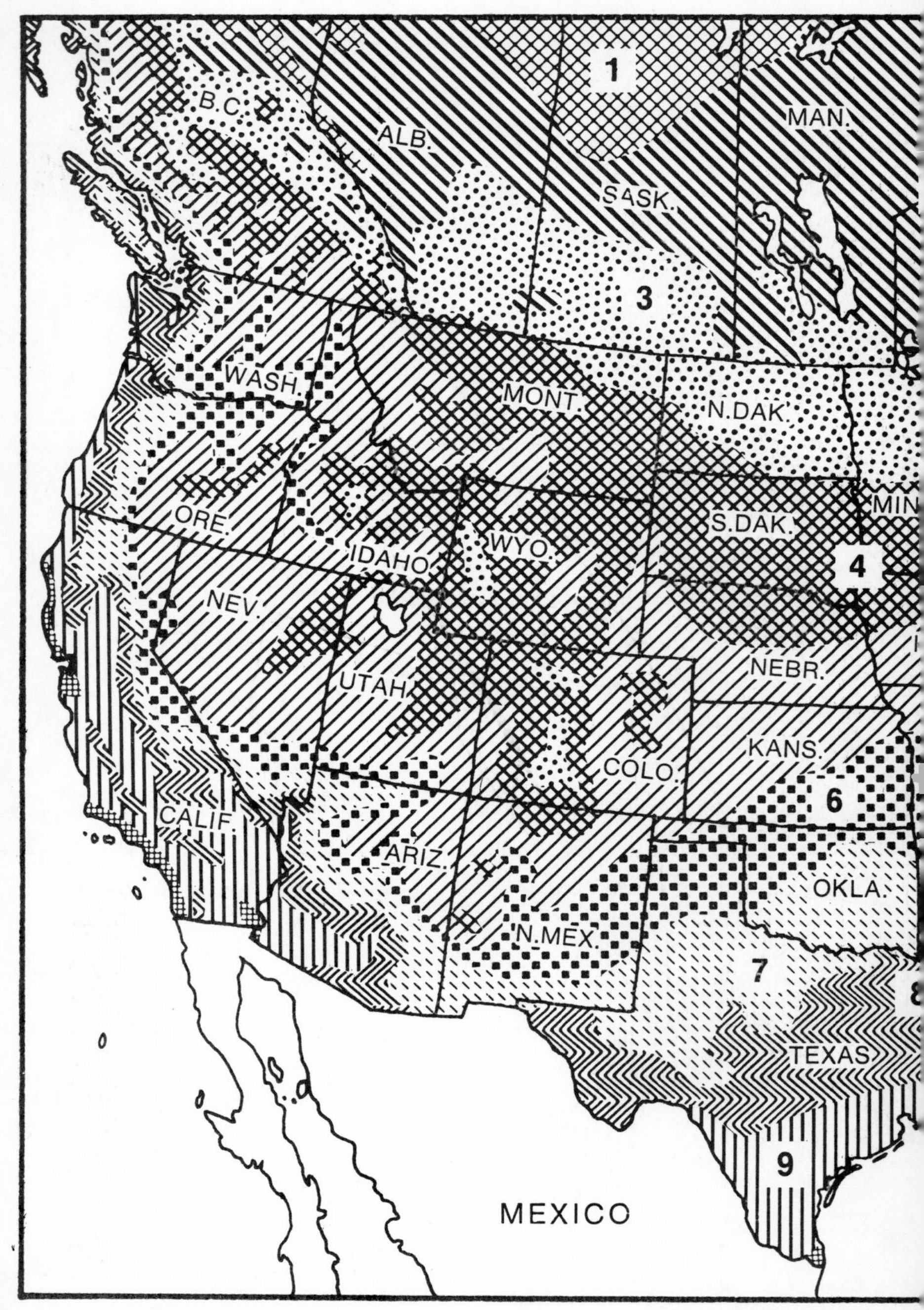

1
B.C.
ALB.
MAN.
SASK.
3
WASH.
MONT.
N.DAK.
ORE.
IDAHO
WYO.
S.DAK.
4
NEV.
UTAH
NEBR.
KANS.
COLO.
6
CALIF.
ARIZ.
OKLA.
N.MEX.
7
TEXAS
9
MEXICO

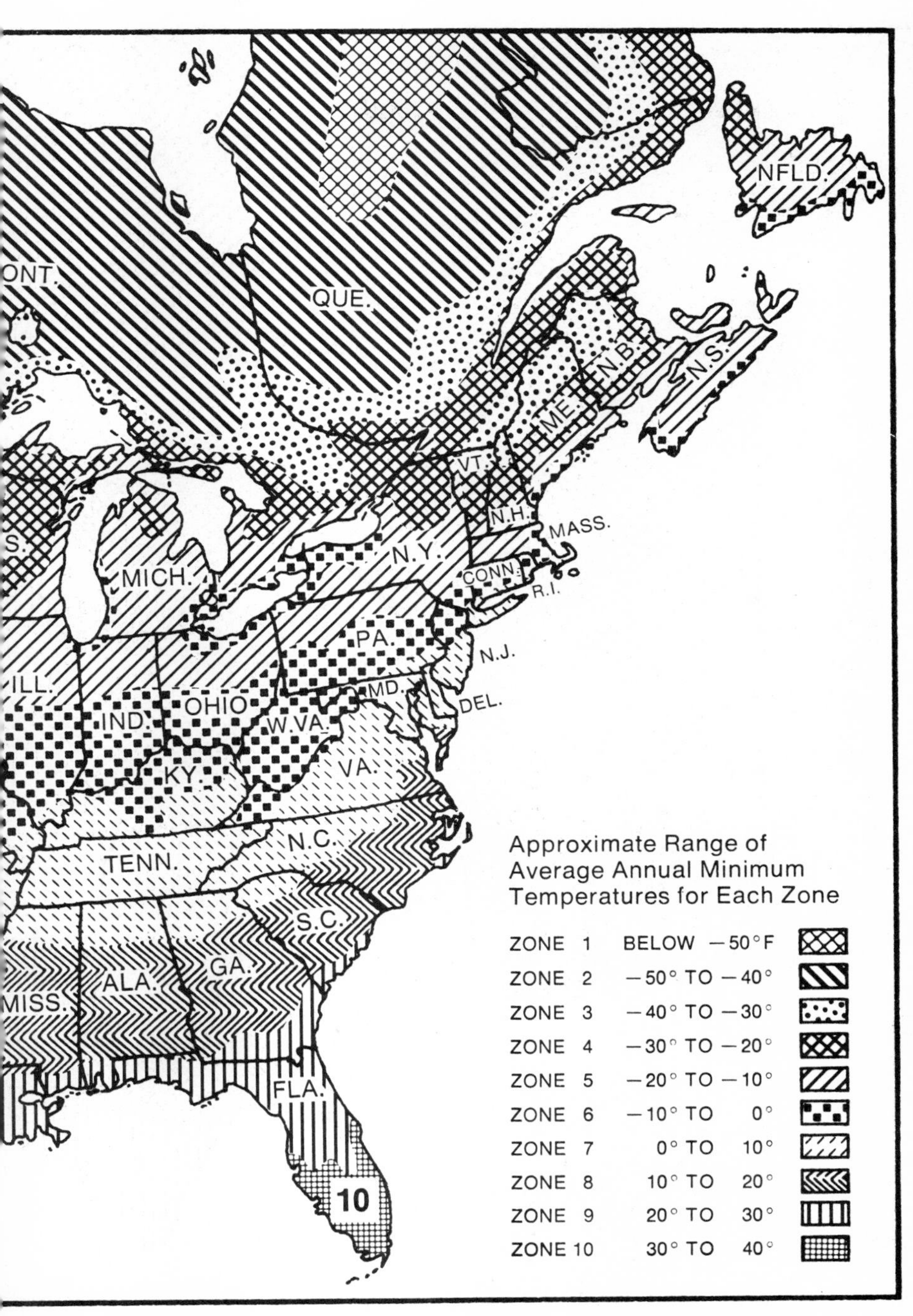
ONT.
QUE.
NFLD.
N.B.
N.S.
ME.
VT.
N.H.
MASS.
N.Y.
CONN.
R.I.
MICH.
PA.
N.J.
ILL.
IND.
OHIO
MD.
DEL.
W.VA.
KY.
VA.
N.C.
TENN.
S.C.
GA.
ALA.
MISS.
FLA.
10
Approximate Range of
Average Annual Minimum
Temperatures for Each Zone
ZONE 1 BELOW −50°F
ZONE 2 −50° TO −40°
ZONE 3 −40° TO −30°
ZONE 4 −30° TO −20°
ZONE 5 −20° TO −10°
ZONE 6 −10° TO 0°
ZONE 7 0° TO 10°
ZONE 8 10° TO 20°
ZONE 9 20° TO 30°
ZONE 10 30° TO 40°

INTRODUCTION

THE JOYS OF A SMALL GARDEN

The small garden can range from a small suburban plot to a backyard patio in the city, but one thing all small gardens have in common is that they provide the maximum pleasure for the minimum effort and space. With imaginative planning the gardener can achieve a wide variety of immensely satisfying results. Anyone who has ever seen a Japanese garden or an Elizabethan herb garden knows how effective a planting in a confined space can be.

Many busy homeowners become almost overwhelmed when they think about what to do with their yard space. They want a beautiful garden but they don't want to devote much of their leisure time to it. Happily, the combination of a sensible plan, the right equipment, and chemical plant controls can give them exactly what they want.

One of the great advantages of keeping things small is that the gardener can afford to use the best plant materials. Planting a garden can be a very expensive endeavor if a large area has to be dealt with, and this often leads homeowners to choose plants that are inexpensive but not what they want. A small garden allows the gardener to use the plants he likes because he doesn't have to buy many of them.

Because the gardener is able to give the small garden the attention it needs without becoming a slave to it, the garden itself is usually more beautiful than a large one and the owner can enjoy it more.

THE SMALL GARDEN BOOK

I

FOR EASIER GARDENING–PLAN

MOST HOME GARDENS are what one might call "a happening." Brought into existence without any planning on the part of their owners, they usually wind up being a nuisance rather than a source of pleasure.

Because they have "happened," rather than having developed from a well-organized plan, their planting and care require hours of unnecessary effort—hours which their owners would rather spend in more enjoyable or useful ways.

If you contrast these unplanned gardens with one designed by my friend, Roy Hay, former editor of *Gardener's Chronicle* and one of the great gardeners of England, you'll see how planning saves time and effort. Hay's garden, which any American home owner would be proud to claim, requires less than one hour of attention a week to keep in apple-pie order.

The story of most new gardens today can be told briefly. They are begun on property that was once a farmland. Years ago, when the former owners of that farmland saw the city gradually creeping toward them, they knew it was only a matter of time until taxes and social pressures would compel them to sell. Facing this inevitable onslaught, they decided it wasn't very wise to spend money keeping up the soil with fertilizers and soil amendments. Finally, they sold the property for a fantastic price to some speculative builder for subdivision purposes.

He began his program by scraping off whatever topsoil was still left and selling it as an extra source of profit. Next, he knocked down all the trees and shrubs, using them for fill so that he could lay out his streets in straight lines on perfectly level land. Not all topsoil was sold, however; enough of it was stockpiled to allow the builder to spread a thin skim of it over a hard clay subsoil.

Once the buildings were completed, common ryegrass was sown on the so-called lawn areas and watered heavily to start germination. At first the ryegrass grew vigorously and made enough of a show to help sell the property to a city couple with children who knew nothing about gardening. Soon after the mortgage papers had been signed, most of this grass struck hardpan and died. Summer rains and the pounding of little feet finished off whatever remained and turned what had been a green lawn into a sea of mud. About that time, a well-meaning neighbor turned up with a bushel basket of discarded iris rhizomes. At least twenty-five years old and full of borers, they were gnarled, knotted, and in poor condition. They were planted gratefully—the beginning of a garden.

From this stage on, the home owner gradually added plants and shrubs—some good, some not so good—and spread them around the yard.

But why go on? By the time our new home owners had acquired some skill in growing, the pattern of their garden had been set in a mold difficult for them or for future owners to break. Yet that pattern should be broken, whether the garden is fairly new or was established years ago by some unthinking gardener.

THE OLDER HOUSE IS A PROBLEM

While it is difficult to simplify gardening in any already-established garden, it's especially hard to do when working with an older property. For one thing, the trees are mature and have acquired value that will be important if the property must be sold later. It would take real courage, for example, to cut down a mature female ginkgo tree—perhaps the dirtiest and most offensive of all trees when in fruit—when it would add at least $1,000 to the value of a house in an area where older trees are scarce.

Yet by cutting it down, the owner could save himself hours of work which he would have to spend keeping the fruit cleared away, not to mention eliminating the stench the fruits give off for nearly a month.

Older shrubs, except in the case of fine specimens of broad-leaved evergreens, are not so much of a problem. Eliminating shrubs doesn't often affect house value. Since most shrub borders tend to become overgrown rather quickly, they need periodic renovation anyway. Originally planted as a "save work" attempt, they are far from a satisfactory solution. Consequently, you can be as ruthless as you please with overgrown deciduous shrubs. Unless they were carefully chosen at the beginning, they are usually best put on a brush heap and burned. Later, we shall have much to say about plant material that can stand neglect and still remain attractive.

Older properties are also likely to contain unwanted buildings and other such features. Think twice, however, before tearing down sheds, garages, and similar structures. At present-day prices, they can be an asset. Even if a building is an eyesore, it can be "planted out," a term we shall meet time and time again later in the text. An abandoned chicken coop or woodshed toward the back of a property can save thousands of steps if used for storing tools necessary for working that particular area.

DEVELOPING THE PLAN

Planning calls for thinking and imagination. If you would like to avoid hours of unnecessary labor in future years, set down on paper what you do want, eliminating any features that do not contribute to your pleasure or convenience.

Even if you consider gardening a pleasant outdoor exercise, planning makes sense. You'll get much more satisfaction out of the time and effort you expend. There is something to be said for taking exercise in a garden where you can see the results of your efforts, rather than on the golf course where only a misplaced divot marks the results of your physical exertion. On the other hand, if you are not about to make a career out of spoon-feeding a garden, it's even more important to do your spading and planting on paper.

Cost is, of course, a consideration. If you can avoid it, never plan to do any work in the garden you don't enjoy which can be done by professional help. For example, if you find the mowing of grass an onerous duty, by all means hire someone to do it for you. You may, however, enjoy snipping and sawing; do your own pruning if that is the case.

Garden work that at first seems much too hard for a sedentary deskworker may not prove too hard after all. I have just walked through our vegetable garden, the first we have had in years. It is not large—about twenty feet by thirty—but it has kept the family well fed all summer long. I spaded this by hand, turning over two rows each evening. Although this took two weeks, the work was done in plenty of time to permit the planting of late crops toward the finish. To me, spading in the cool of the evening is pleasant, with the smell of damp earth and spring flowers to make it even more so. To others, it might be a frightful bore. I know gardeners who enjoy getting down on hands and knees to weed perennial borders; to me this is the most tedious, boring job in all horticulture.

Think before you make major investments in power machinery and tools; the pros and cons will be taken up later, but the problem does enter early into planning. Many a home owner has purchased an expensive rotary tiller to "save work" only to find that it calls for considerable strength to operate and ties up money that could be used to employ a commercial operator who would supply labor as well as the machinery. No investment in gardening requires as much intelligent planning as does the purchase of power equipment. If not carefully planned, finding storage space for such equipment can result in hours of extra labor.

USING THE OUTDOORS

What use will you make of your garden? Is it intended merely to ornament the outdoors, an extension of the interior decoration? Many look upon landscaping in this way—as an effort made to maintain a good front to the neighbors—with no real interest in the process by which that garden develops. There is nothing wrong with this thinking; not everyone really enjoys gardening.

On the other hand, when treated as an outdoor extension of

indoor living, gardening becomes many times as enjoyable. Outdoor living can take many forms. It may mean a place to sit in the sun, to eat a picnic lunch, or to have an evening barbecue. Set down on paper how you would like to use your garden to enhance your pleasure and comfort when living in the open air.

If it is intended for sunbathing, hedges, fences, or screens will be needed to hide you from passers-by, yet they must not cut off cooling breezes. For alfresco dining, picnics, teas, barbecues, or even outdoor cocktail parties, different equipment and structures may be needed.

SPACE FOR OUTDOOR LIVING

Nowadays, paved areas do not increase the labor needed to care for a garden; instead, they reduce garden maintenance. This was not always the case; I can remember the time when a gardener would have to spend an entire day on an average-sized terrace, on hands and knees, rooting out individual weeds by hand. Today, a single spraying once a year with a suitable chemical weed-killer ensures that no plant grows where it is not wanted. As a result, we can use large paved areas to reduce the amount of outdoor space that will need intensive care.

A relatively new development in paving treatments, but one which was copied from the age-old art of Japanese gardening, is the use of ornamental pebbles or stones as a covering for areas around trees, under eaves, or in other places where maintaining vegetation of any kind is difficult or impossible. Unless planned carefully, however, such pebbled areas can be a problem.

Often, an inaccessible area under a bay window is treated in this manner, but is then surrounded by heavy plantings that make access to the area difficult. As a result, it becomes a trap for stray paper, weeds, fallen leaves, and even stray toys—far more unsightly than if it had not been treated at all.

Much is to be said for using brick paving laid on a sand base now that the problem of weeds in joints can be solved so readily. One such paved area I saw in California recently was used for both an outdoor living space and an emergency parking space when large numbers of cars had to be accommodated. In everyday use,

A Japanese-style garden not only reduces work, it is beautiful and satisfying as well.

it was cut off from the driveway by hedge plants grown in containers, which could be moved whenever large parties were being given by the host.

The use to which outdoor living space is to be put will determine its layout, design, and use of plant material. For example, if your planned use is for daytime picnics, Sunday brunches, or afternoon parties, an important tree or overhead trellis to cast a pleasant shade is one of the first features to consider. If it is to be a tree, use of an existing specimen is always a happy answer, unless it happens to be of a species with untidy habits.

When trees are to be planted, remember that they are much easier to move on paper than they are after they have been planted and have made some growth. Once a spot has been tentatively chosen, spend a little time just sitting there. Observe the path of the sun and where the shadows of specimen trees will fall. Keep in mind that in June the sun is high in the sky, but that in September and October, it will be much lower toward the southern horizon. If you plan "frostbite" picnics, with guests bundled up and a brisk fire going, don't locate outdoor living space where it will be shaded from the south by heavy evergreen plantings or by buildings.

A barbecue area used only at night need not be planned with the sun in mind. Here, some shelter from too-cool night breezes might be welcome. Too, much of the pleasure from outdoor living at night comes from the chance to see the stars, which might be cut out of view by a heavily foliaged tree overhead.

What about traffic on nearby walks and streets? If space is limited so that this cannot be "planted out" with hedges or shrubbery borders, consider an ornamental fence, or more interesting, spectacular climbing plants on an ornamental background.

UTILITIES ARE IMPORTANT

Modern garden planners have an easy time installing utilities. Today, it is no trick to lay in water almost anywhere with plastic pipe. By digging a narrow trench with a spade, both water and electricity can be run to outdoor living areas, using underground plastic cable for the latter. Do remember where these are buried, however, marking the trench with finely crushed limestone or sand. If outside help is employed for garden maintenance, laying boards treated with pentachlorophenol over the trench before covering is advisable. Otherwise, you may have trouble when workers cut through pipes or wires when digging.

Since pentachlorophenol (*penta,* for short) is toxic to plants when fresh, do treat the boards two or three weeks in advance of use and allow them to season in the open air. This also holds true for treated woodwork that will come in contact with plants at any time, such as trellises, greenhouse benches, and fences.

With the basic elements out of the way, think of what might be within sight of the area chosen. By all means, avoid a location too close to a compost heap or a garbage can. These should be located so that the prevailing wind blows over the outdoor living space toward them, even if they are at a distance.

Even though ornamental plantings are being reduced to save

labor, do plan to have some flowering plants within view when you are enjoying the open air. Later, various plans for maintaining continuous bloom with minimum effort will be discussed in detail.

Perhaps continuous bloom is not for your family; in this case, save work by eliminating plants that require care when you are not at home. If you spend the summers in a cottage in the woods or by the sea, why keep up a show of summer bloom for the garbageman or meter reader? One of the most delightful gardens I know is practically all green with ground covers as its only display during late June, July, and August because the family spends the entire summer in a mountain cabin. However, when in the city, they enjoy a gorgeous show of spring-flowering bulbs, perennials in June, and a spectacular splash of hardy chrysanthemums in the fall.

If on the other hand, you take winter vacations and spend a leisurely summer at home, then the critical months of June, July, and August must be considered. Although not the easiest period in which to keep up a good show, there are easy-to-grow plants which require little labor.

What about other uses for outdoor space? A children's playyard, surrounded by a protecting fence, is a wonderful convenience for a busy mother. Children do grow up, however, leaving a substantial area which gets little use. At this moment, I am struggling with the problem of removing a too-substantial swing which I erected when my children were small, burying the three-inch upright steel pipes in huge blocks of concrete. It will take hours of work to remove this now useless bit of equipment.

One idea to consider is the possibility of doing something ornamental with a sandbox, perhaps making it free-form or in some other interesting style, with the idea of turning it into a garden pool later. This would justify using more space for what would otherwise have been a temporary feature, and for putting more work into its construction. This would also require having a second plan for the area, for the time when it is no longer to be used for its original purpose, which would take into consideration such things as setting out important trees or shrubs so that they will not shade the pool at maturity.

A clothes-drying yard seems almost an anachronism in this day of electric and gas dryers, yet there are people who insist that the fragrance of clothes dried in the sun will never be matched by the fragrance of those dried in any artificial device. Another argument for drying in outdoor space is that the sun costs nothing—when it is shining.

An important consideration when planning a garden is storage space for tools. This may be a shed, a corner in the garage or a place in the basement. The basement is perhaps the poorest of all solutions to the problem because it calls for dragging needed tools and equipment up and down stairs, usually at a considerable distance from the work to be done. Garages are seldom ideal for tools needed in caring for the rear of a suburban or city property because they face the street. Another problem is the ever-increasing length of American cars, which leaves less space for storage. Perhaps a good argument for the small European compact!

Don't overlook the possibility of saving both time and effort by dividing the tool inventory—have one set in the garage for working the front of your property and the other in a shed or other storage facility in the rear. This may call for buying duplicate sets of rakes, spades, etc., but in figuring your time at even a dollar an hour, it won't take long to pay off the investment.

If the front lawn is small, only a hand mower might be needed, leaving the larger power mower for the back lawn. Another hint: When buying a larger mower, pass up the relatively small value of a trade-in and keep the old mower for the less expansive area.

DRAWING THE PLAN

There *are* gardeners who, after years of experience, can picture in their minds exactly where certain plants and various landscape features belong, but this is an ability we do not all share. Planning on paper, setting down details of each major feature, helps visualize the finished effect. More important (at least for the purpose of this book) is that it promotes efficiency.

In such a plan, trees can be moved, terraces and fences juggled for better traffic patterns, storage for tools and materials located for easier handling, and in many other ways, the work load lightened.

To do a good job of planning, start with a steel tape 50 to 100 feet long, a pencil, and a pad of graph paper. Graph paper pads are sold by most school supply stores, stationers, and stores that serve architects and engineers. This paper is ruled in small squares, each representing a unit in whatever scale you choose.

Some pads are ruled uniformly, while others divide the individual squares into blocks of either ten or twelve squares. Unless you are working on the metric system, use the one with twelve squares to the block: you can then use individual blocks as feet. The number of blocks is not too important when drawing the big plan of the entire property (which might be on a scale as small as one sixteenth of an inch equals a foot), but is most helpful when laying out smaller details.

Also cut some stakes about two feet long to mark spots where certain features are to be placed. If you have a table saw, these can be ripped out of scrap lumber, or you can buy some one-inch furring strips at a lumber yard. Paint these (at least the tip) the brightest color you can find. The new fluorescent paints in red or orange, which are visible for nearly a city block, are ideal for this purpose.

The next step is to set down on graph paper any existing features you do not plan to move, such as the garage, swimming pool, drives, etc. These can be readily located on paper by measuring from two known points. When indicating a tree, show its trunk as a spot, but also show how far out the branches spread by drawing in a dotted circle.

An important phase of garden planning and one often neglected is making provision for proper drainage. Attention to this detail is one mark of the professional landscape architect, as contrasted with the neglect of this factor by amateurs. Try to imagine if you were to upset a barrel filled with water on any given spot on your property. Would it flow down the drive and into the garage? That sounds like an impossible situation, yet a neighbor who did not plan for drainage once had the end of *his* garage pushed out by the ice that formed on the floor following a thaw. He had not run into this difficulty when his drive was paved with gravel, but when it was blacktopped, the surface formed a perfect flume leading right under the doors.

Major changes in drainage usually call for professional help but now is the time to spot them for attention. Often, cutting away a bit of soil or building a low ridge to divert drainage in a new direction is a simple matter. True, this represents work yet a few hours spent in preventing future trouble means a net gain in the end. Devices for making small changes in grades will be discussed later under lawn making, but can be applied to other areas as well as the lawn.

This brings up another point of importance on properties with sharp slopes. Unless properly planned, such slopes can consume hours and hours of labor in future years. The worst possible way to treat such areas is as mowed turf. Not only does this require strenuous efforts to mow, but in addition, it can be dangerous. Having control of a power mower on a steep slope is far from child's play.

Terracing is an expensive, and not always a successful, solution. Unless the terrace is paved (adding still further to costs), it will cut up the area into small patches of lawn, increasing the labor needed for maintenance. The simplest solution, involving the least physical effort, is to "plant it out." By that is meant giving over the slope to permanent planting which will require little or no upkeep. If too heavy, such treatment can cut up a property into small cells or rooms, but by keeping the planting low, vistas and air movement can be preserved.

Mention of "vistas" does seem a bit extravagant when discussing most city and suburban properties, however. One of the weaknesses of most books on home landscaping is that they discuss treatment of home grounds as though they were vast country estates with distant vistas to frame. If you do happen to have a pleasant view, by all means, don't plant it out. In designing most properties, however, the problem is not one of preserving views outside the lot line, but of hiding the neighbor's garbage can or blotting out an obtrusive telephone pole.

On nine out of ten suburban properties, first attention should be given to confining the view of landscape features within the lot lines. Inside larger cities, there is practically no alternative to looking inward instead of out. For this reason, particular attention should be paid to hedges and fences: if they don't exist, plan to put them in.

Once major features of a planting are in place on graph paper, the next step is to plan for new features that will not contribute too much to the work load. These should not be sketched in permanently at first. They can be indicated lightly in pencil, but a much better idea is to sketch them on sheets of thin, transparent paper. If you can't find regular architect's tracing paper, buy thin onion-skin paper in a stationery store. Over the years, I have accumulated rolls of a transparent negative paper used in an office duplicating machine which is ideal for this purpose—a tip for those who have access to similar material.

Trees, hedges, and other features drawn on such paper (to scale) can be moved about at will over the basic plan until they exactly fit your ideas. Next, try them on the actual site for "fit." Use the stakes mentioned earlier to indicate a tree or shrub. Stand off and see how it matches your mental image. Often moving the stake just a few inches will improve your original idea.

2

SOIL—THE BASIC "STUFF" OF GARDENING

IF WE REALLY WANT TO SAVE TIME AND EFFORT in gardening, we cannot afford to ignore soil—the basic "stuff" of gardening. What I am about to say may seem to be strange advice to be included in a book designed to eliminate effort, yet it is in the initial treatment of soil that we have our greatest opportunity to avoid both work and expenditure of time. At least half the energy expended in gardening is devoted to turning over earth, to cultivating it, and to manipulating it in an effort to better mold it to our purposes.

A problem arises here because about 995 out of every 1,000 gardens must be made on soils that are not well adapted to this use. In spite of the assumption made by garden writers (and in particular by authors of bulletins put out by state and federal agencies) that home owners have an unlimited choice of sites for gardening, practically everyone is compelled to begin with what clay, sand, loam, or marl exists on his own property.

Open almost any book or bulletin on growing vegetables, for example, and you will most likely read a paragraph something like this: "Select a site for growing vegetables on a rich, sandy loam in the open, but one which is sheltered from strong prevailing winds. Be sure it receives at least six hours of direct sunshine daily. The soil should be well drained and free of large stones."

This is excellent advice, if you are fortunate enough to have such a combination of conditions. It means little if you are saddled with a stiff, unyielding clay that refuses to dry out in the spring or a sterile, droughty sand that dries out so rapidly that the need of plants for water cannot be met. Glib advice of this sort assumes that a prospective buyer of property goes around with spade in hand, investigating the quality of lawns and gardens that surround the house he is about to buy. This is difficult to imagine.

Although I am personally far more interested in soils that most home owners would be (and have written a book on home garden soils), never once in the four homes we have occupied since marriage have I made such an examination. Among my thousands of gardening friends in North America and Europe, I know of only one man who made his choice of a home on the basis of its gardening possibilities.

As desirable as an ideal soil would be, we must face facts—we are all saddled with the soils which already cover our future gardens. If we are to avoid unnecessary effort and wasted time, we must deliberately manipulate existing earth to allow plants to do their best without requiring constant attention from us.

A second fallacy which needs to be exploded is the one that says success in gardening is the result, not of our own efforts, but of that mythical creature—Mother Nature—being allowed to have her way without interference from us. Those who follow this theory all too often wind up with a tangle of brush and weeds requiring more effort to subdue than had we battled natural forces from the beginning.

Whether we are working at farming in the open field or are dealing with the far-less-expansive area called a garden, we are *not* cooperating with nature, but are rather trying to circumvent it and to neutralize its adverse effect on plants. What we are really after is *disciplined* and *controlled* growth. No matter how hard cultists and nature enthusiasts try to convince us we should allow plants to grow without restraint, subject only to the vagaries of native soil, we must be masters of our plants to be successful, not mere observers.

Although gardening is the finer, the more intensive art, even the less-careful farm cultivation is a far cry from the natural check-and-balance system which limit growth in uncultivated fields and woodlands to mere survival. No farmer would tolerate for a moment subjecting his plants to the competition they would be compelled to face in the wild. He is striving, not for the amount of productivity possible when the plant must compete with other species for survival, but for the maximum growth and production of which it is capable under his protection.

In his eagerness to produce more with less effort, he has not only created genetic weaklings, which would be unable to survive were they allowed to exist without protection, but has deliberately sought to perpetuate such weaklings when they possess other good qualities. A corn plant, for example, capable of producing from ten to twenty times the weight of grain borne by its primitive ancestors, can do so only if guarded from competition with weeds and if nourished lavishly by artificial fertilization. Modern field corn is a man-made mongrel sired by exotic parents, which is incapable of surviving winter temperatures that occur over the region where corn is a dominant crop.

Modern flowers, vegetables, and fruits grown in home gardens are, if anything, less fitted for survival. Perhaps the best example of this lack of innate stamina in a plant is the modern hybrid tea rose. As one leading rose authority expressed it, "the modern hybrid tea rose is a damned poor excuse for a shrub." It must be blanketed for winter protection against temperatures lower than twelve degrees above zero and coddled with sprays or dusts against insects and diseases. Left to its own devices in the average winter of the northeastern quarter of the United States, it would be dead by spring.

Gardening is, therefore, an avocation based, not on requiring us to accept conditions as they exist, but rather on forcing Mother Nature into a pattern better suited to our wants and desires. In no single aspect of the growing of plants is this realization as important as it is in the case of soil. To a considerable degree we might even say that gardening *is* soil management. When it is done wisely and effectively, some of our most important savings in time and effort can be made here.

Ours is not just "field dirt." Instead, it is a substance for which the name *gardener's loam* has been suggested. Surprisingly enough, it is perhaps the most complex substance with which we will ever have to deal. Although its basic elements seem quite simple—clay, sand, and other minerals, when these are combined with microorganisms and humus into soils that lie in climates as diverse as those found from the subarctic to the tropics, in which altering a single element affects all the others, we are faced with two worlds capable of infinite variation—the microcosm and the macrocosm we call soil.

This is no place for an elaborate treatise on the infinite phases of soil.* One illustration of its complexity, though, can be had in a book by Dr. Selman Waksman, the scientist who contributed so much to medical progress with his discovery of streptomycin. As a soils scientist, he wrote a masterly book entitled, simply, *Humus*. This tome ran to nearly 900 pages discussing a single fraction of soil, yet in the end, it probably left unanswered as many questions about humus as it cleared up. As much more could be written about the properties of clays, sand, subsoil water, contained air, and other mechanical and chemical systems at work under our feet.

The subject becomes more complicated when we begin to consider the biological aspects involved. Perhaps the most important single fact to keep in mind is that soil is *alive*; it is an organism on which all other animate matter on the face of the earth depends. Pick up a handful of rich garden loam, and in your palm you will probably hold as many living organisms as there are human beings in the entire world. Although they are so minute that a powerful microscope is needed to see most of them, without their activities all life on the face of the earth would grind slowly to a halt. They enter into two systems—the carbon cycle and the nitrogen cycle—vital to the survival of every organism that breathes.

Since few busy home owners and weekend gardeners can spare the time needed to become soil experts, let us divide the subject into a few simple elements.

*Those interested in further information on soils are referred to the following books:

Lyon and Buckman, *The Nature and Properties of Soils* (New York: Macmillan, 1943), which calls for a working knowledge of modern chemistry and physics to read.

Charles E. Kellogg, *Our Garden Soils* (New York: Macmillan).

R. Milton Carleton, *Your Garden Soil* (Princeton, N.J.: Van Nostrand, 1961).

MINERAL ELEMENTS

The first fact to understand about soil is that while its "bones" are mineral, it is more than just a simple mixture of chemicals and minerals. A skeleton must have flesh to function—in the case of soil, the flesh is the organic elements.

It is true that in the beginning, eons ago, what is now soil was a simple mixture of pure minerals and soluble salts and acids. As life crept out of the sea, however, primitive organisms, such as molds and lichens, lived and died on sterile rocks. As they decayed, they left behind acids which gradually dissolved the basic rock, impregnating the rock debris with organic matter.

Students of soil origins agree that true soil was not developed before this admixture occurred, yet mineral elements were the original skeleton around which it evolved. The smallest particles of such minerals (which we class as *clay*) are so fine that ordinary microscopes cannot reveal them. It was not until the development of the modern electronic microscope that their forms and actual sizes could be established. These ultrafine particles are colloidal—that is, they tend to adhere to each other and form a gel or gum.

In pure form, the colloidal nature of clay is a nuisance because it prevents the free movement of air and water in and out of the root zone. When diluted with other forms of minerals, however, clays perform an important function: they suck up and hold plant food nutrients, preventing them from escaping in drainage water. For this reason, gardener's loam must have a certain amount of clay in it.

When a soil is too high in this element and refuses to dry out in spring, we do have a trick or two that will overcome this tendency. We can either separate the particles mechanically by the addition of sand, cinders, or other coarse material (of this, more later) or we can *flocculate* the colloids, a technical way of saying we can make them form larger grains. If we introduce finely ground limestone or even hydrated lime into a clay soil, we add a chemical which has an electric charge opposite to that of clay. Each particle of lime (in theory at least) will attract from five to eight particles of clay, thus making the soil from five to eight times as permeable to air and water as it was before treatment. Actually, this extreme correction would be all but impossible to bring about because of the tremendous number of particles that would have to be clumped in pure clay, yet the addition of limestone is one of our better tricks for improving heavy soils.

In general, clay soils in the South need less lime to bring about this effect, but because they remain unfrozen for longer periods of time, chemical interactions are going on which permit them to return to their original state more quickly.

Just how much limestone to add is a question easy to ask but difficult to answer accurately. If you are faced with an unmanageable clay soil, try applying enough finely ground limestone to cover the garden plot to a depth of one inch, working this in to a depth of six inches. If it is still stubborn and sticky after treatment, try another inch.

In suburban areas close to farm supply outlets, ground agricultural limestone is readily available and is the best material to use. Because of its extremely fine particle size, this goes to work almost at once. In areas where this finely ground stone is not readily available, use the grade of limestone used for top-dressing stone drives. This is coarser and takes a little longer to become effective, but for this reason, lasts longer.

One advantage to using this method of opening up clay soils is that it also solves the acid soil problem. Most clays in the United States are acid in reaction. Alkaline clays do exist, but are not commonly found where anyone wants to garden.

One recommendation for improving clay soils—the addition of sand—must be taken with several grains of salt. This recommendation seldom carries with it information on *how much* sand to use. I have seen many gardens where this prescription was followed only to have the soil turn harder and less permeable than it was before treatment. This method for opening up clay soils fails to consider the tremendous differences in size between even the largest particles of clay and those of sand. The latter are at least 500 times as large (a million times in the case of the colloidal fraction) as those of the finest sands.

When we add small amounts of sand to clay, the fine particles merely fill the interstices between the coarser grains, forming a substance like concrete. Thus, instead of separating the clay as intended, the sand becomes the aggregate, cemented together with a colloidal glue. This method of improving heavy soils will work only if the percentage of clay is relatively small, or if at least one-third as much sand is added as the amount of clay to be treated.

SAND AS A PROBLEM SOIL

Pure sand itself is a basic material which causes as much trouble as does clay when used for garden purposes. Actually, the amount of work needed to correct its faults is so great that few home owners are willing to undertake the job. Fortunately, when cost is not an important factor, we can use modern power equipment to remove the sand, treat it, and return the soil to its original position.

Once the correction has been made, practically no further effort will be needed: modified sands are among our best garden soils. The operation consists of digging out the soil to a depth of twelve to fifteen inches over the entire area and laying down a barrier of plastic film or tar paper. A layer of humus or other vegetable matter is placed over the barrier and the sand returned to its original position.

Now moisture and plant foods, instead of being sucked away by the sharp drainage of sand, can be trapped long enough so that plant roots can use them. Gradually, dead roots and other organic matter accumulating over the barrier will build up the humus content of the soil until plants can survive. In the meanwhile, the paper or plastic may rot, but a stable soil will have formed that can maintain itself under cultivation.

Although using organic matter in the form of compost, peat moss, and similar materials is the best way to modify most soils, it does not pay to try this with pure sands. Any added material of this type is rapidly drained away by rain and never gets a chance to reach plants. On the Indiana sand dunes I have seen a fairly small lawn suck up a ton or more of humus every year for years without showing any improvement until a barrier was installed.

Such drastic treatment is, of course, unnecessary on sandy loams, which contain enough organic matter to retain moisture and plant foods.

SILT

Although a fairly good garden soil could be made from a mixture of sand and clay to which organic matter had been added, most of our better garden loams are a mixture of these two minerals combined with an intermediate-sized ingredient called *silt.* In texture, silt particles range in size from the microscopic to those that can just be seen with the naked eye.

Silt has some of the characteristics of clay in that it produces tight soils which do not permit water to enter freely. One soil, about which the owner had complained as being so full of clay that it cracked when it was dried out, was found to contain less than 20 percent clay but about 45 percent silt. In this proportion, the clay and silt particles intermeshed so completely that a cement was formed.

Soil that contains too much sand can be corrected to produce one of our best garden soils, as this Maine seaside garden indicates.

Mention of this particular problem soil presents an opportunity to discuss another material for modifying clays and silts. Since this owner's soil was quite alkaline, the addition of limestone was not desirable. Fortunately, though, he had burned hard coal for years before converting to gas and had piled the ashes behind an old barn. Here they had weathered for years, so that all the harmful sulfur compounds had been leached out. The addition of a layer of two inches of these weathered ashes did wonders for this particular soil.

Where "home-made" ashes are not available, investigate possible sources of so-called steam cinders—the kind produced when coal is burned in high-pressure boilers at high temperatures. This forms a clinkerlike ash which is highly porous. If such steam cinders are allowed to weather out of doors for at least one winter, they can be used in quite large amounts to loosen heavy soil. One of the best lawns I ever grew was sown on a heavy clay soil into which I had plowed a three-inch-deep layer of weathered steam cinders. They are usually available for the cost of hauling.

Unlike sand, cinders improve soil when added in almost any quantity. They work partially by separating particles of clay, but also by providing porous passages for water and air. Almost any porous, fluffy mineral of the right pH can be used to lighten soil.

Our English friends used ground-up old plaster for this purpose, but this was not the lime product we often use by mistake. Instead it was calcium sulfate, or gypsum, which is neutral in reaction. Old gypsum plaster is useful in the Middle West and other areas where the strongly alkaline, old lime plaster would not do. In the acid soils of the East, though, the latter is a highly desirable material.

Vermiculite, now widely sold as an insulating material, is a useful soil amendment, and a special horticultural grade is available for this purpose. However, I prefer the wall-fill type, which has larger particles and is usually cheaper.

An odd-ball material which I prefer above all others is the calcined clay sold as a cat and dog litter. This is highly absorbent and loosens soil beautifully. It is too expensive to buy especially for this purpose, but after Old Tom has filled it with organic matter, don't waste it: use it on the compost heap or flower border.

Incidentally, this material is sold commercially at a lower price for absorbing oil on garage floors and for other industrial processes. For a limited job of soil amendment, it is well worth its cost.

ORGANIC MATTER

With this all-too-sketchy outline of what mineral elements go into a garden soil, it is time to discuss what is perhaps the most important ingredient of all—organic matter, particularly that form of organic matter which has gone through its more rapid stages of decay and reached a fairly stable condition. We call this element *humus*.

Unfortunately, this word is misused by uninformed peddlers of almost any form of organic matter that is black and crumbly. I have even seen an outworn farm soil, high in carbon but practically devoid of organic matter, sold as humus.

Although it is difficult to define by specification, once you have had a handful of this substance, its characteristic "feel" and odor are unmistakable. It is the smell of moist earth in spring, not quite musty, not quite green, but somewhere in between.

Humus is the heart of gardener's loam, the ingredient which is missing in all too many soils. Except for a few areas where old swamps have been drained, leaving beds of almost pure semi-decayed organic matter, practically any soil can be improved by the addition of well-rotted organic matter which was originally of animal or vegetable origin. Sources of organic matter are many, but nothing beats a well-run compost pile, unless it be the possession of a stable of saddle horses or a dairy herd. Since few gardeners who would be interested in this book fall in the latter class, a discussion of composting is definitely in order.

A compost pile is really a culture of soil bacteria and fungi that are capable of feeding on waste materials, using some of the food elements they contain for their own life processes, but leaving behind a mellow, clean-smelling "duff" which eventually becomes true compost. Beginning gardeners often question whether this step is necessary: why not apply the organic matter directly to the garden? This can be done, but there are reasons why composting is the better practice.

For one thing, during the initial stages of decay, products harmful to plants are released, which are either gradually dissipated as gas or are consumed by soil organisms. For another, organisms which cause plant diseases often survive on fresh decaying material, living off the starches and sugars they contain. By the time organic breakdown has been completed, these starches and sugars are gone, leaving behind a soil "sponge" which serves as an absorbent for soluble plant foods, as well as a home for beneficial bacteria.

Although making a compost pile does call for a little physical effort, actually the labor involved is all but offset by that saved in hauling plant wastes to a dump or in disposing of table wastes. Begin by finding a level spot in an inconspicuous corner—even the best compost pile is not a thing of beauty. The soil underneath should be well drained so that water will not make the pile soggy. On heavy soil, a layer of wood chips, gravel, steam cinders, or almost any fluffy material can be laid down as a base.

A four- to six-inch-deep layer of almost any kind of organic matter should be laid down first. Fallen leaves, weeds, table wastes, spoiled flour, wood chips or sawdust, and many other materials from once-living organisms will do. Over this, sprinkle a good mixed fertilizer (an exact formula is not too important) about as thickly as you would put sugar on strawberries. The purpose of this is to supply bacteria and fungi with plant foods: they are plants just as much as are other vegetable organisms except that they lack green coloring matter. Fertilizing them helps speed the breakdown of organic matter into humus.

This fertilizer will not all be wasted since when these microorganisms die (they have a very short life cycle as a rule), most of it will be returned to the soil as their cells decay. In fact, the finished compost is usually richer than the original organic matter, due to a small amount of nitrogen gained during the process of organic breakdown.

Next, sprinkle a thin layer of good garden loam over the first layer. This is to "seed" it with microorganisms necessary for proper functioning of the pile. Build up the pile in this way layer by layer to a height of two to three feet. A deeper pile is not desirable because the weight of the mass of the upper layers tends to force out air from the lower layers. This permits bacteria that live in the absence of oxygen to work: their effect is harmful.

Turn the pile every couple of weeks to thoroughly mix all the ingredients and to aerate the inside material. If rain does not fall, wet down the pile, but don't overdo this.

Within three to four months in warm weather, organic matter ought to break down into a soft, fluffy duff—the well-rotted compost of which gardeners write.

The time has come to introduce a term from which many gardeners shy because it sounds mysterious—*pH.* A proper understanding of this term can make the difference between a poor garden that always needs attention and a super garden that grows almost without attention. True, the theory of the hydrogen-ion concentration of soil solutions *is* complex, but so are the laws of thermodynamics governing our producing steam heat, reading a thermometer, or drawing hot water out of a tap. Yet we do all these things without any knowledge of the technical complexities involved in their operation.

This term merely has to do with measuring the relative acidity or alkalinity of soils. Reading a pH scale is even less complicated than reading a thermometer, which has *two* reference points—freezing and boiling. In the pH scale, 7.0 is the midpoint, meaning that acid and alkaline elements are in balance. Any reading from 0 to 6.9 is acid; from 7.1 to 14.0 is alkaline.

The readings can be made with simple test kits that can be had for a dollar or two at most good garden supply houses. They contain papers that react to the chemicals in soil and can be read because they change color to match a scale. Much more accurate, but hardly necessary for the home gardener, are the electric meters which read directly. Your county farm adviser should have one of these and can make readings for you.

But why is pH so important? Because it determines what will happen to both the native fertility in the soil and the fertilizers you apply. To simplify the whole subject, the important fact to remember is that all the fertilizer elements in soil will be available to plants if the pH is no lower than 6.0 and no higher than 6.9. Most of the plants grown in home gardens do best within this range. Exceptions are largely acid-loving species, such as azaleas, rhododendrons, laurel, and hollies. For these, a pH of below 6.0 is best.

Soil test kits carry directions for raising or lowering soil reaction, so these need not be repeated here, but they are important when you want to grow plants with better results and less effort.

Well-rotted compost—contents of the pile after four months of warm weather or over winter—can be applied to the garden at any time, either as a mulch or worked into the soil. Its effect after a year or two of regular use will be to produce a soil that almost always weighs less than it did originally, works more easily, and holds both moisture and fertility. The heat of decomposition usually destroys all weed seeds, reducing work from this source.

The mention of weed seed brings up the question of buying so-called good black dirt to fill in low spots, to improve an otherwise poor existing soil, or to top-dress lawns. Avoid doing so whenever possible. In spite of advertised claims, whether verbal or printed, I distrust every claim for "weed-free" soil.

For one thing, the only way to really destroy weed seed in soil is by steaming or chemical fumigation, an expensive process which commercial florists must use, but which is practically never employed by black dirt peddlers. Nor can much faith be put in the richness of soils simply because they are black. True, in nature, most black soils tend to be rich, but after a century or so of cropping, this richness can be completely exhausted, leaving behind carbon residues which give these soils their color.

When soil simply must be purchased, pile it long in advance, if possible, and watch what types of weeds grow in it. If these are the easy-to-kill annuals, such as smartweed, lamb's-quarters, and purslane, further treatment may not be needed.

If, however, the pile is infested with quack grass, bindweed, nut grass, and similar hard-to-kill species, spreading it on a lawn or garden without further treatment will merely add hours and hours of work to your garden program. There are soil fumigants which can be used by the amateur. If you are near a florist's supply house, investigate Dowfume, a liquid that turns to gas and penetrates deeply into piled soil. It is not exactly weak tea and needs careful handling, but by the use of a heavy plastic cover and an injection tube, it can be used without any real danger.

Perhaps the most readily available chemical for this purpose is Vapam, a liquid which is applied to the surface of the soil after it has been spread. It is handled by most large garden centers.

While the use of these chemicals does involve some work, the end result should be a saving in both time and physical effort.

FERTILIZERS

Fertilizers and soils are associated with each other in the minds of most gardeners, but with a misunderstanding of their relationship. Most of us think of feeding plants as a process much like making a deposit in a bank, which may be drawn out later with interest. This leads us to believe that all we have to do to get better results is to pour on more chemicals or manures.

Actually, the use of fertilizers is more aptly compared with investing in a business enterprise and, by judicious management of all its elements, finally making a profit. Practically nothing of the chemical elements you apply, or which are released by the decay of organic fertilizers, is used directly by plants.

Instead, except for a miniscule amount absorbed directly by roots, dissolved fertilizer elements follow one of three paths. Some are absorbed and adsorbed on clay and organic particles in soil, to be stored until plant roots reach this reserve of nutrition. This explains one reason for increasing the organic and clay content of sandy soils. In porous soils, much fertility is washed down with drainage waters, to be lost forever to that particular garden. Most important, in rich soils most of these vital nutrients are absorbed and digested by such soil microorganisms as bacteria, fungi, and protozoa. It would seem at first that once nutrients were absorbed by such organisms, they would be lost forever, but this is not the case. Fortunately, the life span of these minute forms of life is so short that they soon die and decay, releasing whatever food elements their cells contain to plant roots which, in the meanwhile, have expanded into new areas of the soil.

Plant roots, even of the most vigorous species, are unable to fill the total volume of the soil in which they live. Microorganisms ordinarily occupy the greater part of that volume—there are millions of them in a single handful of gardener's loam. This explains why organic matter and aeration—factors which favor the multiplication of all beneficial soil organisms—are so important. Practically all the advantages claimed for organic fertilizers can be credited to their function as carriers and conservers of soil organisms.

Here is a good place to take up the much-debated arguments for and against the use of organic plant foods and the equally hot blasts, pro and con, on the subject of chemical plant foods. Each source of fertility has its place: good plants can be grown with either type as the sole source of nutrients, yet for the gardener who is interested in saving time, labor, and money, using a combination of the two is the only sensible program. Let us look at what plants need in order to grow and develop. We hear a great deal about the "big three" elements—nitrogen, phosphorus, and potash, and much less about the so-called minor elements, such as calcium, magnesium, iron, sulfur, and others, yet each of the latter, while required in lesser amounts, can be as critical *in absentia* as any of the big three.

In the end, both types of nutrients wind up in near-elemental form—a "nutritious soup" containing plant foods in completely soluble form. If you are an organic gardening enthusiast, think for a moment. Where are the teeth of a plant? Plants cannot eat hamburgers, nor any other solid food. Meat scraps, bits of roots and stems, natural fertilizers of all kinds, must be broken down by the activities of complex communities of soil organisms before they can be taken up and used for growth. These steps are quite involved. For example, breakdown of organic protein into nitrogen which can be absorbed by plant roots involves at least three such groups of soil organisms. Since these organisms do not work actively at temperatures below forty-two degrees and are relatively sluggish until soils warm up to above sixty degrees, nutrients from organic sources simply cannot feed plants until some time in late May or early June, at least they can't north of the Ohio River.

What is important to appreciate is that after breakdown has taken place, the end products of digestion by microorganisms are the same nitrogen, phosphorus, and potash chemical found in mineral plant foods. Plants are unable to distinguish between them in any way that science has been able to detect. True, it is easier to overload a soil with high concentrations of salts when chemicals are used, thus causing injury to plants, but this represents the abuse, not the use, of plant foods.

Nor are organic fertilizers and manures innocent of producing injury by "burning"—the argument most frequently used against mineral forms of fertilizer. In the past a common experience on golf courses, before greenskeepers learned how to use sewerage sludge safely, was a condition called delayed nitrogen burn. Sludge would be applied at a recommended rate early in the spring, but because soil bacteria were still inactive at this time, nothing would happen. Anxious to have greens in playing condition early, greenskeepers would make another application, often followed by a third feeding in early May, just as soils were beginning to warm up.

After a few hot days, bacteria would go to work at a rapid pace, releasing nitrogen at such a rate that it actually oozed out of openings in the leaf blade. I have applied test solutions to grass in this condition and have seen it turn red at once, indicating that highly concentrated solutions of nitrogen were present. A single afternoon in the hot sun would often kill out the entire green. The effect was a burn just as disastrous as a heavy overdose of ammonium sulfate would produce, but occurring so long after the overdosing with sewerage sludge that the true cause was difficult to appreciate. A fact to keep in mind is this—If it can feed plants, any substance is capable of burning foliage and roots, unless in solution.

The slow availability of organic fertilizers is both good and bad. It is good when you as a gardener want to do all the fertilizing at once without having to make repeated applications during the season. Favorable effects from a liberal application of barnyard manure have been recorded as long as fifty years afterwards, although when used at rates recommended on commercial brands, practically all the nutrients are either used up or converted to unavailable forms in a single season.

Slow availability is a drawback, however, when your purpose in fertilizing is to feed woody plants early in spring or late in fall. This is particularly important to consider when feeding trees and shrubs in early spring, the most critical period in the growth of such plants. A mature elm, for example, is called upon to produce an acre or more of new leaves in early spring, long before nutrients from the soil become available. Most of this new growth is nourished by foods stored the previous fall, but in the case of newly planted specimens, much of the boost needed for a good start must come from the soil. For this purpose, only fully soluble chemical fertilizers are of any value.

This early-spring availability is also important in the case of lawns, since grasses make their best growth long before natural nitrogen is available from soil.

In an effort to reproduce the slow availability of organic fertilizers in chemical sources, new long-feeding chemical plant foods have been developed, designed to slow up release (principally of nitrogen—the most elusive of our nutrient elements) to a rate equal to that of the plant's demands on the soil for nourishment. Perhaps the most widely available of these slow-release fertlizers is ureaform, which is made by reacting urea—a high-nitrogen fertilizer—with formaldehyde. This forms a soft, slowly soluble plastic which breaks down partially by chemical and partially by bacterial action. It contributes only nitrogen, but it can be combined with other fertilizer elements to make a complete plant food. A single application of one of these mixed ureaform products will feed a lawn an entire growing season when it is made either in early spring or in fall. This represents a big saving in time and effort when compared with the four or five applications of lightweight lawn fertilizers, analyzing about 20-10-5 that are necessary. Dollarwise, savings are equally attractive since packaging and shipping costs are reduced, even though pound for pound, ureaform fertilizers seem more expensive. It is sold under various trade names, either as a straight nitrogen fertilizer or in mixtures.

The gardener who wants to save work should take a long, hard look at these same widely sold 20-10-5 lightweight lawn fertilizers for another reason. Although fertilizers for lawns will be discussed in detail later, these materials do illustrate how a faulty formulation can increase the amount of effort needed to maintain turf in good condition. As one who did much to popularize this ratio of lawn food elements, I can speak from experience. When I tested these fertilizers for three years, test lawns showed excellent growth responses. After it had been on the market for about three years, however, reports of failing lawns, which had previously been kept at a high level of growth with it, began to trickle in.

Soil analyses of affected lawns showed serious deficiencies of potash in better than 75 percent of the complaints. Suddenly, the reason why lawns were failing struck me. A basic rule on agronomy is that for every pound of nitrogen used by grasses and grasslike plants, from one-half to one pound of potash is needed to allow plants to utilize the nitrogen. Although our Midwest soils are high in native potash, this supply is not inexhaustible. So long as grasses could draw on this natural reserve, they did well, but when it was depleted to a point where more nitrogen was applied than could be balanced by potash, roots began to fail and disease organisms found them easy to invade.

When you are in doubt as to what formulation to use on a vegetable garden, flower border, or lawn, try to find a product in which the nutrient elements—the "big three" of nitrogen, phosphorus, and potash—are equally balanced. This would be one marked with a 10-10-10, 12-12-12, 20-20-20 formula. In this way, you can be almost certain that if enough fertilizer is applied and if it is completely dissolved, plants will have available all the elements they need.

What about liquid fertilizers? As quick pickups for plants that are not doing well, they are useful, but their effectiveness lasts for only three or four days at most. Because they are in liquid form, they are completely soluble and are thus easily washed away. By the same token, though, they can be taken up by plants at once and so go to work the minute they are applied. When sold already dissolved in glass or plastic bottles, they are extremely expensive for the amount of actual plant food they contain; far better are the completely soluble salts that do not need expensive water shipped with them.

One difficulty in the frequent use of light doses of liquid plant foods will be solved in 1971 with the introduction of a low-cost applicator which is widely used in commercial green houses. It is the Hydrocare Liquid Applicator, containing a pump with four cylinders that injects measured amounts of solutions of fertilizers into a hose stream. It has proved so easy to use that I have switched to this method of feeding my own lawn. It can be left attached to the hose and put into use with the simple push of a button. If not on display at dealers, write the HYDROCARE CORP., 1739 Harding Road, Northfield, Ill. 60093.

When considering fertilizers, don't overlook the vital importance of water to dissolve them; for every *ounce* of nutrients absorbed, plants need at least five to six *pounds* of water before they can be used.

3

KNOW YOUR CLIMATE

"WHAT IN HEAVEN'S NAME does climate have to do with easier gardening?" Being puzzled over that relationship is understandable because the two ideas don't seem to be too closely related. Actually they are—by understanding what *kind* of a climate you have, you can avoid trying to grow plants which require constant care to keep alive as well as the labor and expense of having to replace them when they die.

Many of the problems gardeners face do relate to climate, at least indirectly. Much of the blame for this lies in the time-hallowed custom of writing garden books by reading those of the past, which were in turn copies (chances are) of some earlier British work. I am not an Anglophobe: I have great respect for the skills and knowledge of my many English friends who garden exceedingly well. The trouble occurs, though, when we try to transport British gardening practices to America.

This practice fails because it does not take into account the important differences between the maritime climate of Great Britain and that of most of the United States. There is a small section of northeastern United States beginning on Cape Cod in Massachusetts and continuing down to Long Island where we can ape the British to our profit horticulturally. When, however, we extend that copying to the Piedmont climate of our south Atlantic coastal plain or to the continental climate of the Middle West with its violent temperature variations, we are courting trouble.

My friend George Kelly once wrote an excellent book entitled

Rocky Mountain Gardening is Different, a title which is certainly true. So are the climates of our arid Southwest, the cooler regions along the Canadian border, and the fickle weather of the Great Plains. Each section has its own peculiarities which must be learned from experienced gardeners within its borders.

Perhaps a couple of examples will help demonstrate how climate affects what you do and how hard you must work at it. The most conspicuous example is the method recommended for growing perennials from seed on this side of the Atlantic, an exact copy, even to the time of year, of the culture used by Englishmen for generations. It calls for sowing seeds after the rush of spring work is over in late June or early July. The resultant seedlings are then transplanted as fairly mature plants into permanent positions in late August or early September. The effectiveness of this method can be seen in the magnificent perennial borders of English gardens—great waves of color that fill every available inch of space in June and July. By this method even the humblest cottager can raise enough outstanding perennials from a shilling packet of seed to stage a gorgeous show.

Think for a moment, however, about climatic differences between England and the United States. Anyone who has shivered in the fifty- to sixty-degree temperatures experienced on England's summer nights will readily see how unlike our warm nights they are. Here, we expect readings in the seventies and eighties as a matter of course. Many of our finest perennials—delphiniums, for example—will not germinate in warm soil. Once soil temperatures go much above sixty degrees, they will either rot or lie dormant until cooler temperatures occur. On this side of the Atlantic they must be sown as early as the soil is workable to take advantage of the residual coolness of winter. Because our soils are likely to be wet in spring, it is good practice to prepare the beds or frames for sowing without further digging or raking. Even better, sow the seed in fall covered with a light mulch so that they will lie dormant until suitable temperatures occur in early spring.

The winter that follows England's cool summers is another instance of our climatic differences. Here conditions are exactly reversed. We expect frozen ground over most of northeastern United States from Thanksgiving on, with killing freezes even before then. In England, unfrozen soil permits the planting of

Extremes in temperature throughout much of the United States must be carefully considered in planning gardens, and the well-planned garden can be almost as beautiful in winter as at other times.

dormant and semidormant plants all winter long. I recall the shocked look on the face of Harry Wheatcroft, that bearded high priest of the rose in Britain, when I told him that I did not recommend fall planting of roses north of a line drawn from Indianapolis to Philadelphia. "Heavens," he exclaimed, "when *do* you plant? At least ninety percent of our new plantings are in the ground before March."

A consideration of climate is particularly important when selecting woody plants—trees, shrubs, and vines that survive above ground and do not renew their tops from the ground up. Plants of this type have definite requirements as to minimum and maximum temperatures, moisture, day length, etc. Many beginners believe that the farther north the area from which a plant comes, the more likely it is to be hardy. Yet if we take an apple tree from Minnesota and plant it in Florida, it will go into dormancy in fall as usual, but will never start growth again—it will not have had enough cold to condition it for regrowth.

Although the dedicated gardener, anxious to beat out his neighbors, may be able to grow rare and unusual species outside their natural range, he who is interested in saving time, money, and labor will do well to stick to species which fit the climatic conditions of his particular locality. This subject will be discussed in detail later.

For many years I have urged the officers of the American Horticultural Council and its successor organization, the American Horticultural Society, to consider making a survey of plant hardiness, a costly operation which we all recognize as important but cannot find the funds to finance. This is one of the major needs of American horticulture and one which would cost about as much to finance as would the development of some miniature control gadget on a rocket to the moon. Apparently, it is far more important politically to know what the climate is on the moon than to evaluate it on earth, even though the latter knowledge might benefit millions of gardeners and farmers.

The first step in making such a study would be to set up climatic analogues—descriptions of climates all over the world from which our plants come. Such analogues do exist, compiled for the benefit of explorers for *agricultural* plants, but they need to be interpreted for use by horticulturists.

In the meanwhile, thoughtful gardeners can set up their own analogues—crude, of course, yet effective in sorting out from the botanical richness of the world those plants which will grow best without coddling. In general, because many plants are sensitive to the length of day during the summer, try to select species from the same latitude as your own. The amount of rainfall and the season during which it falls should be matched as closely as possible. Maximum temperatures in summer are just as important as minimum readings in winter.

Here the value of being able to place confidence in a nearby well-run nursery or garden center should be emphasized. Supplement their recommendations with the study of a reliable reference work. Perhaps the best available for the amateur is *Hortus Second*. The original edition was edited by the famous Liberty Hyde Bailey and published by Macmillan. It not only lists all plants known to be in American nursery trade, but gives facts on their origins to serve as a guide.

For a guide to climatic similarities and differences within the

United States, buy a copy of the Hardiness Zone Map compiled by a committee of the American Horticultural Society and published by the United States Department of Agriculture. It is for sale through the government printing office at fifteen cents a copy.

One of the knottiest climate problems is the existence of the so-called microclimates—minute variations in conditions which occur within every recognized climatic zone. These variations can occur as close together as the distance between the north and south or east and west sides of a house. A hillside may have an entirely different climate than does the flat land at its base. Some parts of the United States show substantial variations within a few miles of each other. In the area of New York City, for instance, Long Island is only a few miles from Nyack geographically, but climatically, it is at least 300 miles farther south.

In Oakland, California, the east slope may have a climate more like that of a community 100 miles north than like that of the west slope less than half a mile away. In the Chicago area, North Shore gardeners are usually able to enjoy their dahlias and other tender plants for at least a month later in fall, and can plant them out three weeks earlier in spring, than can those living in the western suburbs. Too, there are substantial specimens of boxwood on some North Shore estates which would never survive in communities west of the city.

Microclimates are the result of variations in wind currents (a windbreak can often raise your hardiness zone rating one full zone), sun exposure, protection by large bodies of water, etc. To be effective as a modifier of winter temperatures, a body of water must be at least a mile across and the area to be affected must lie in the path of prevailing winds. Water effects can be spectacular. One of the most dramatic examples was that of the planting of California redwood trees in Geneva, New York, about the middle of the nineteenth century, by the famous old nursery firm of Elwanger & Barry. They were protected heavily the first two years, then exposed to normal winter weather. They survived until the test winter of 1940–1941, when a temperature drop of sixty degrees in twenty-four hours, following a very warm fall, finally killed them.

Even the most ardent advocate of labor saving in the garden hates to be limited to the plants which everyone in his neighborhood grows. We all like to have at least one "gee-whiz" exotic specimen that will make the neighbors sit up and take notice. By studying the elements which make up microclimates, you can often place a single spectacular tree or shrub so that it will not be injured by winter winds or sun. True, heavy winter protection can be provided for valuable specimens, but since they are located in conspicuous spots as a rule, such covering does not add to the beauty of the winter landscape. Two or three winters of study may be needed to select the best location for an expensive plant.

Microclimates also can play a role in the selection of a site for herbaceous plants. For example, a site protected from cold winter winds and exposed to warm spring sunshine can often permit planting the vegetable garden two to three weeks earlier. Just the opposite location might be desirable for planting tulips or lilies which are often apt to poke shoots above ground too early in spring. When this happens, the foliage may survive, but the flower bud inside can be damaged or killed.

An excellent example of the need to study the right spot for a plant in terms of climate is in the planting of Dutch, Spanish, and English irises, all of which tend to make early fall growth if planted too early. If planting is delayed until the onset of winter when the bed will be heavily shaded, these will not be as likely to make such premature growth.

In analyzing climatic effects on plant growth, it is important to study shadow patterns, both in summer and in winter. Most gardeners never give this a thought, yet a knowledge of areas that will be shaded at various seasons is most useful. A plant in winter shade is far less likely to be winterkilled or damaged than is one in full sun. For example, winter sun in the Middle West is more intense than in the humid areas along the eastern seaboard. As a result, rhododendrons and azaleas are difficult to keep alive there, even though acid soil and proper humidity are provided. If, however, they are planted in a spot so that their stems are in full sun in mid-June, July, and August, but so that some solid object shades them the rest of the year, they are much more likely to survive.

For the gardener who would like to know more about weather and how it affects plants, an excellent reference work is the 1941 yearbook of the United States Department of Agriculture entitled *Climate and Man*. It is available in most public libraries.

4

GARDEN TOOLS

WHEN IT COMES TO GARDEN TOOLS, many gardeners are veritable packrats, buying them only to stow away in a basement or garage after a trial run or two. Even if they prove impractical, they are seldom discarded, but are looked upon as our wives look upon antiques—items to own, not to use.

I can speak from experience. My tool shed is full of weird and useless devices, most of them forced on me by enthusiastic inventors or salesmen, all of whom were certain that once I had their gadget in my hands, I would become a lifelong booster. For example, mine is perhaps the only tool shed in North America that can boast a machine from making peat pots. This dust-catcher, forced on me by a disillusioned salesman just before he left for home in Germany, has been sitting there since before World War II.

Today, peat pots are an everyday product, with over half a billion in use in the United States alone. This doesn't alter the fact that I have never turned out a single pot on this excellent piece of machinery, but it seems too fine a piece of engineering to toss on the junk pile.

In addition to this white elephant, I must have fifty or more garden tools of little or no value. Most of them are so-called multiple-use devices, such as a hoe which becomes a rake when turned over or a spade with cultivator teeth on the back. Inventors are fond of turning out such combinations, which invariably fail because they violate a basic principle of garden tools—they must be as personal as a tooth brush. Even if by some miracle two purposes could be served on a single handle, one or the other would not fit either the physical abilities of the user or his psychological relationship to that particular bit of equipment.

Although the tool collector has his faults, he is usually much better off than is the incompetent gardener struggling with inadequate devices—the rake whose head and handle part company, dull spades with back-breaking handles, a hose that allows only a thin trickle to come through, and similar inefficient bits of cheap junk.

Good tools *do* save time, money, and human effort. How much that saving totals is astounding. I look back on over half a century spent in gardening and am delightfully surprised. Between modern chemicals and present-day tools and equipment, the physical energy required to care for a modern suburban property has been reduced to about one-fourth of that which we once had to expend during the earlier years of this century. To double-trench our vegetable plot alone, then, called for the lifting by hand of over a ton of soil, without the effort of replacing it. Today, a Rototiller does almost as good a job in fifteen minutes. Yet not all labor-saving tools are new. Take, for example, the common garden hoe.

HOES

Perhaps the best example I know of a tool having to fit the garden and the gardener, the tool, is the English scuffle hoe. This is one device for which we can thank the British, even as we look askance at the ill-advised transfer of some of their cultural practices to the United States. Mine is now some thirty years old and is worn to a razor's edge by years of contact with soil.

If you do not know the English scuffle hoe, it is high time you made its acquaintance. It is deceptively simple—a wide, flat blade fastened to the handle by a horseshoe-shaped loop. It works along the surface of the ground, cutting off any weeds in its path and stirring the soil lightly. I know of no other tool which is as safe to use in weeding around shallow-rooted plants and shrubs, particularly azaleas and rhododendrons. In using a scuffle hoe, the operator pushes rather than pulls. He can walk either forwards or backwards. By walking backwards, he avoids stepping on soil he has just cultivated, perhaps the most useful feature of this tool.

Once the knack of using it has been acquired, most gardeners give up all other cultivating tools for a good scuffle hoe. The big problem is in finding a well-made one: the best are British, usually made in Sheffield. American versions are often clumsy and badly balanced.

Not everyone likes this device, however. I once had a handyman, a refugee from an Alabama cotton field, who had been raised with a conventional cotton hoe in his hands. I have never seen anyone who could manipulate this heavy, cumbersome tool with greater skill. He could flick out a weed growing between two plants barely a couple of inches apart without disturbing either plant. When, however, I tried to teach him to use my idea of a proper hoe, he managed to cut down several feet of lettuce row before he threw it down in disgust.

Those interested in saving effort but who are addicted to the old-time field hoe would do well to invest in what is called an onion hoe in the United States. The onion hoe is made in the same shape, with the same swing, as its more cumbersome prototype, but with a blade only one-third as deep. With this narrower blade, it can cut just as many weeds, but because it pulls less soil with each stroke, it uses less muscle. The term *onion hoe* comes from its being used to thin seedling onions in the row with the narrow side of the blade.

A tool that ought to be in the collection of every gardener who plants vegetables is a well-made Warren hoe, useful in both opening and closing a seed row. It is heart-shaped or, perhaps more accurately, lance-shaped. The upper edge of the blade forms two "mule ears" while the lower edge terminates in a triangular point. Held with the "ears" upright, it opens a row for sowing seed. It can then be reversed to pull soil from each side, closing the row. Although some gardeners use a Warren hoe for cultivating as well as for sowing seed, it is not well balanced enough for continued use and is tiring.

When using any hoe, unless you are anxious to get in some physical exercise, don't exert too much effort. It works just about as well (except in soils that are too hard to be worth cultivating at best) when raised about a foot from the soil as it does when raised shoulder high. Here is where the scuffle hoe is the greatest labor saver of all—it is never lifted off the ground.

RAKES

There are rakes and rakes—most of them heavy users of human energy. Because rake teeth dig in and the loose material is pulled toward the user, raking requires the expenditure of considerable physical effort.

The poorest excuse we have for a rake is the cheap flat-headed cast-iron type sold at bargain prices in outlets that are not primarily garden merchandisers. Even if the head stays on (not likely in this type), it pulls badly and does a poor job of raking. Instead, for preparing seed beds and similar garden tasks, insist on a bow rake fastened to its handle by a stirrup-shaped bow. Since such rakes are not cast, but are made from high-grade metal, a well-made bow rake will last a lifetime if well cared for.

This rake calls for real skill in its manufacturing: the art is often passed on from father to son. Nowadays, few sons want to take up the trade, so bow rakes are not usually sold in chain stores. Most good garden centers do offer them. Every gardener needs at least one such tool, or better yet, a small and a large size.

Far from expensive and certainly not long lasting is a rake made out of bent bamboo in Japan. Even the best of these cannot be expected to last more than three or four years in use, yet they do such an outstanding job that they are worth replacing often. I have tried all sorts of American versions of this rake (fancy Americans copying the Japanese!) but none has proved as efficient as the Japanese product. The Yankee imitations are made from spring wire or flat steel fingers and either don't rake well or collapse in use.

The bamboo rake is a "must" for cleaning off leaves from a lawn (unless a lawn sweeper is available). Even when a sweeper is used, a light raking by hand will remove trash left behind by the mechanical device. Don't limit its use to the lawn, however. No other tool can give as fine a finish to a newly made flower border or vegetable bed. It pays to buy this tool in two or three widths, using the narrower widths where the wide ones will be unnecessarily heavy.

On the West Coast, where most professional gardeners are Japanese, dealers often sell a very narrow bamboo rake, about eight inches wide, dubbed a "Japanese hand." On a long, slender handle, this is invaluable for flicking out leaves, paper, and trash from under shrubs and evergreens. Once you get accustomed to this tool, it is almost indispensable.

A rake which should be relegated to limbo is the type used for pulling up crab grass. Its only users nowadays are organic gardeners who decry the use of chemical weed-killers and innocent beginners who are often lured into buying this device. I know of no rake that calls for expending as much physical effort as does this man-killer. Crab grass clings tenaciously to the soil and a real jerk is needed to loosen it. Since this rake is unable to grasp the plant until it is quite mature, with seed heads already formed, it usually scatters enough seed to perpetuate the crop *ad infinitum*. A crab grass rake saves neither effort nor time in the end.

SPADES, SHOVELS, AND SPADING FORKS

Another British contribution which has had an adverse effect on our gardening habits is the D-handled spade with its short wooden shaft. If you will examine a statue of St. Fiacre, the supposed patron saint of true gardeners, in his hand you will see a wooden-bladed spade almost identical mechanically to the back-breaking type favored by English gardeners since the sixteenth century.

This tool was a necessity for digging in a ditch, where there was little room for a longer handle to be used, but it requires almost twice as much energy to lift a given amount of soil than does a modern long-handled spade (or more properly, a shovel). It is the difference between using a short lever and a long one. Imagine you are hand-digging a vegetable plot twenty by fifty feet. With a long-handled spade, you would have to lift approximately a quarter of a ton of soil, but if one with a short handle is used instead, you would have to lift the equivalent of half a ton.

My favorite tool is a long-handled diamond-pointed spade which is forged with a heavier backbone but with a thinner razor edge. Because of this thinner edge and its diamond point, it can be used to chop hard soil more easily than a square-edged old-time spade with a D-handle. This makes an excellent scoop, too, when loose soil must be moved, although for this purpose I usually use a retired coal scoop.

We can thank the British for this next tillage tool—the square-tined spading fork. Unlike the thin, flat-bladed American fork, this has tough tines so strong that they are practically unbreakable in use. A fork is almost a necessity when digging in stony or gravelish soils. It also saves effort when cultivating clay because the tines are easier to drive down into heavy moist soil.

There is a small version of the spading fork, a so-called ladies' fork, which is useful for digging between established plants in the perennial border and in other spots where you want to avoid disturbing surrounding soil.

HAND CULTIVATORS

The short-handled cultivator is almost a thing of the past, although there are gardeners who don't mind kneeling to make closer contact with the soil. ******** The stars represent a pause when I left my typewriter, walked over to a drawer marked Hand Garden Tools, and threw out nine such gadgets which had not been used in years. Most of them came as parts of sets of hand tools, of which the only useful units were the trowels.

There is a cultivator which *is* quite useful—the type which has three or five curved teeth attached to a long handle. This is a surface scratcher, handy for destroying small weeds. It actually functions as a hoe. It may not be of much use in good garden loam when a scuffle hoe is available, but used in a soil filled with stones and gravel, it will avoid dulling the hoe's edge. Never use a toothed cultivator with a chopping motion: this ruins the teeth.

TROWELS

We still have no adequate substitute for a good hand trowel, even though this means stoop labor when transplanting. This is one tool where quality is beyond price. The blade should be welded onto the shank in one piece and not stuck on with rivets, and should not be bent out of light sheet metal. Select a trowel by imagining you are using it in every possible position. The handle should feel comfortable in all positions. Stainless steel is practically a "must." Beware of cast aluminum trowels: although they are sturdy and often well balanced, in my experience they corrode even worse than steel or cast iron and the corrosion is extremely difficult to remove. Most people prefer the old-fashioned wooden handle, which is good provided it is of tough wood and is well made.

DIBBLES

May the devil take all dibbles: they compact soil too much, form a hole difficult to close, and in general are a nuisance. In my experience, a much better tool for opening a hole when transplanting seedlings can be made by splitting off a piece of cedar shingle and whittling this to the size desired. This makes a flat hole rather than a round one, which is easier to close once the seedling has been inserted by pushing this stick down close to the first hole.

SHEARS AND PRUNERS

Grass shears can be dismissed with a one-line recommendation: forget them. Nowadays, chemical edgers have eliminated the need for laborious hand snipping of grass. The same can be said for lawn edgers. Pruning shears are another story. Here the most important step in selection is feeling the fit in your hand. Most garden centers have a few old branches around on which to try a shear. By all means, do so. Notice how the latch works that keeps the shear closed when not in use. These devices have a habit of catching and bruising your hand. Watch, too, where the cutting edge really takes hold. Some blades don't really begin to work until you are halfway through a branch or twig.

Hedge shears might almost be left out of any discussion which is concerned with saving labor: to plant a trimmed hedge to begin with is to sign up for years of regular snipping and pruning. At the same time, even a hedge allowed to grow naturally does need a little discipline from time to time. Any shear you do buy should be equipped with rubber bumpers that take up the shock of each cut when the blades close. This seems a small detail, yet if you have ever whacked away at a long hedge, you will be grateful each time the shear closes that there is no metal-to-metal bump.

WHEELED TOOLS

Whether hand-propelled or driven by power, wheeled tools are important on the larger place. Over mechanizing a small city or suburban property, on the other hand, can result in more time and effort being wasted on machinery than would be needed to do the necessary work by hand. A small riding tractor, complete with mower, sweeper, garden cart, and half a dozen other gadgets on an eighty-foot lot may be fine as a status symbol, but as a work saver, it is a delusion and a snare.

No one can decide for you just how much power equipment you need, if any, except that a power mower is usually not needed on a lawn area of less than 2,000 square feet. Power does have its disadvantages. For one thing, it means more weight on a lawn, which in turn means soil compactions. Since compaction is a worse enemy than crab grass today, any equipment that adds to it is to be considered carefully. Use of such equipment would necessitate more frequent soil aeration and perhaps renovation.

These factors should be considered when choosing a mower, a riding tractor, a power lawn sweeper, and any other heavy power units. In my own case, I switched from a twenty-four-inch power mower to one which was eighteen inches wide and found my grass doing better for the change. True, this meant more trips back and forth, but it also meant less weight to swing on the turns or when moving the mower from lawn to storage.

Mowers will be discussed later under "Lawns" and are mentioned here only because they are the most widely used type of power equipment.

The number of small rotary tillers sold nowadays is astonishing —astonishing because this is a power tool of limited use on any property under an acre in extent. It is used principally for the initial preparation of lawn areas (a one-time job), for working up the soil in annual beds (once in spring each year), and for tilling the vegetable garden, again only once a year. Usually, a tiller can be hired or the work done by a custom operator for less than the annual interest on the price of a tiller owned outright. Use of a custom operator has another advantage—his muscle, not yours, does the work. This is something to keep in mind—whenever it is possible to have work done, by all means do so. There are more enjoyable tasks than running a lawn mower. Be sure, however, that the operator you hire is able and will do a good job, even if you must instruct him.

DUSTERS AND SPRAYERS

These are necessary evils, to be used only when necessary, yet they are vital to healthy plants. The first problem to settle is whether to spray or dust. Entomologists all agree that an effective chemical applied as a spray at the proper time is much more effective than the same chemical applied as a dust, even if the latter is timed perfectly.

Where the problem arises is in the difference in preparation for dusting and spraying. In the former, present-day broad-spectrum products permit their use right out of the package, usually combining fungicides and insecticides in a single product. The home owner, just before catching his train into the city, can pick up a duster—kept filled at all times—and treat his roses in five minutes. This is a job he is much more likely to do than he would if he must open a bottle of spray, measure out the proper amount, fill a sprayer, and go to work. He knows that to keep his sprayer working properly, any unused solution will have to be dumped out and the entire mechanism thoroughly cleaned and drained. As a result, he neglects the job. Consequently, for the man interested in saving time and effort, dusting is the more practical method for controlling garden pests.*

Here again, the individual preferences of the user are all important: any equipment purchased should suit the gardener's strength, habits and problems.

*The above comments apply to insecticide-fungicide application only. See chapter 10, "Chemical Control of Plant Growth," for additional comments on sprayers.

WATERING EQUIPMENT

Since plants are largely water, this is the most important of all growth elements, more so than are all the fertilizers you apply. True, its availability is often left to natural rainfall, yet proper application of water artificially at the right time can mean saving plants which otherwise would have to be replaced or nursed back to health.

When we think of water, our first thoughts are about a hose, yet today this is far less important than it once was. With the advent of plastic pipe, the hose has become only the terminal distributing mechanism rather than the entire system. This is all to the good, since the minute water is turned into a hose, it begins to lose pressure. This does not mean that piping introduces no pressure drop, but rather that underground piping is usually relatively straight, without kinks or restricted areas. Too, it can be laid in diameters sufficiently large to reduce pressure loss to a minimum.

Today, an entire underground system, even with sprinkler heads, can be installed for about the cost of a good bicycle, if the gardener does the work. An important factor in the successful laying of such a system is having an appreciation for mathematics. Most of us feel that a half-inch pipe will carry at least half as much water as a one-inch pipe. Actually, the ratio is closer to 1 to 4. To be exact, the area of a half-inch pipe is 0.19635 square inches whereas that of a one-inch pipe is 0.7854.

The minimum underground pipe size should be three-quarters of an inch, but one inch is better. This will permit the use of more efficient sprinklers that will apply water faster and take less time to do the job. Another important factor is the number and distribution of outlets on the water line. These should be located so that twenty-five feet of hose would be the maximum needed to reach any area in the garden or lawn.

Use the largest-diameter hose available (usually three-quarters of an inch, but all too often not more than five-eighths of an inch) to take advantage of the volume of water available. Scorn the half-inch hose of the price-merchandisers: this is a complete waste of time.

An important factor in selecting sprinklers is to pick those that apply water accurately without wasting it in overlapping. My preference is for the oscillating type that weaves back and forth, covering a rectangular or square pattern. This can be set for a full rectangle or for a half-coverage either right or left. Circular sprinklers must overlap in order to get complete coverage, which means that more time and effort must be spent moving sprinklers.

WHEELBARROWS AND CARTS

Except that it does permit wheeling through narrow rows, a wheelbarrow is a device wished upon us by the ancient Chinese, where narrow streets and country lanes demanded such a vehicle, which has no practical excuse for existing today. A much better carrier of garden necessities is a two-wheeled cart. By that I do not mean the type made by a former baby-carriage manufacturer who wanted to put his idle equipment to use. Instead, I mean a solid box mounted on two wheels at least as large as twenty-inch bicycle wheels, with rubber tires. Such a cart will not only carry more materials but will do so with less effort.

MATERIALS

In the current age of plastics, gardeners must be suspicious of all materials from which garden tools and equipment are made. True, many of the high-impact plastics can give superior service under hard use. The better grades of plastic hose will last longer than old-time rubber products. Plastic garden labels, properly marked, will often remain legible longer than will those out of the old-time gardeners' favorite—lead.

The reverse is, of course, true. Cheap plastic hose seldom outlasts the first year of use. One of the most ridiculous products I ever tried was a plastic garden cart, with a companion plastic spreader, both of which were broken before the summer was over.

Aluminum, too, has proved to be a disappointment in use. It seems to have a strange affinity for soil acids, which produce a hard corrosion which is all but impossible to remove. Magnesium tools seem to have the same defect.

The most satisfactory material I have found is expensive, yet well worth its extra cost—stainless steel. It can be wiped clean with a rag or wisp of straw at the end of a full day's work. Even if cleaning is neglected for days, serious corrosion does not seem to occur. The one danger is that because stainless steel is expensive, manufacturers are likely to cut down the weight of the metal used, so the tool is not adequate for the job it is intended to do.

TOOL CARE

Although cleaning tools is a bore, in the end it will save more work than it makes. To care for wooden handles, rub off any dirt that has accumulated and then rub them with a rag dipped in boiled linseed oil. This same rag is excellent for removing dirt on lawn mower blades.

Before storing tools for the winter, rub them with an oiled rag to prevent winter rust. Soak the attachment of the handle to the working part of the tool in oil also: this prevents the separation caused by shrinking wood.

Spades and hoes are usually self-sharpening, yet a light touch with a carborundum scythe stone is desirable to remove any big nicks.

Always drain hoses and sprinklers for the winter: they can be damaged by water freezing in them.

5

TREES AND SHRUBS FOR EASY UPKEEP

Some day, gardens of all-plastic flowers will become a horrible reality. Anyone who has watched the way these slippery imposters have taken over the cut-flower field cannot ignore the possibility of their use becoming universal, even in landscaping.

Even today, they have made a beginning: only recently I changed my route to the office to avoid the daily shock of passing a motel which has its entrance drive ringed by strident, scarlet, synthetic geraniums. No one believes they *are* geraniums—they are about as convincing as is rouge on the cheeks of a corpse.

Until that humiliating day arrives, however, gardeners must face the task of choosing their basic materials from a vast array of living plants. Correct selection is vital when a saving of time, labor, and money are limiting factors.

In advising readers to avoid planting species which involve extra effort, I am in the position of a doctor who says, "Do as I say, not as I do." Looking out of my breakfast room window, I see five weeping willows on a remote corner of our property, under which is a mat of brittle twigs and fallen leaves nearly a foot deep. After every high wind, large limbs must be hauled to the trash pile.

Fortunately, out of the four black walnuts that once stood on the property, only one remains: the rest were felled without any sense of loss on my part. If it were not for the fact that the remaining specimen shades the west side of the house, it too would go.

Under our west foundation are roots of an ancient mulberry

that once threatened to push over that wall until it, too, felt the ax. Looking out toward the street, I see three elms lining the parkway, fortunately spared the ravages of Dutch elm disease. Three other elms that stood on the lot away from the street (and so not protected by our village forester) have already succumbed.

Across the line on my neighbor's property to the south stands an enormous honey locust, beautifully formed, but as fruitful as a healthy rabbit. Each spring, I must rake up several bushels of fallen pods. Not a hundred yards away stands another beautiful but messy tree—an American plane tree, or sycamore. It is a mess producer, spring, summer, and fall. Its brittle twigs and branches are constantly falling, leaves litter the ground both summer and fall, the fruits blow everywhere, and in the spring, its unfolding leaf buds shed a fuzzy coat of forked hairs that are irritating to eyes and throat.

To the north, fortunately out of sight of our window, are half a dozen box elders that every summer spawn thousands of box-elder bugs.

The existence of so many undesirable species on a single property illustrates two important facts. The first is that trees are long-lived—permanent elements in the landscape picture—and, once in place, must be tolerated. The second is that few of us are willing to cut down mature trees and to replace them with better species. Hence the most important consideration in planting new trees is careful selection.

Perhaps the first thought should be given to regional adaptation. Among the thousands of species which might be able to survive in a given spot, less than 20 percent will be fully adapted. What is not commonly appreciated is that a garden in America is actually the terminus of a long, long caravan bringing to it plant materials from climates as diverse as the subtropics and the subarctic. In a single border planting in one Chicago park, I was able to identify species which had originated on a subtropic seashore, others on a semi desert, and still others in Canada, Japan, Mexico, northern Europe, and the U.S. Great Plains.

Under the care of several skilled gardeners, all these were growing beautifully. Had they been neglected, however, as they almost certainly would have been in the garden of a busy commuter, the results would have been quite different.

Well-placed crabapple trees add shade and beauty to a small backyard garden.

The following list of plants has been deliberately limited: it is by no means a catalog of the thousands of species available to the American gardener. On the contrary, it has been studied several times in an effort to eliminate every species which involves extra effort and expense. Although each plant listed might fare better with a little tender loving care, it should survive in spite of neglect, at least for a time. Of necessity, this guideline must eliminate many beautiful but temperamental species which the dedicated gardener would insist on having. Even this culling will not reduce garden labor to zero, but it will eliminate many hours of labor spent in fighting insect pests, cleaning up litter, and caring for fussy trees, shrubs, and flowers.

Perhaps the most noticeable loss will be in the list of annuals and perennials. It is unfortunate that these require more work than do woody plants, or at least they call for attention being given on a stricter schedule. If we do not snip spent flower spikes from lilacs today, we can do it next week or even next month. If, however, marigolds or other annuals are neglected and are permitted to set seed, they are finished as garden ornaments.

This insistence on toughness—on the ability to survive in spite of use—may force us to make some not-so-pleasant choices while rejecting beautiful but demanding alternatives. For example, one of my favorite trees is the horse chestnut, certainly one of the loveliest of all woody plants when in full bloom. To recommend it to a busy suburbanite would, however, be unkind, condemning him to spending many hours picking up twigs and branches broken after strong winds, to fighting fallen nuts for weeks in the fall, and to treating rot in the wood bared by breaking branches.

Problematic environmental conditions (a sooty urban garden or a planting near a pollution-producing mill) might actually call for planting a tree as tough but as undesirable as the tree of heaven, or stinkweed. Thus you will not find such lovely things as the paper bark birch, the silver maple, or the black locust in the following list: they have been eliminated for the reasons just given. See the zone map on p. vii for hardiness zone numbers.

TREES FOR SHADE AND STREET

Proper selection of woody plants is particularly important since they are not easy to uproot and replace. The following list is limited to those species which are long-lived, are subject to practically no serious diseases or insect pests, and are able to survive under neglect. Exceptions are noted.

Abies concolor: White fir. Zone 4. To 120 feet.

With the longest needles of any of the firs, this desirable evergreen, with its stiffly horizontal branches, forms a rather narrow pyramid. Because of its long needles, the effect is much softer than that of the more rigid blue spruce. It will grow to about 30 feet in most locations in twenty years.

Acer ginnala: Amur maple. Zone 2. To 20 feet.

Upright with a rounded top, this is one of the most desirable small maples because of its brilliant scarlet fall color. It is practically carefree. For hedge purposes, *Acer campestre,* the hedge maple, is similar, but has no fall color.

Acer negundo: Box elder. Zone 2. To 60 feet.

Although this is an arboreal weed not worth planting where better trees will grow, it is a godsend out on the Great Plains. There is a silver-variegated form of it, called the ghost tree, which makes a spectacular specimen, even in the East.

Acer pseudoplatanus: Sycamore maple. Zone 5. To 90 feet.

Because it lacks fall color, other maples should be used if possible. Its one virtue, though—it can tolerate salty sea breezes—makes it one of the few deciduous trees suitable for seashore planting.

Acer saccharum: Sugar maple. Zone 3. To 100 feet.

This is a tough, vigorous species with perhaps the most gorgeous autumn color of any native tree. Its shape is that of a rounded oval, but there are columnar varieties available for planting where a narrow tree is wanted.

Ailanthus altissima erythrocarpa: Tree of heaven. Zone 4. To 60 feet.

This is the "tree that grows in Brooklyn." It will grow anywhere, even on the grounds of oil refineries, steel mills, and on wastes from mines. It will survive even if its roots are covered with salt water for short periods of time. For all its toughness, it is an arboreal weed, for use only where nothing better will grow. Some find the odor of its male flowers sickening—they give off an overpoweringly sweet, sticky perfume, but this lasts for only a short time. Its wood is weak and breaks easily, although shaping by pruning helps reduce this difficulty.

Amelanchier canadensis: Shadblow serviceberry. Zone 4. To 50 feet.

Its nodding clusters of airy white flowers appearing in late April and its yellow or red foliage in fall make this a highly desirable species. New leaves have a grayish cast.

Amelanchier grandiflora: Apple serviceberry. Zone 4. To 25 feet.

It has larger flowers than the previous species, but is otherwise similar.

Aralia elata: Devil's walking stick, Japanese angelica. Zone 3. To 45 feet.

This is just the tree to plant for closing a gap where trespassers insist on walking. Its vicious spines will discourage all forms of life—human and otherwise—from making close contact with it. With its compound leaves, often two feet long, it is excellent for tropical effects. Tolerates city smoke.

Araucaria araucana: Monkey-puzzle tree. Zone 7. To 90 feet, but lower at north limits of its growth.

Although this is a real "gee-whiz" plant that makes visitors sit up and take notice, it is a bit too exotic for good landscape effects. Its twisted branches and spiny needles are responsible for its common name.

Araucaria excelsa: Norfolk Island pine. Zone 10. To 100 feet in the South, but often sold in pots as an indoor Christmas tree.

This pine is a useful ornamental in frostfree parts of the country.

Arbutus menziesii: Pacific madrone. Zone 7. To 60 feet.

A beautiful species valued much more highly in England than it is here, this tree does not do well in the East, but on the Pacific Coast and in Great Britain, it is probably our finest broad-leaved evergreen. It should not be planted on lawns, however—it sheds bark, leaves, fruit, and flowers throughout the year.

Arbutus unedo: Strawberry tree. Zone 8. To 25 feet.

A much cleaner tree than the above, it is equally attractive. The fruits resemble strawberries and cling to the tree for months.

Bauhinia variegata: Buddhist bauhinia, mountain ebony, orchid tree. Zone 10. To 20 feet.

The lavender-purple flowers scattered throughout the foliage of this tree resemble small orchids. It will lose some of its leaves in the winter.

Carpinus caroliniana: Blue beech, ironwood, American hornbeam. Zone 2. To 35 feet.

This tree has perhaps the hardest wood of any native tree and will often form several trunks. Its autumn foliage is orange to red.

Carya glabra: Pignut. Zone 4. To 100 feet.

This is a slow-growing tree, which does well on poor soils. Because the falling nuts are a nuisance (they are of no edible value), don't plant where they will fall on lawns, walks, or drives. Squirrels attracted by the nuts can also be a nusiance.

Carya ovata: Shagbark hickory. Zone 4. To 100 feet.

This is the best hickory to use as an ornamental. Even though the nuts are excellent, see remarks under *Carya glabra.* If nuts are to be harvested, select instead one of the many improved, named varieties. It is hard to transplant.

Carya pecan: Pecan. Zone 5. To 125 feet.

This is a noble tree, fast-growing, and for many, bearing the best-flavored of all nuts. Some nurseries offer hardy strains of it which will bear nuts as far north as central Illinois and Ohio. It has good yellow autumn color. Don't try to grow on dry soils, though—it is a tree of the rich bottom lands.

Castanea mollissima: Chinese chestnut. Zone 4. To 60 feet.

Not the shapeliest tree in existence, but if carefully trimmed when young, it will form a rounded, dense head. It is the only chestnut resistant to the bark disease which kills native species. Bronzy yellow autumn color.

Castanospermum australe: Moreton Bay chestnut. Zone 10. To 50 feet.

Its seeds are edible, but it is most desirable because of its clean evergreen foliage and striking yellow flowers. It forms a broad, spreading top.

Castanopsis chrysophylla: Evergreen chinquapin. Zone 7. To 100 feet.

Although its spiny burrs are a nuisance when planted where these can drop into shrubbery or tall grass, this is a beautiful specimen tree with airy spikes of ivory white flowers.

Casuarina equisetifolia: She-oak, Australian pine, horsetail pine, Australian beefwood. Zone 9. To 45 feet.

This is a tree that will grow on miserable soils (including brackish sands), will survive salt spray, and can be clipped for use as a hedge. Otherwise it is an ugly thing with an open habit that provides poor shade. In its native habitat it is said to grow to 70 feet, but I have never seen a specimen larger than 45 feet.

Casuarina stricta: Coast beefwood. Zone 9. To 30 feet.

Similar to the preceding, this one has a slender habit and drooping foliage.

Catalpa bignonioides: Indian bean tree, cigar tree, common catalpa. Zone 5. To 50 feet.

This species has the most refined foliage of any catalpa, but it is still a bit coarse. The long pods are not ornamental, but a catalpa in bloom, with its large trusses of whitish flowers, is like a good-looking hussy. But beware of the umbrella-headed version of this tree, beloved by Victorian gardeners because it could be used as a vegetable punctuation point. Growing to only 7 or 8 feet, a single specimen this size with branches allowed to grow until they touch the ground can be a useful accent specimen *if* used discreetly. Leaves of both types are ill-smelling if bruised.

Catalpa speciosa: Western mahogany, northern catalpa, catawba tree. Zone 5. To 90 feet.

Although quite similar to the preceding, the leaves of this tree are not ill-smelling if bruised. It shares all the common names of *Catalpa bignonioides,* and the two species are, as a result, badly mixed in nurseries.

Cedrus atlantica: Atlas cedar. Zone 6. To 60 feet.

This is a difficult tree to rate as to hardiness: I have seen specimens growing in Rhode Island and Connecticut near the sea, but it is probably not reliably hardy much north of Philadelphia. A dramatic evergreen, it is perhaps too overpowering for smaller properties, but lovely at a distance. The blue atlas cedar, a variety, is best. It is pyramidal in habit.

Cedrus deodara: Deodar cedar, incense tree. Zone 7. To 150 feet.

This tree is like the preceding, but is less stiff in habit, with the ends of branches drooping.

Cedrus libani: Cedar of Lebanon. Zone 5 (but see comments). To 60 feet.

Solomon's temple is said to have been built from the wood of this tree. Although it forms a somewhat broader pyramid than the above, it is more open in habit. Ordinary strains are not hardy much north of Philadelphia, but the Arnold Arboretum strain will grow as far north as Massachusetts.

Celtis laevigata: Sugarberry, sugar hackberry, Mississippi hackberry. Zone 5. To 90 feet.

All hackberries are susceptible to attacks by a mite that carries a fungus. This causes the ends of branches to sprout clumps of small twigs called witches'-broom. Some consider these disfiguring (they are visible only when the tree is dormant), but in my experience, they merely give the tree a denser appearance in summer. Because of their similarity to elms in general appearance, hackberries are useful for replacing dead elms on streets where surviving trees are of that species. *Celtis laevigata* is the most resistant species to witches'-broom.

Ceratonia siliqua: St. John's-bread, carob, wild locust, desert bread. Zone 9. To 50 feet.

Said to be the biblical "wild honey and locusts" on which St. John fed in the wilderness, this is an outstanding evergreen tree for dry soils. Trees are of one sex only: if fruit is wanted, both male and female trees must be planted. Conversely, if the pods are a nuisance, be sure that only male trees are used.

Cercidiphyllum japonicum: Katsura tree. Zone 4. To 60 feet.

Why this outstanding tree with its clean, open foliage and resistance to disease and insect pests is not more widely used is a mystery. Its habit of growth, usually with several trunks, many prejudice gardeners against it, but a fine specimen with its broad, spreading, oval form is a beautiful sight. Its autumn color is yellow to bright red.

Cercis canadensis: Judas tree, redbud. Zone 5. To 40 feet, but usually much lower.

The brilliant cerise flowers of the redbud coming at any other season of the year would normally be too garish to please most gardeners, but in early spring, they are delightful. The small pealike clusters of flowers often mask an entire branch. There is a white variety which needs to be planted against a dark background to be seen at its best, when it will appear as delicate as fine lace.

Cercis chinensis: Chinese redbud. Zone 6. To 40 feet in China, but I have never seen a specimen taller than 15 feet here.

In trying to grow this in Zone 5, I have had the tree killed to the ground about every five or six years. Its flowers are larger and even more conspicuous than the preceding.

Chamaecyparis lawsoniana: Port Orford cedar, Lawson false cypress. Zone 5 (but see comments). To 100 feet.

This evergreen, native to a small area in the Pacific Northwest, is widely grown in Australia, England, and New Zealand, but only in areas where the air is quite moist. Outside a small section of the West Coast, it does not thrive. There are several attractive varieties, columnar to broadly pyramidal. It is an excellent tree where it will grow.

Chamaecyparis obtusa: Hinoki false cypress. Zone 3 (but see comments). To 100 feet.

This tree is much like the preceding, somewhat hardier as to cold, yet demanding a moist climate.

Chionanthus virginica: American fringe tree. Zone 4. To 30 feet.

To really appreciate this tree, it should be seen for the first time in bloom in its native habitat—from New Jersey south through Georgia. Its daintily fringed flowers smother the tree in early June. Two drawbacks, though, are that it needs acid soil and it is sometimes attacked by the same scale that infests lilacs.

Cinnamomum camphora: Camphor tree. Zone 9. To 40 feet.

A clean, shapely evergreen with dense glossy foliage, it makes a perfect street tree if the lower branches are trimmed up.

Cladrastis lutea: Yellowwood, gopherwood, Kentucky yellowwood. Zone 4. To 40 feet.

The wisterialike fragrant flowers appear in pendulous clusters in early June on this tree. Although it forms a handsome round-headed tree, on the northern limits of its range it is not a reliable bloomer. Its autumn color is from orange to gold.

Cocos nucifera: Coco palm, coconut. Zone 10. To 80 feet.

Yankees moving south are fascinated by coconuts and plant them everywhere, but a falling nut can be a lethal missile. This should never be used as a street tree or planted along walks and drives. They are best planted from seeds (it will bear in about six years if in good soil). It will tolerate some salt spray.

Cornus controversa: Giant dogwood. Zone 5. To 60 feet in its native Japan.

Although it is often passed over for its more striking relatives, it is an outstanding tree with a picturesque horizontal habit. Flowers are in white umbels, followed by conspicuous black fruits in early fall. It is resistant to the blight that often injures other dogwoods.

Cornus florida: Flowering dogwood. Zone 4. To 35 feet.

This is the one flowering tree (along with the American fringe tree) which British gardeners admit is as lovely as anything they can grow. Its shining white bracts (they are leaves rather than true flowers) light up the woods of northeastern United States from early to mid-May. The bright red berries make it conspicuous again in fall. It is perhaps the most useful of all the low-growing flowering trees within its range. Unfortunately, though, it cannot be grown west of Michigan since it is definitely not a tree for the prairies and plains because of its need for shelter from harsh winds and its higher moisture requirements.

Cornus mas: Cornelian cherry, gold of spring. Zone 5. To 15 feet.

Why this lovely tall shrub or small tree is not grown by every American gardener is a mystery. One of the earliest blooming trees, it opens its tiny yellow clusters of flowers during February thaws, unless cold weather refuses to break in which case it waits until March. It does well everywhere, even in smoky cities. The cherrylike scarlet fruits are edible, with a clean tart taste.

Cornus nuttallii: Pacific dogwood. Zone 7. To 60 feet.

This is the western counterpart of *Cornus florida,* except that its flowers have six bracts instead of four and the tree is a giant in comparison. If only it would grow in the East! It often blooms again in fall.

Corylus corlurna: Turkish hazel. Zone 4. To 60 feet.

This is hard to find but worth planting. Its catkins are borne very early in spring, it tolerates dry soils, and it is a well-shaped healthy tree producing edible fruits in August and September.

Corylus avellana: European hazel. Zone 4. To 15 feet.

Although usually a shrub, this can be trained as a small tree. The variety *C. avellana fuscorubra* is one of our better small trees with purple foliage. The fruit of the regular type is the filbert of commerce.

Crataegus, various species: Hawthorns. Practically all hardy to Zone 4. From 15 to 35 feet.

These small trees, quite beautiful when in full bloom in spring or in fruit in fall, *are not for the gardener who wants to avoid work.* All hawthorns are quite sensitive to a number of insect pests and diseases. Unless you are willing to give them special attention, they will not survive. Because the hawthorns are promiscuous, they are so badly mixed in the nursery trade that it is not safe to buy by description: see the actual specimen you want before you buy.

Cryptomeria japonica: Temple cedar, sugi, Japanese cedar. Zone 5. To 125 feet.

This stately tree so often portrayed in pictures of Japanese temples must have high humidity and rich soil to thrive.

Cupressus macrocarpa: Monterey cypress. Zone 7. To 75 feet.

Visitors to Monterey in California rave about the beauty of specimens of this tree which have been shaped by the persistent Pacific winds. It makes an ideal windbreak or hedge for California seaside areas, tolerating salt air.

Cupressus sempervirens: Italian cypress. Zone 7. To 70 feet.

This is the tree most often meant when cypress is mentioned. The variety *stricta* is used as a vegetable punctuation point since it is four feet or less in diameter, but twenty feet tall. The wood is among the most durable in the world.

Davidia involucrata: Dove tree. Zone 6. To 50 feet.

A most erratic bloomer in colder climates, but when its flowers do open, it is a spectacular sight. They are formed around a ball of golden stamens, white bracts, or wings, often 7 inches long. The tree itself is hard to Zone 4, but does not bloom there.

Delonix regia: Royal poinciana, flame of the forest, flamboyant. Zone 10. To 40 feet.

Many consider this the world's most spectacular flowering tree, with its flamboyant scarlet and yellow blossoms. It is a rapid grower in almost any soil.

Elaeagnus angustifolia: Russian olive. Zone 2. To 20 feet.

This tree is as conspicuous in a quiet way as the preceding species is flamboyant. It has soft gray foliage and interesting bark, brown and peeling in winter, on picturesque crooked trunks. It survives everywhere.

Eriobotrya japonica: Japanese plum, loquat. Zone 7. To 20 feet.

Sometimes grown for its edible fruits (which I find hardly worth the bother), this tree, as a specimen tree, is outstanding because of its handsome leathery evergreen foliage. It does best in full sun on rich, moist soils.

Erythea armata: Blue fan palm, Mexican blue palm. Zone 9. To 40 feet, but usually much lower.

The stem of this tree is covered by a shaggy "petticoat" and it has waxy blue foliage. Unlike many palms, this one prefers rich soil, moisture, and an occasional feeding.

Eugenia paniculata: Bush cherry, Australian jelly tree. Zone 9. To 40 feet.

An excellent evergreen tree with rosy-purple fruits that are used in making jelly, this tree is often sheared for use as a topiary specimen.

Euonymus bungeana: Winterberry. Zone 4. To 18 feet.

This is a tall shrub that can be trained to a single trunk. The variety semipersistens is better than the original type because it retains its fruits for weeks after frost has removed the foliage. Like all *Euonymus* species, it is attacked by Euonymus scale.

Euonymus europaeus: Spindle tree, broken-heart tree. Zone 3. To 20 feet.

This is another shrub sometimes trained into a tree. If it were not for its susceptibility to scale, it would be a wonderful small tree when so trained. A well-grown specimen which glows with a reddish fire in autumn is worth the trouble it takes to keep it sprayed.

Fagus grandifolia: American beech. Zone 3. To 90 feet.

Perhaps the most majestic of shade trees, its only competitor would be a perfect specimen of pin oak. It forms a dense pyramid with rich, dark green foliage in spring and summer, turning a golden bronze in fall. In winter no tree has handsomer bark, which turns a steely gray. Because of its long sweeping branches, it is not at its best as a street tree, but makes a noble specimen when viewed across a stretch of lawn.

Fagus sylvatica: European beech. Zone 4. To 90 feet.

If only the original type of the European beech were available, it could be ignored in favor of its American relative. Through the centuries, however, some of the world's most magnificent ornamental trees have evolved from it. If asked to name the world's finest shade tree, many would nominate the copper beech or the purple beech. Others would nominate the magnificent weeping beech. For those looking for vigor and active growth, without fuss, the tricolor variety should be avoided in spite of its flamboyant white, green, and pink foliage.

Ficus carica: Common fig. Zone 6. To 25 feet.

Having one's own fig tree is common up to the Carolinas at low elevation, but by protecting them in winter (which, of course, involves some labor), they can also be grown to the southern tip of Long Island. No tree casts a denser shade, and if care is used in planting on poor soil, fruit too can be enjoyed. On rich soil, fruiting is poor.

Ficus macrophylla: Moreton Bay fig, big leaf fig. Zone 9. To 70 feet.

Perhaps no other tree has sheltered as many people from the sun as the famous specimen of this fig in Santa Barbara, California, which covers several acres and even excels in size the famous banyan tree (another fig) which sheltered 7,000 men of Alexander's army.

Fraxinus americana: American ash, white ash. Zone 3. To 120 feet.

Because this tree is not fussy as to where it grows and seeds vigorously, experts are inclined to belittle it, yet it is the perfect tree for the home owner who wishes to save time, effort, and money. Its habit of shedding its leaves early is counted against it, yet this removes foliage in time to allow the owner to enjoy the warming autumn sun and to get rid of fallen leaves when temperatures are still above bone-chilling readings. It leafs out rather late in spring, again permitting the sun to warm the gardener as well as allowing grass underneath to get a start. Its autumn coloring, a deep purple, is unique.

Fraxinus ornus: Flowering ash. Zone 5. To 60 feet.

Far more appreciated in Europe than America, this tree blooms profusely: the fragrance of its blossoms is intense and lovely. The sap that exudes from the bark when injured is edible and used as chewing gum. It is, perhaps, the parent of the Moraine ash.

Fraxinus pennsylvanica: Green ash, river ash, red ash. Zone 3. To 60 feet.

Everything said about the American ash applies here: in addition, this species is hardier. Autumn foliage is yellow rather than purple. It is an excellent tree.

Ginkgo biloba: Maidenhair tree, ginkgo. Zone 4. To 120 feet.

This tree is a living fossil which has outlived all its enemies and acquired no new ones. Perhaps the best example of this I have seen is in Urbana, Illinois, where all the elms on one fine old property were killed by Dutch elm disease, leaving a magnificent specimen of ginkgo standing alone—sufficient in itself to ornament a large home. But be sure that you buy this tree from a reputable nursery who will guarantee that it is a grafted or budded male tree. Female trees bear foul-smelling fruits that will offend the neighbors and are a filthy mess if they fall on a mowed lawn.

Gleditsia triacanthos: Honey locust. Zone 4. To 100 feet.

Widely planted as a substitute for the American elm as a street and lawn tree, only the improved varieties of this tree, such as the Moraine locust, should be planted—those that do not bear fruit. My neighbor has a fruiting specimen that shares its pods with me—I collect some five bushels of them when they fall in spring. This is one tree under which a fairly satisfactory lawn can be grown—the light, airy foliage permits filtered sunshine to reach the grass.

Gordonia alatamaha: Franklin tree. Zone 5. To 20 feet.

This is a choice small evergreen for growing in warmer areas. Its principle feature is its late-blooming habit. The fragrant cup-shaped white flowers, 3 inches across, appear in autumn.

Gordonia lasianthus: Loblolly bay, bastard magnolia. Zone 8. To 60 feet.

Nearly an evergreen with baylike foliage, this tree has cup-shaped fragrant white flowers which bloom from July to August.

Grevillea robusta: Silk oak. Zone 10. To 150 feet.

Although an intriguing species, it is mentioned here only to warn newcomers to southern California against planting it as a street tree: it is messy because of its brittle wood which breaks in a heavy breeze.

Gymnocladus dioicus: Kentucky coffee tree. Zone 4. To 80 feet.

Its greenish white flowers are followed by ten-inch-long brownish pods that were used as a substitute for coffee in colonial days. But don't try it: the flavor is far from satisfying. Because of the pods, it is considered a dirty tree, but if planted where these will fall in shrubbery, it is worthwhile for its interesting shape on the winter landscape.

Halesia carolina: Carolina silver bell. Zone 4. To 30 feet.

Its unusual bell-shaped white flowers that appear in early spring are so fugitive that the value is low. It does best in sheltered woods and has good yellow autumn color.

Halesia monticola: Tisswood, mountain silver bell. Zone 5. To 45 feet in cultivation; wild trees often much taller.

A far more dramatic tree than the preceding, with larger flowers and more of them, this species is a favorite in England. It is practically free from disease and insect threats.

Hippophae rhamnoides: Sea buckthorn. Zone 3. To 30 feet.

This tree is grown principally for its bright yellow-orange berries which are not relished much by birds and remain, therefore, on the plant well into fall. Both male and female plants must be present if fruits are to be produced. It tolerates salt spray and has interesting gray-green foliage.

Hymenosporum flavum: Sweet shade. Zone 10. To 50 feet.

Characterized by its delightful fragrant flowers, yellow in color and appearing in June, this is a rapid-growing evergreen shade tree with no important insect or disease enemies.

Ilex aquifolium: English holly. Zone 6. To 70 feet, but usually much lower in cultivation in the United States.

This is *the* Christmas holly of tradition for which the American species is only a fair substitute. Unfortunately, it is not easy to grow north of Philadelphia except in favored locations. It needs an acid soil and both male and female plants must be planted if berries are wanted. Growth to tree size is slow.

Ilex opaca: American holly. Zone 5, but some selected varieties hardy in Zone 4. To 45 feet.

Improved varieties are tougher than you think: a plant sent to me in October by Paul Bosley of Mentor, Ohio, was carried around in a car for two weeks before it was planted hastily in unprepared soil. It has since survived and thrived through two winters. Where true English holly cannot be grown, some of these improved varieties are well worth considering.

Jacaranda acutifolia: Violet tree, Jacaranda. Zone 9. To 50 feet, but often grown as a tall shrub.

This is one time I personally envy those who live in warm climates and can grow this tree. Its violet-purple flowers, funnel-shaped and about 2 inches long, are borne in great masses in early summer. Almost evergreen, losing its lacy foliage for a short period in March, this tree is listed by some nurserymen as *J. mimosifolia.*

Juglans species:

The walnuts are listed here only to caution against their use by those who wish to save work. The nuts are a nuisance (and rarely edible) which only attract squirrels who then sit in the tree and husk them, dropping brown juice that stains clothing, concrete, and anything else it falls on. Even worse, fallen leaves are toxic to most vegetation, and growth under walnut trees is always poor. Far better trees are available.

Juniperus species:

One caution is needed about most junipers. When they grow in the vicinity of members of the rose family (crab apples, pears, hawthorns, etc.), they act as a sort of Typhoid Mary in one of the strangest of all plant diseases, juniper rust. In spring, small orange bits of matter growing on the juniper suddenly begin to sprout horns, and the entire mess swells into a bright orange blob of jellylike matter. These cedar "apples" then produce spores which are borne by the wind to nearby quinces, apples, pears, and hawthorns, where they produce the summer stage of this fungus. Slightly swollen areas on these plants turn orange and ooze an orange juice, then turn black. Severe infestations will defoliate entire trees, and if this continues for three years, they may die. Because of this complication, don't plant junipers if labor saving is important. They can be kept clean, of course, by following a strict sanitation program. Some species are immune.

Kalopanax pictus: Castor aralia. Zone 4. To 80 feet.

Why this tree is not more widely grown is puzzling. It is clean growing, vigorous, and has no insect or disease enemies. Its foliage resembles that of the maples or the sweet gum. Its autumn color is not distinctive—reddish—and its fruits are eaten so freely by birds that they are available for only a few days.

Lagerstroemia indica: Crepe myrtle, crape myrtle. Zone 7. To 20 feet.

Welcomed by Northerners who move South and miss the lilacs,

its huge trusses of bluish-violet, lavender, white, and red flowers create a lilac effect. The foliage resembles that of privet or the Persian lilac. One improtant difference: the bare trunks exhibit an interesting flaking pattern in winter.

Larix species:

Avoid the larches: While among the loveliest of trees when in spring foliage, they are attacked by so many disfiguring insects that they are a constant chore.

Laurus nobilis: True laurel, bay-leaf tree. Zone 8. To 25 feet.

Dense evergreen aromatic foliage makes this one of the choicest of all small trees. The strong essential oil in the leaves (the characteristic odor of bay rum) repels insects. Leaves when dried form the bay leaf of commerce.

Ligustrum lucidum: Glossy privet. Zone 7. To 30 feet.

Although usually thought of as a shrub (which it is when so grown), the glossy privet, when grown to a single trunk, develops into a most attractive small tree with nearly evergreen leaves up to 6 inches long. Its blue-black fruits in winter add to the picture.

Liquidambar styraciflua: Sweet gum, autumn flame tree, star gum. Zone 4. To 125 feet.

The home owner with a property big enough to support a mature specimen of this beautiful tree is to be envied. Give it room and it will be the glory of the autumn landscape. The fall color is not mere color: it is a chromatic explosion. The basic hue is a brilliant orange-scarlet, shaded with copper, gold, bronze, and hints of green. No two leaves are alike in color, but all blend to form a glorious whole.

Liriodendron tulipifera: Tulip tree, white poplar, whitewood. Zone 4. To 150 feet.

One specimen, estimated to be over 200 years old, has been measured at nearly 200 feet in height. A valuable landscape tree, it needs a rich, moist soil to grow well. The flowers do resemble tulips, but because they are greenish yellow with a slight touch of orange, they do not stand out as prominently as one might expect. These trees need the same care as magnolias in transplanting because of their fleshy roots.

Macadamia ternifolia: Queensland nut. Zone 10. To 30 feet.

This is another of the many fine evergreen trees available to Southern gardeners which, if grown with several trunks, each developing foliage from the ground up, becomes shrublike in appearance. To develop multiple trunks, nip out the growing tip on young specimens. Its one advantage is its ability to survive in dry climates. The nuts are edible and are a commercial crop in Hawaii.

Maclura pomifera: Osage orange, beau d'arc, prairie orange, bow dart. Zone 4. To 40 feet.

This tree is a complete nuisance if planted where its ball-like fruits, wrinkled and chartreuse green in color, can fall on drives and walks. As an impenetrable barrier hedge that is "horse-high, bull-strong, and pig-tight," nothing can equal it. Fruits and foliage contain a natural insecticide, so it is not troubled by pests. The fruits are collected eagerly by flower arrangers, but in order to have fruit, several trees must be planted together because the sexes are separate (if fruits are wanted).

Magnolia acuminata: Cucumber tree. Zone 4. To 80 feet.

Although the hardiest of our native magnolias, its flowers are not conspicuous. Since its large leaves are often disfigured if wind can whip them, plant in a sheltered spot. The common name comes from the resemblance of young fruits to cucumbers. A similar, but much lower, tree (to 30 feet) is *Magnolia cordata,* which has smaller leaves. It is hardy to Zone 5.

Magnolia salicifolia: Anise magnolia. Zone 4. To 30 feet.

Much more graceful than most magnolias as a tree, it has narrow leaves and flowers at an earlier age than other species do. Fragrant white flowers are nearly 6 inches across, with a purple base. Foliage has a lemony scent.

Magnolia soulangeana: Saucer magnolia, tulip tree. Zone 4. To 25 feet.

A well-grown specimen of this tree in full bloom in spring is as fine as anything in the floral kingdom. Its large flowers, like huge Darwin tulips, five to ten inches across, vary in color (in different varieties) from pristine white to deep purple. They appear before the leaves unfold. Its one fault is that it often blooms before the danger from frost is over, so that flowers are ruined.

Magnolia stellata: Star magnolia, water lily magnolia. Zone 4. To 15 feet.

Like the preceding, it often flowers too early and is nipped by late frost. If planted where it is shaded from the south in spring, it will flower later. The many-petaled pure-white flowers (pink in the variety rosea) open out flat. This is a real gem, best when treated as a specimen plant and set against a dark evergreen background.

Malus species:

Although flowering crab apples are among our most valuable small flowering trees, only a few species are mentioned here because of their susceptibility to disease. In general, the American natives are omitted because of their susceptibility to two diseases, cedar rust (described under *Juniperus*) and fire blight, a disease which can kill the entire tree. The Asiatic species are preferred because of their disease resistance.

Malus arnoldiana: Arnold crab. Zone 4. To 20 feet.

This is effective at two seasons. In spring, its rosy red buds and fragrant pink flowers are delightful. In fall, its yellow and red fruits hang on through September and October and are eaten eagerly by migrating birds.

Malus baccata: Siberian crab. Zone 2. To 40 feet.

The hardiest of all flowering crabs, its flowers are white. Its fruits are similar to those of the preceding, but mature earlier and are better for making jelly. Because it is grown in nurseries from seed, seedlings vary in many characteristics: chose it when in bloom and move it later with a ball of earth.

Malus "Dolgo": Zone 3. To 35 feet.

No crab has more jewellike fruits than does the Dolgo; they are vivid scarlet in color and glow like rubies in the sun. The fruits, which ripen in August, make excellent jelly.

Malus "Dorothea": Zone 4. To 25 feet.

This is *the* variety to replace the beautiful but disease-ridden variety, Bechtel's double-flowering crab. Dorothea drops clean, whereas the faded flowers of Bechtel's crab cling and form an unsightly mess. Another advantage is that Dorothea produces fruit, unusual in a double variety. Most double varieties are sterile. The blossoms are a bright pink or rosy crimson. Although of American origin, it is quite resistant to cedar rust.

Malus floribunda: Japanese flowering crab. Zone 4. To 30 feet.

A sure-fire variety that will please everyone, this tree has no serious faults. Its rich pink buds open and then gradually fade to white. The yellow and red fruit clings until October unless eaten by migrating birds.

Malus "Hopa": Hopa crab. Zone 4. To 25 feet.

Another dual-purpose crab, this tree is both ornamental and good for jelly. Hopa jelly is particularly attractive because the fruit flesh is purplish which imparts to it a beautiful burgundy tinge. Foliage has a purplish tinge also; the flowers are purplish pink.

Malus hupehensis: Tea crab. Zone 4. To 20 feet.

Some nursery catalogs still list this as *Malus theifera.* If allowed to grow without pruning, it forms a perfect vase-shaped tree. It has deep pink flowers, fading to white, and its leaves are used for tea in China: after trying them, I wonder why! It is mainly valuable for its picturesque form and free bloom.

Malus purpurea aldenhamensis: Aldenham crab. Zone 4. To 25 feet.

One of the best of the so-called purple crabs for smaller properties, this tree sometimes repeats flowering in late fall if the weather is favorable. The purplish fruit is not conspicuous but clings until mid-October.

Maytenus boaria: Chilean mayten tree. Zone 9. To 35 feet.

It differs from the many fine evergreen trees available in California in that it has *light* green foliage and is hardier farther north. With its drooping branches, it makes an interesting specimen plant.

Melaleuca leucadendron: Cajeput tree, bottle brush tree, tea tree. Zone 9. To 35 feet.

This tree yields an essential oil used in medicine, and like so many other trees that produce such oils, insects rarely attack it. Foliage is evergreen. Flowers are bottle brush in form in spikes to 6 inches long. The bark peels off in thin gray strips. It tolerates salt spray in seaside plantings.

Melia azedarach: Chinaberry. Zone 7. To 40 feet.

This is mentioned only to damn it, but with faint praise. Short-lived, dirty, and ugly in form, it is, yet, a dependable shade producer. Perhaps my opinion is colored by the first specimen I ever saw—a scrawny specimen growing in front of an unpainted sharecropper's shanty with the ground underneath littered with fallen fruits and leaves.

Metasequoia glyptostroboides: Dawn redwood. Zone 5. To 100 feet.

This is the zone rating given by several experts, but this tree is also growing well in Zone 4 in several instances. This, like the ginkgo tree, is a living fossil, known for years by botanists only from rock imprints but discovered and identified in 1945. It resembles the true redwood from California in leaf but is somewhat more pyramidal in early growth. Although this is a fascinating conversation piece, I am not particularly impressed with its landscape value: it is an upright, rather narrow tree with widely spaced branches. How it will look a hundred years from now, nobody in America knows. The only mature trees are in a remote section of China. Perhaps a specimen on a large property would be desirable, but certainly not as the only fine tree on a smaller lot.

Morus species: Mulberry.

Avoid all mulberries as you would the plague. They are dirty trees, dropping fruits that stain clothing and cement, are easily broken in high winds, and are hard to prune to graceful forms. Their only value is as a source of food for birds.

Myrica californica: California bayberry. Zone 7. To 25 feet.

This is another of the fine small evergreens available to Pacific

Coast gardeners, but with bronzy foliage. The purple berries are attractive in early winter, but trees of both sexes are needed to produce them. It has practically no pests.

Myrica cerifera: Wax myrtle, tallow tree, bayberry tree. Zone 6. To 30 feet.

This is better grown as a tall shrub than a tree, but it can be pruned to a single stem. Its small gray-green berries can be used to make bayberry candles, though the yield of wax is small. It tends to be an evergreen from the Carolinas south.

Nyssa sylvatica: Black gum, sour gum, tupelo, pepperidge tree. Zone 4. To 90 feet.

Like the sweet gum, this tree becomes a glorious pillar of fire in fall, turning from brilliant orange to fiery scarlet. Needs careful pruning when young to shape the top. Tolerates seaside conditions.

Oxydendrum arboreum: Sourwood, sorrel tree. Zone 4. To 50 feet.

Largely a tree of the Eastern seaboard, it is found only on acid soils. It is a quality tree for landscaping which has foliage like that of its mountain laurel relatives, flowers which are bell-shaped, white, and in racemes, and brilliant autumn color, ranging from vivid scarlet to bright crimson.

Parrotia persica: Iron tree. Zone 5. To 15 feet.

In Persia, this tree is a giant of 50 feet, but is smaller when grown in the United States. Its foliage resembles that of the witch hazels and it has interesting horizontal branching. It is at its best in autumn when its foliage turns bright scarlet, gold, and orange. The bark peels off in interesting patterns.

Paulownia tomentosa: Empress tree, royal paulownia. Zone 5. To 50 feet.

This is sometimes called the violet catalpa because its clusters of bright violet flowers are borne in clusters like those of the true catalpa and closely resemble them in appearance. Although coarse in appearance, it can be forgiven its faults because of the glorious appearance of the tree when in full bloom. Not usually a reliable bloomer north of Philadelphia, some specimens have survived along the Hudson for decades, without flowering.

Phellodendron amurense: Amur cork tree. Zone 4. To 40 feet.

A much-neglected tree of moderate stature, it has few enemies. The rugged bark at one time was considered as a source of cork, but when this failed to prove economical, the species lapsed into the background. It also throws a fine shade, and is fairly rapid in growth.

Phoenix canariensis: Canary Island palm. Zone 9. To 60 feet.

Although one of the hardiest of all palms, it does need a rich soil to do well. It is a favorite street tree in California. The enormous leaves, sometimes 20 feet long, would seem to be a hazard if they dropped on the heads of passers-by, but I have seen no reports on this possibility.

Phoenix reclinata: Senegal date palm, Spiny feather palm. Zone 10. To 20 feet.

Not as hardy as the preceding, it tends to form multiple trunks. Fruits are not edible.

Picea abies: Norway spruce. Zone 2. To 150 feet, but much lower in cultivation.

If you don't care what happens to a planting after twenty-five years, this is a good evergreen, but if you are planting for posterity as well as for your own pleasure—don't buy it. Sooner or later, the upper branches thin out, most of the lower ones die off, and those that are left droop in a funereal manner. Everywhere you can see the unfortunate effect of using this species for planting near the front door of a home. It is a forest tree which cannot, by any known method of pruning, be kept down to manageable height.

Picea glauca densata: Black Hills spruce. Zone 2. To 40 feet.

Naturally lower in habit than most spruces, this is one of the best, particularly if a seedling with good color is selected (it does vary in color).

Picea pungens: Colorado spruce. Zone 2. To 100 feet, but lower in cultivation.

The variety Moerheim spruce is more compact and denser growing than this type. Unfortunately, none of its varieties age gracefully. Again, look down any street in an older community in northeastern United States and you will see dozens of horrible examples of its misuse as a dooryard tree. It belongs in the background where its form and color can be seen as a whole.

Pinus bungeana: Lace bark pine. Zone 4. To 60 feet.

Desirable for its striking bark which peels off in interesting patches to expose a cream-colored inner bark, this tree is best when grown with several trunks, a common form of this evergreen. It is slow-growing, an advantage in that it does not grow too large for its place rapidly, as do too many pines.

Pinus canariensis: Canary Island pine. Zone 9. To 75 feet.

The needles are bluish green when young and are about 12 inches long. It grows well on the drier soils in southern Texas and California.

Pinus cembra: Swiss stone pine. Zone 2. To 60 feet.

This tree grows very slowly: it should be planted as an older specimen if possible. It is more formal in habit than are most pines.

Pinus nigra: Austrian pine. Zone 4. To 80 feet.

If it were not for borer attacks, this would be an excellent evergreen, one of the best for making tall, tight windbreaks and background plantings. It is also a rapid grower.

Pinus resinosa: Red pine, Norway pine. Zone 2. To 70 feet.

Check with a local tree man to see if the pine bud moth is a pest in your area: if it is, don't plant this species, or be ready to spray annually. A handsome, upright tree with reddish bark that is particularly attractive when snow is on the ground, this is a more graceful tree than the Austrian pine.

Pinus thunbergii: Japanese black pine. Zone 4. To 80 feet.

Although it is not at all attractive, it is included here because of its ability to tolerate salt spray—it is the only pine safe to plant near exposed beaches. It quickly takes on picturesque forms when windblown.

Pistacia chinensis: Chinese pistachio. Zone 9. To 40 feet.

This is not the tree that produces the edible nut of commerce (*Pistacia vera*), but it is still a desirable shade tree. Striking red fruits borne in clusters are produced only by female trees. This species is deciduous. Seeds can be squeezed for an edible oil. Some people seem to be sensitive to the foliage, although in the Orient, leaf buds are sometimes boiled for food. A tree in full leaf is handsome. It has no known insect or disease pests.

Pittosporum rhombifolium: Diamond leaf, Queensland tree. Zone 10. To 40 feet in America.

Excellent glossy evergreen foliage and clean growth make this a highly attractive tree. The ivory-colored flowers are fragrant and are followed by orange-yellow fruits.

Platanus acerifolia: London plane tree. Zone 5. To 100 feet.

An excellent tree for city streets, it is not subject to the twig blight which makes our native sycamore undesirable. All *Platanus* species, however, shed hairs in spring which cause nasal and throat irritation in some individuals. The peeling bark is picturesque, but the ball-like fruits can be a nuisance, although they are not produced as freely as those of the sycamore.

Platanus orientalis: Oriental plane tree. Zone 5. To 90 feet.

If it were not so large, this would be a desirable street tree, but its huge trunks can present a problem on narrow parkways. It is quite similar to the London plane tree.

Platanus occidentalis: American plane tree, sycamore, buttonwood. Zone 5. To 120 feet.

This is much too messy a tree for anyone who wants to save work, although its huge trunk and towering branches make it a striking tree "along the Wabash."

Podocarpus macrophyllus: False yew. Zone 7. To 50 feet.

Its needles resemble those of the yew, but are much coarser. This is a desirable evergreen for tall screens or sheared hedges in the South.

Populus species:

Unless you live on the Great Plains or in other areas hostile to tree growth, forget the poplars. The first tree I could recognize was a Carolina poplar, which had been planted on the streets of a nearby subdivision. Twenty-five years later, not a single tree was alive. All poplars are weak-wooded, dirty when in fruit, and when the "cotton" begins to blow, a complete nuisance.

Prunus species:

Although there are some lovely small flowering trees among the cherries, plums, and apricots, it is my duty to warn you against them if you are not interested in spending extra time on their care. Like other members of the rose family, they are susceptible to scale, borers, and canker worms. In addition, all are short-lived.

Pseudolarix amabilis: Golden larch. Zone 5. To 120 feet.

If it were only smaller in stature, this would be a marvelous landscape subject. It is attacked by no known insects or diseases. The foliage is a lovely soft green in spring, turning a clear golden yellow in fall. Unfortunately, it spreads out forty to fifty feet in width, hardly a tree for a suburban lot, but give it room and it is magnificent.

Pseudotsuga taxifolia: Douglas fir. Zone 4. To 300 feet.

This is one of America's tallest native trees, but even in its native Northwest, it will only grow about a foot a year for the first half of its life. There are two forms of this—the coast variety which is only hardy to Zone 6 and the mountain form which survives in Zone 4. This is the perfect species to plant near the front of your home to use as a living Christmas tree. It will hardly reach 75 feet in your lifetime.

Pyrus calleryana: Chinese sand pear. Zone 4. To 50 feet.

Largely used as an understock for grafting other pears, it is still a fine ornamental in its own right. The variety Bradford, introduced by the USDA, is the most uniform type in growth. A peculiarity of this fine tree, with its fresh glossy green foliage, is that its autumn color varies with the region in which it is grown. I obtained twenty-five trees from the original tree in this country, which stands on the grounds of the Glenn Dale station of the USDA. That tree had the most glorious autumn color I have ever seen—pure gold inside, shading to orange, and on the outer layer of leaves, an incandescent scarlet. Yet not one of my trees has ever shown any good autumn color. If frost holds off until late, a few leaves may turn a dull maroon, but that is all. But trees from the same lot as mine, grown in California, repeat the color show of the parent tree. This species and the following are never affected by fire blight. Fruit is worthless. Probably at its best along the East Coast and in California.

Pyrus ussuriensis: Manchurian sand pear. Zone 4. To 50 feet.

Much like the above in every way, it is slightly hardier. Also, its flower buds are pink before opening.

Quercus alba: White oak. Zone 4. To 90 feet.

Perhaps the most majestic tree you can hope to see is an ancient "pasture" oak—a tree left standing in a field when the rest of the forest had been destroyed or that grew naturally in the open. It is particularly fine in winter when its branches seem to defy wind and snow. But don't expect to produce such a tree from a sapling in your lifetime: the white oak is not in a hurry. A five-foot sapling will grow to about 15 to 18 feet in twenty years, too slow for a man in a hurry. For the "feel" of the white oak, with none of its sluggish growth, consider the pin oak.

Quercus borealis: Red oak, northern red oak. Zone 4. To 75 feet.

An excellent shade tree and one that transplants readily, it is the fastest growing of all the oaks.

Quercus laurifolia: Laurel oak. Zone 7. To 60 feet.

One of the better street trees for the South, its clean, dark green foliage is practically evergreen. It is also faster growing than most oaks.

Quercus palustris: Pin oak, swamp Spanish oak. Zone 4. To 80 feet.

As easy to transplant as a box elder, the pin oak is perhaps our most desirable species. It has no taproot. It prefers a deep, moist soil slightly on the acid side. It can be kept from developing chlorotic (yellow) foliage in the Middle West by regular feeding with a solution of ferrous ammonium sulfate or with a chelated iron compound. It is worthless as a street tree unless a parkway at least 40 feet across is to be planted. Its low sweeping branches would make passage impossible otherwise. This species grows faster than an American elm.

Quercus virginiana: Live oak. Zone 7. To 60 feet.

This is the tree that supplied our colonial navy with stout timbers for keels and ribs. It forms a tremendous mound at maturity, about half again as wide as it is tall. Thus a mature 60-foot tree would have a spread of at least 90 feet, something to consider when placing it. Evergreen in the South, where it is a favorite street tree, it is deciduous farther north.

Roystonea regia: Royal palm. Zone 10. To 70 feet.

This lovely palm epitomizes the tropics for many Americans—a graceful yet stately column of grayish ivory that gleams in the sun and is topped by a canopy of feathery foliage.

Salix species:

The willows as a group should be shunned by anyone trying to reduce hours spent in yard work. I estimate that my own five willows (plus one pussy willow) require at least five hours of work each during the growing season, the equivalent of two lost weekends. Spring finds the lawn underneath littered with fallen twigs. A windstorm calls for an inspection to discover broken branches, often several inches in diameter. Trimming off drooping branches so the lawn can be mowed underneath is another chore. Worst of all—fighting aphids and other insect pests which adore willows. For some time, I kept them pest free by treating with a systemic insecticide (samples given me from various manufacturers of such products), but now that I must buy this, I find the cost prohibitive. Still, the sight of golden twigs in spring, flushed with a faint chartreuse lace of new leaves, is worth the physical effort to me. But be warned!

Salix caprea: Goat willow, sallow, pussy willow. Zone 4. To 25 feet.

I would make an exception of this one willow—although it makes a poor tree, everyone needs the lift that comes from the sight of the golden stamens filming the gray underneath of catkins in early spring. Best procedure for growing this is to buy a bunch of pussy willows from a florist in the spring and plant one of the twigs in damp soil: it should be a full-sized tree in two or three years. The reason for actually seeing the catkins before you plant is that only male trees produce the attractive ones: female catkins are greenish gray and less attractive.

Sassafras albidum: Sassafras, tea tree. Zone 4. To 50 feet.

Although a difficult tree to transplant, the sassafras belongs in any planting designed to display autumn color at its best. Its mitten-shaped leaves turn the most brilliant scarlet imaginable, with an underglow of golden orange. Give it room and it will make a fine specimen, a far cry from the crowded trees usually seen in the wild. Like most trees that produce aromatic oils, it does not suffer from insect pests.

Schinus molle: Mastic tree, California pepper tree, Peruvian mastic. Zone 9. To 30 feet.

Newcomers to warm climates need to be warned of the faults of this tree, which may not be apparent in well-cared-for specimens. Although a strong grower and able to thrive under neglect, it is a dirty tree, shedding twigs and leaves freely. Its worst fault is that it acts as an incubator for black scale. If you have citrus trees anywhere near, beware!

Sciandopitys verticillata: Japanese umbrella pine. Zone 5. To 120 feet.

One of the slowest-growing needled evergreens of dense habit, this is a neat tree that does not get out of hand. It is popular when trained as a bonsai specimen—typically Japanese in form. In the United States, I have never seen a specimen taller than 25 feet, but in Japan this would be a forest giant.

Sequoia gigantea: Big tree, giant redwood. Zone 6. To 300 feet.

Botanists have kicked this around from one genus to another (in England, they still call it a *Cunninghami*), but it is usually catalogued under the name I am using. Correctly, it is probably now *Sequoiadendron gigantea.* Whatever its name, it is one of the glories of the tree world, but not for the small estate. A single tree needs at least two acres to be displayed properly. It probably would not survive much more than a hundred miles from the sea: damp winds seem to be necessary to permit its tremendous vascular system to function.

Sequoia sempervirens: Coast redwood. Zone 7. To 365 feet.

The world's tallest (but not bulkiest) tree, this is somewhat less hardy than the preceding species, but otherwise quite similar.

Sophora japonica: Chinese scholar tree, Japanese pagoda tree. Zone 5. To 50 feet.

Why this handsome tree is not more frequently planted is a mystery. A clean tree with no important insect enemies, surviving in city smoke (up to a degree), its greatest asset is its late-flowering habit. In late summer it is covered with spires of ivory white pealike flowers. They are followed by seed pods that remain on the tree late in winter.

Sorbus species:

As much as I admire a fine specimen of the mountain ash, I always pity the owner, who has probably spent hours probing the trunk for borers. So susceptible are these trees to borers that unless they are treated at least twice a year, they are not safe. In addition, San Jose scale is a constant menace.

Stenolobium stans: Yellow bells, Florida yellow trumpet. Zone 10. To 18 feet.

Related to the trumpet vine, this bears similar flowers which are about 2 inches long and bright yellow in color. It flowers in fall.

Syringa amurensis: Japanese tree lilac. Zone 3. To 30 feet.

Don't plant this expecting to have lilac-fragrant flowers on a tree: the flowers are not pleasantly fragrant. Blooms in July. In some areas, lilac borers and scale are a problem, although its value as a conversation piece makes it almost worth the effort needed to keep it healthy.

Taxus species:

While the yew trees of England are legendary, for all practical purposes yews are shrublike in the United States. See under "Evergreens." If you expect to live for 100 to 200 years, you can, of course, grow this as a tree. There is an outstanding specimen in Colonial Williamsburg.

Tilia cordata: Lime tree, little-leaf linden. Zone 3. To 75 feet.

This is the lime tree so often mentioned in English literature. It forms a densely conical tree with thick foliage—a perfect shade tree. It is one of the best street trees, except that it is somewhat slow-growing.

Tilia europaea: European linden. Zone 3. To 90 feet.

Except for its habit of suckering,* this is almost as good a tree as the preceding, and since it is faster growing, it is even more desirable when quicker effects are wanted.

Tilia tomentosa: Silver linden, white linden. Zone 4. To 90 feet.

One of the finest of all shade trees, it has a neat, disciplined outline —a broad, dense pyramid. The fine hairs on the leaves show white when stirred by a breeze. They do, however, catch soot, making this a poor tree for sooty cities. The blossoms, unfortunately, contain a poison that will kill bees. A related species, *Tilia petiolaris,* is even more beautiful, with delicately drooping branches, but is rarely offered by commercial nurseries. It is somewhat difficult to propagate.

Tsuga canadensis: Canadian hemlock. Zone 3. To 50 feet.

If this tree would only tolerate drier air, it would perhaps be the most widely planted species in America. Its graceful cone form, with softly drooping branches and delicate green foliage, makes it a picture of the ideal evergreen tree. This is (within its natural range) the perfect plant for evergreen hedges. It tolerates shearing as only one other species—*Taxus*—can do. In Canadian woods it sometimes attains a height of 90 feet.

Tsuga caroliniana: Spruce pine, Carolina hemlock. Zone 4. To 40 feet.

In addition to meeting all the requirements of the Canadian hemlock, this species is more tolerant of city conditions. It is, however, slightly less hardy and lower in height.

Ulmus species:

Under present-day conditions, with Dutch elm disease endemic over most of the eastern half of the United States, only the foolhardy would plant trees of this genus. True, the disease can be stemmed by constant preventive spraying, but this brings the wrath of the bird

*A plant which "suckers" produces shoots from its roots which are near the surface when these have been bruised or cut, usually by a lawn mower.

lovers who fail to realize that once the trees are dead, the birds will also disappear. The exceptions to the rule of not planting elms are noted below.

Ulmus parvifolia: Chinese elm. Zone 5. To 40 feet.

Not to be confused with the Siberian elm, this is a hardier, but less attractive, tree. The Chinese elm, particularly the evergreen variety grown in California, is fast growing, clean, and does not break up as readily as the more brittle Siberian variety. Both will grow on rather dry soils.

Ulmus pumila: Siberian elm. Zone 4. To 60 feet.

This tree is most useful as a windbreak on the Great Plains, even though high winds will snap off its branches readily. It is a fast-growing tree and easy to establish. Both it and the Chinese elm, although somewhat resistant to Dutch elm disease, can be infected by the causative fungus. Unfortunately, it takes several years to die, during which time it acts as a source of infection for hundreds of yards around.

Viburnum lentago: Nannyberry, wayfarer tree. Zone 2. To 20 feet.

Usually grown as a shrub, this is a useful small tree when trained to a single trunk. A fine specimen which is growing on a neighbor's property—but in sight of our windows—gives us great enjoyment for a short period of the year when migrating cedar waxwings fly over, soon stripping it of every black berry. The white flowers, which form in flattish clusters, are handsome in spring.

Zelkova serrata: False elm, Japanese zelkova. Zone 5. To 90 feet.

Because its foliage resembles that of the American elm (it is closely related), it is often recommended to replace that species lost to the Dutch elm disease, especially when a long line of trees must be filled out. Unfortunately, it differs in shape, and although its lower limbs can be trimmed up, it is not a perfect substitute. It is, however, an excellent shade tree in its own right. Older trees shed their bark in patches. In Japan, the wood is preferred for building jinrikishas, and as a base for lacquered objects.

PLANTING TREES

One of the best ways to save future work is to spend a few extra minutes making the original planting. The future growth of a tree is determined largely by its first few months in a new location. Too, if not kept moist, wood surrounding the vascular bundles that transmit water will harden and reduce flow of nutrients to the branches and foliage. This hardening is irreversible. If it is checked then, it will seldom produce a satisfactory root system and will be permanently stunted. Here are steps that professional landscapers (who must guarantee what they plant) take care to do right:

1. Provide proper drainage: Except for a few species, such as willows and alders, that have special root structures enabling them to survive with their roots in water, trees cannot survive without air. The most common mistake is failing to provide a way for water to get out of the hole dug for the tree. If the surrounding soil happens to be a tight clay or even a rich loam, that hole, often quite ample in size, when filled with looser soil will merely act as a sump into which the drainage from surrounding surfaces will run. Consequently, always be sure there is an outlet for subsoil water, even if you must lay a line of drain tile from the hole to a lower point to furnish this.

2. Be sure the soil used for filling the hole is thoroughly prepared so that it is loose, rich, and adequately supplied with plant food. Remember, once a shade tree is planted, the soil around and beneath it may not be exposed again for a hundred years or more. Here is one place where long-lasting fertilizers, such as phosphorus and potash, must be supplied, once and for all. Phosphorus in particular is important, since it does not move downward in soil, but remains where placed originally.

Before filling in the hole, be sure the bottom contains enriched soil. This is difficult to do when planting balled-and-burlapped stock because if the enriched soil is loose, the ball may sink and the tree will be standing lower than it should, below the enriched soil. A trick I use to prevent this is to give the ball a small but solid base by erecting a small column of eight bricks (four on each tier) onto which the ball is set. Now soil can be pushed under the ball and washed in around the roots without fear of that ball sinking.

3. Provide solid support for the top and trunk of all newly set trees. Even bare branches offer some resistance to wind, which causes the entire top to sway. As tiny hair roots form, vital to future growth, this swaying will break off many of them. For young saplings, a single stake driven alongside the trunk will be sufficient, but for larger specimens, this is useless. I prefer to use three pieces of something solid (such as pieces of old electrical conduit I have salvaged for this purpose) which I set in the form of a tepee with its apex at least halfway up the tree.

4. Settle the soil around the tree with plenty of water, but avoid water-logging it. From now on, the biggest factor in success will be keeping that soil constantly moist, but never drowned out. Dig down

occasionally to see how moisture conditions are six inches or more below the surface: don't judge solely by surface appearance.

5. Wrap the trunk with one of the creped kraft-paper tree wraps. This serves two purposes. First, it keeps the bark moist and cool, which helps the tree move water and food up the trunk more freely. Dry bark cannot transport these vital elements. Perhaps most of the losses of newly planted trees are the result of the drying out of the vascular system of the plant. Second, it prevents borers and other insects from attacking the bark at a time when it is particularly vulnerable.

6. Avoid applying fertilizers until the tree has had a chance to form a new root system. If the soil was properly enriched in planting, no further feeding should be needed until the following year.

7. When planting trees in full leaf with a ball of earth, use one of the antidesiccant sprays that prevent excess water loss through the foliage.

SHRUBS FOR EASIER MAINTENANCE

In a misguided effort to eliminate labor and expense in home landscape upkeep, many a gardener has filled up his property with shrubs only to find that he has not only taken on more than he had bargained for, but that he had so filled the available space with woody plants that no room was left for the beauty of flowers.

Nonetheless, shrubs are the backbone of a good landscaping scheme, and their careful selection will determine for years to come the hours of labor that will be needed to keep them presentable.

Again, as in the case of trees, my purpose has been to eliminate those species which are time-consuming and which require special attention to keep them growing well. At times, the choice will be difficult. For example, who would want to eliminate the glory of spring shrubbery which results from the lavish use of lilacs? Yet against their inclusion in the landscape picture must be weighed their need for constant attention to eliminate scale, their lack of resistance to borer invasion, and their need for removal of faded flowers, and their sensitivity to mildew infection in fall.

Thus every list of easy-care shrubs must make some concessions to beauty, to personal preferences—and this one will be no exception.

Abelia grandiflora: Bush arbutus, glossy abelia. Zone 6. To 3 to 6 feet.

Immediately, I am faced with a conflict between my personal taste and the need for making a disinterested evaluation. My attempts to grow abelia—the struggle to keep the plant alive, to prune out winter-injured wood, and to see the feeble showing of bloom for all this effort—has hardly been worth the effort. When, however, I have seen this plant in the South, with its glossy evergreen foliage and almost continuous bloom, I cannot fault it too much. If I have any criticism of it, it would be the weakness of the color of the blooms—they are neither a good pink nor a clean white. Yet it is a non-demanding, easy-to-grow shrub in the South.

Acanthopanax pentaphyllum: Angelica shrub, five-leaved aralia. Zone 4. To 8 feet.

This is a stiff, awkward shrub, but it is so undemanding that it must be listed herein. It has bold five-parted foliage resembling that of the aralia and is an excellent shrub for city use because it tolerates smoke and dirt. It survives well in shaded situations.

Acer japonicum: Japanese maple, full-moon maple. Zone 7. To 12 feet.

Although less commonly seen than the true Japanese maple (see below), this is a useful shrub because of its normally low growth. It can be sheared to a height of 3 or 4 feet and will still thrive. The variety *filicifolium* has beautiful threadlike cut foliage. The variety aureum is a clear yellow until midsummer, then turns green. Both varieties turn a gorgeous scarlet in fall.

Acer palmatum: True Japanese maple. Zone 5. To 20 feet.

One of the gems of the shrub world, it has many varieties ranging in color from soft light green through pink, scarlet, crimson, and purple to bronze. It will do well in sheltered positions in Zone 4 if not exposed to winter sunshine.

Aesculus parviflora: Bottle-brush buckeye. Zone 4. To 12 feet.

This is a bold, majestic shrub for properties where it can be given room. Often spreading to a width of 20 feet, it produces candles of tiny white flowers in July and August, when other shrub flowers are scarce. Some consider the foliage coarse, but it is in scale with the size of the shrub.

Alnus incana: Speckled alder. Zone 3. To 20 feet.

The alders are particularly lovely in spring when the delicate lettuce-green foliage contrasts with the fading catkins. In the wild, this can grow to a 60-foot tree, but it can also be maintained at shrub height if wanted. It must have soil that is constantly damp to do well.

Amelanchier canadensis: Shadblow, shadbush, apple serviceberry. Zone 4. To 20 feet.

For many New Englanders, spring does not arrive until the shadblow blooms. The flowers come before the foliage, wreathing the branches in a cloud of white. The fruit is a maroon-purple berry, edible, but rather tasteless.

Amelanchier stolonifera: Running shadbush, running serviceberry. Zone 3. To 8 feet.

This is a good shrub to bind loose sand banks because it suckers freely. It is worth growing for its tremendous crop of sweet, purplish black berries which once formed a staple food for the American Indian.

Aralia spinosa: Devil's walking stick. Zone 5. To 15 feet.

Similar to the species listed among trees, this species is easier to maintain at shrub height. With its heavier, stouter thorns, it is the perfect shrub to use where an impenetrable barrier must be set up—even the boldest trespasser would avoid this species. Ivory white flowers are produced in tremendous panicles in August.

Ardisia crispa: Coral berry. Zone 8. To 1 foot.

Grown principally for its bright coral-red berries which resemble those of holly but last longer, this makes an excellent edging plant for shrub borders in the South. Its evergreen foliage is glossy with wavy margins.

Aronia arbutifolia: Red chokeberry. Zone 4. To 8 feet.

A showy-fruited shrub with no major enemies, it is at its best in September.

Aronia melanocarpa: Black chokeberry. Chokecherry. Zone 4. To 6 feet.

Although its fruits do not last as long as those of the preceding, it is equally attractive.

Aucuba japonica: Gold-dust tree. Zone 7. To 10 feet tall.

The scarlet berries of this shrub are produced only on female plants, but the males are just as attractive in foliage—a fresh green color dotted with golden spots. They prefer a half-shaded situation.

Azalea species:

The azaleas are properly rhododendrons, although in commerce the two groups are separated. Because they generally require special care which complicates the schedule of a busy gardener, they are not covered here.

Benzoin aestivale: Spicebush, Benjamin bush. Zone 4. To 10 feet.

Sometimes catalogued as *Lindera benzoin,* it is one of the first heralds of spring, sending out its tiny greenish white flowers on leafless branches in March. It is equally interesting in fall when its foliage turns golden yellow. The spicy red fruits ripen in October. An old-fashioned favorite, its berries were used as a spice during the Civil War, the flavor is similar to that of allspice).

Berberis aggregata: Salmon barberry. Zone 6. To 8 feet.

A densely branched spiny shrub, deciduous with salmon-colored berries in fall, this makes an excellent hedge plant as an alternate (where it is hardy) to the much-overused Japanese barberry.

Berberis buxifolia: Magellan barberry. Zone 7. To 8 feet but usually lower.

An evergreen shrub with purple berries, it is grown mainly along the Pacific Coast.

Berberis darwinii: Darwin barberry. Zone 8. To 6 feet.

A striking evergreen barberry with deep green foliage, it has yellow flowers which are followed by purple fruits.

Berberis julianae: Wintergreen barberry. Zone 5. To 6 feet.

The hardiest of the evergreen barberries and a handsome shrub, it is the parent of several modern hybrids. It has dark glossy foliage and its fruit is a dark blue berry with a conspicuous bloom.

Berberis mentorensis: Mentor barberry. Zone 4. To 3 to 5 feet.

A semievergreen hybrid between the preceding and the Japanese barberry, this shrub forms a stiff, impenetrable hedge.

Berberis thunbergii: Japanese barberry. Zone 3. To 6 feet.

If it were not so widely planted as to be almost banal, this would be a choice shrub. Its bright red fruits cling until March (birds either do not relish them much or are unable to reach them through the thorns). The plant can be sheared like boxwood. Many varieties of it are available.

Buddleia davidi: Butterfly bush, summer lilac. Zone 5. To 5 feet in the North; 10 feet in the South.

In the North, this dies to the ground by freezing every winter, but south of the Ohio River, its tops remain alive and attain a greater height. No other shrub blooms so abundantly over so long a period of time. A well-grown plant will be at least as wide as it is tall, so allow plenty of room. The name *summer lilac* describes the flowers, which come in white, purple, red, pink, and lavender shades.

Buxus japonica koreana: Korean boxwood. Zone 4. To 2 feet.

Usually catalogued under the name given, it is botanically known as *Buxus microphylla koreana.* A well-grown specimen in summer is the equal of the finest English box of the same size, but in winter, this species turns a dull olive-green which is not at all attractive. The color change can sometimes be prevented (if this is necessary) by spraying with one of the latex antidesiccants.

Buxus sempervirens: Common boxwood, English boxwood. Zone 6. To 25 feet, but only after a century or more.

This is one of the world's most treasured shrubs, although some object to the odor of the dark, glossy evergreen foliage, calling it catlike. The box-leaf miner, once considered a serious drawback to its culture, is now easily controlled with a systemic insecticide. The cost of such controls, however, is fairly high and should be considered before selecting boxwood for the home landscape.

Callicarpa americana: French mulberry. Zone 6. To 6 feet.

This is a native species in spite of its "French" common name. Its fruits are a reddish violet, but are not as striking as those of the following.

Callicarpa purpurea: Hardy beautyberry. Zone 5. To 4 feet.

To those seeing its violet-purple berries for the first time, this is an amazing shrub, particularly in September and October when they shine like jewels.

Callistemon lanceolatus: Bottle brush, Lemon bush. Zone 8. To 15 feet, but usually lower.

The distinctive flowers that resemble a bottle brush, the lemon odor of the leaves, and the ease with which they grow on lighter soils make this a species for special situations. The one objection to it are the unsightly seed capsules that cling to the plant for a year or two.

Callistemon speciosus: Zone 8. To 15 feet.

This is the showiest of the bottle brushes, but in other respects like the preceding except that it is more difficult to keep low. It can be trained as a tree.

Calluna vulgaris: Scotch heather. Zone 5. To 3 feet.

This shrubby perennial is worth testing wherever full sun, moist air, and sandy soils make other plants difficult to grow.

Calycanthus floridus: Carolina allspice, sweet shrub, Strawberry shrub, sweet Betsy. Zone 5. To 8 feet.

An old-fashioned shrub dating from colonial days, it was loved for its odd chocolate-colored flowers which emit a spicy fragrance when crushed. When Southerners mention "shrub" without any qualification, this is the plant they mean. It grows best in partial shade.

Camellia japonica: Camellia, Japonica. Zone 7. To 25 feet, but usually much lower.

Those looking for pestfree shrubs should know the camellias are susceptible to a petal blight, to scale, and to mealy bugs. For this reason, they are not covered here. The oldest specimens in the United States, in Middleton Gardens, Charleston, South Carolina, are 45 feet tall after two centuries.

Caragana arborescens: Siberian peatree, pea shrub. Zone 2. To 20 feet.

Although often grown as a tree, this is best as a many-branched shrub. Its flowers are bright yellow, pealike, and borne freely in June. Almost indispensable in exposed plantings of the Great Prairies, it tolerates drought and blistering heat as well as subzero cold. At the same time, it is a delightful tall shrub in less rigorous climates.

Carpenteria californica: California mock orange. Zone 8. To 10 feet.

This is an excellent shrub for hot, dry places where the eastern mock orange cannot be grown. Its flowers are larger than those of the mock orange, but otherwise similar and fragrant.

Caryopteris incana: Bluebeard, blue spirea, verbena shrub, Chinese beardwort. Zone 6. To 6 feet.

Two things commend this shrub to the gardener—it has blue flowers, not too common on woody plants and it flowers late (in September as a rule). Its common names describe its flowers. It must have well-drained soil and a position in full sun at the northern limit of its range.

Ceanothus americanus: New Jersey tea, Jersey tea. Zone 4. To 3 feet.

The eastern representative of a beautiful group of "California lilacs," this shrub is much less spectacular than are its western cousins, yet it remains a desirable shrub in its own right. Its white flowers are small, grown in ball-like clusters, and are borne from June to October.

Ceanothus thrysiflorus: Blueblossom, California lilac. Zone 7. To 20 feet.

The great waves of blue that cover the California hills are a result of the flowering of this shrub. White varieties are in commerce, but are much less spectacular than the vivid cerulean of this species.

Chaenomeles speciosa: Flowering quince. Zone 4. To 3 feet.

Kicked from pillar to post by botanists, this is listed in most catalogs as *Cydonia japonica.* The type has brick-red flowers, but some of the new hybrids are as lovely as roses in soft apple-blossom pink, white, ivory, salmon, and deep crimson. Blooming in April in most of the United States, their flowers are particularly welcome, although they are susceptible to fire blight, as are all flowering quinces.

Chaenomeles lagenaria: Japonica, Japanese flowering quince. Zone 5. To 5 feet.

Like the above but taller, this species is a bit lax in growth, but if a wire is stretched along a hedge line through which its branches are woven to each other, a splendid colorful hedge is produced. The two species flower at the same time at a season when there are not too many shrubs in flower.

Chaenomeles sinensis: Chinese flowering quince. Zone 6. To 15 feet.

Although hard to find, this is worth searching out. It can be trained into a graceful, lax-branched small tree. Its flowers are pale pink and are followed by 5-inch-long lemon-yellow fruits that make tasty quince jelly.

Chilopsis linearis: Flowering willow, desert willow, Mexican catalpa, willow shrub. Zone 8. To 20 feet.

The lilac-colored flowers of this tree resemble those of the catalpa or the trumpet creeper in form. It is a valuable and beautiful shrub for semidesert conditions.

Chionanthus retusus: Chinese fringe tree. Zone 6.

Not as hardy as the following and with less-showy flowers, this shrub is not quite as demanding of acid soil. It blooms a week later.

Chionanthus virginicus: Fringe tree, old man's beard. Zone 5. To 30 feet.

In May and June, it wreathes its branches in panicles of white. It must be grown in acid soil.

Choisya ternata: Mexican orange. Zone 9. To 10 feet.

This shrub is a relative of our citrus species. Its intensely fragrant white flowers grow in large clusters in the spring. The foliage is evergreen. In irrigated areas, it can be thrown into bloom by withholding water, then irrigating.

Citrus trifoliata: Hardy orange, three-leaf orange. Zone 7. To 15 feet.

A fine specimen of this shrub or small tree stands on the grounds of the USDA in Washington, where visitors are often tempted to taste the orangelike fruits, only to shiver as they discover how bitter they are. An excellent evergreen, a very spiny shrub, it makes a "boyproof" hedge. It will survive temperatures as low as ten above zero.

Clerodendrum trichotomum: Harlequin glory bower. Zone 6. To 20 feet.

A late-flowering shrub with unusual flowers—white with reddish brown calyxes that gradually turn red—it is valuable for its September bloom. This shrub is rather coarse in foliage and it suckers, but it is vigorous and relatively troublefree.

Clethra alnifolia: Summersweet, sweet pepperbush. Zone 3. To 10 feet.

Growing in damp, lightly shaded places, this is a lovely thing, flowering from July to September. White candles of fragrant bloom cover the entire plant. It must have acid soil to survive.

Colutea arborescens: Bladder senna. Zone 5. To 10 feet.

Yellow pealike flowers in clusters open on this plant from summer to autumn. The bladderlike fruits make a satisfying pop when squeezed. Will grow well in light shade. A graceful, useful shrub because of its long season of bloom at a season when few other shrubs are in bloom.

Comptonia asplenifolia (Comptonia peregrina): Sweet fern, sweet shrub. Zone 2. To 2 to 3 feet.

An excellent species for planting half-wild areas, this is not a fern, but it has fernlike foliage. When crushed, it gives off a pleasing pungent odor.

Cornus alba siberica: Coral dogwood. Zone 3. To 10 feet.

This is one of the most valuable shrubs for winter effects because of its colored bark. The color will be better if old branches are cut off within 6 inches of the ground every third year. The bark is a bright coral red.

Cornus alternifolia: Pagoda dogwood, blue dogwood, pigeonberry. Zone 2. To 25 feet.

A favorite food for many birds is the berries of this shrub. It has interesting horizontal branching, pale yellow flowers that open in May, and bluish black berries on red stems which follow.

Cornus amomum: Silky dogwood, squaw bush, kinnikinnick. Zone 2. To 10 feet.

Purple branches make this plant interesting for winter color. It can also be trained as a small tree by pruning it to a single stem.

Cornus baileyi: Red dogwood. Zone 3. To 10 feet.

This is not as bright in color as *Cornus alba,* but it will thrive on poorer soils, even on sand dunes.

Cornus canadensis: Bunchberry. Zone 1. Below 9 inches.

It is hard to imagine this being a shrub, yet it is woody. It is a tiny gem for acid soils in the shade. A patch of this, half an acre in area, on my summer home in Maine glows like living coals in August and September.

Cornus mas: Cornelian cherry. Zone 4. To 20 feet.

Why this charming shrub is not more widely planted is a mystery. Perhaps the reason is that it flowers in early March, a time when few gardeners are willing to brave cold and snow to see their tiny golden petals against gray skies. The fruits, however, would sell this plant to anyone—small scarlet "plums" that ripen in August. They are edible, but the birds usually take them first.

Cornus racemosa: Gray dogwood. Zone 3. To 10 feet.

Although this is not a striking shrub, its clean gray silky bark and shiny white fruits are attractive.

Cornus stolonifera: Red osier dogwood. Zone 3. To 10 feet.

This is much like *Cornus alba* except that this species suckers, making it excellent for holding banks. There are yellow-twigged and green-twigged varieties that add color to the winter landscape.

Cotoneaster species:

Of late, I have seen so many shrubs of this genus attacked by a variety of rusts, by fire blight, and by other diseases that I feel it advisable to omit any recommendations for it, even though there are many handsome shrubs among the cotoneasters.

Cyrilla racemiflora: Leatherwood, black titi. Zone 6. To 20 feet.

Its long racemes of white flowers, which resemble lilies of the valley, appearing in June and July, make this a most desirable shrub. Add to that lovely autumn foliage of orange-scarlet and crimson, and this plant has an added attraction.

Cytisus species:

The brooms are curious but interesting plants on which the leaves have been reduced to tiny scales (on some species). They are largely plants for areas near the coast: they do not do well in the continental climate of the Midwest. They prefer slightly acid soils that are not too rich and that are well-drained. They are hardy in Zone 6, (except for *C. cananriensis*), but must have a sheltered spot in full sun to thrive.

Cytisus albus: Dwarf white broom, pale broom. Zone 6. To 18 inches.

The flowers of this plant form a crowded head of yellowish white. It blooms in June.

Cytisus canariensis: Genista. Zone 8. To 6 feet.

This is the yellow-flowered shrubby plant pushed into blooming for Easter in the North, but grown in the open in California, where it flowers in spring and summer. Called *Genista* by florists, it is not a true member of that genus. It has a delightful sweet pea fragrance.

Cytisus nigricans: Spike broom, black root. Zone 6. To 3 feet.

The flowers of this broom are produced in terminal clusters and are bright yellow and fragrant. In the northern edge of its range, it may freeze to the ground in winter, but it will flower on new wood the following summer.

Cytisus praecox: Warminster broom. Zone 6. To 8 feet.

This is perhaps the most free-flowering of all the brooms, producing great masses of light yellow flowers in May. It is a great favorite in Germany.

Cytisus purpureus: Purple broom. Zone 6. Semiprostrate to 24 inches.

An untidy mass, yet striking when in full bloom, the purple broom is valuable for its different colors. There are white, pink, and purple varieties. Sometimes, stems of this species are grafted on a tall upright species to produce a weeping specimen, a real conversation piece.

Cytisus scoparius: Scotch broom. Zone 6. To 8 feet.

This quite-leafless shrub with its large pealike yellow flowers is perhaps the best known of this genus, and the hardiest. It has become naturalized on several offshore islands of New England, but I have had no luck establishing it on my summer place on Natinicus, off Maine.

Daphne species:

The taller species of daphne present a problem in that their fruits are poisonous, and there have been a number of fatalities recorded caused by children eating the bright red berries. The low *Daphne cneorum* is not as much of a hazard. Too, it seldom sets fruits under garden conditions, but the possibility cannot be overlooked.

Daphne cneorum: Rose daphne, garland flower. Zone 5. To 1 foot.

Intensely fragrant rose-pink flowers bloom on this plant in late April and early May. Although it is difficult to establish—best moved with a ball of earth—it is well worth a little extra trouble at first. One caution: when used as cut flowers, the blossoms are so cloyingly sweet that they are objectionable to many people.

Deutzia gracilis: Slender deutzio. Zone 5. To 4 feet.

The arching branches of this shrub are covered with sprays of white flowers forming a good background for tulips. Its tips, however, are likely to kill out and require pruning in spring.

Deutzia lemoinei: Zone 4. To 7 feet.

Except that it is taller and somewhat hardier, it is much like the preceding.

Diervilla lonicera: Gravelweed, bush honeysuckle. To Zone 2. To 3 feet.

Not to be confused with the species of lonicera which is also called bush honeysuckle, gravelweed is an extremely hardy shrub which bears yellow flowers in June and July. Rather coarse and suckering freely, it is a good subject for naturalizing. It will grow well in full sun or light shade. The flowers deepen to red as they age.

Diosma ericoides: Buchu, breath-of-heaven. Zone 10. To 2 feet.

This heatherlike shrub bears tiny star-shaped white flowers, which are intensely fragrant. Needing a peat or acid soil, this was once a popular greenhouse plant in Victorian days.

Dombeya wallichii: Pink snowball, pink ball, Cape wedding flower. Zone 9. To 30 feet.

A treelike shrub from Africa, this bears flowers like the northern snowball, but they are showy pink, 5 inches in diameter, and are produced throughout the winter in California. One objection: the flowers do not drop after fading and must be snipped off.

Duranta repens: Florida lilac, skyflower, pigeonberry, golden dewdrop. Zone 9. To 18 feet.

Its flowers, forget-me-not blue in color, are produced in August and are followed by golden orange berries. It is one of Florida's most popular flowering shrubs.

Elaeagnus angustifolia: Russian olive, oleaster. Zone 3. To 20 feet.

A charming gray-leaved tall shrub or small tree, this survives subzero winters on the Great Plains. Fragrant yellow flowers, silvery on the outside in June, are followed by an olive-shaped yellowish fruit which is covered with silvery scales and is edible, but mealy and insipid.

Elaeagnus argentea: Silverberry, wolf willow, Missouri silver tree, buffalo berry. Zone 3. To 10 feet.

Perhaps the most silvery shrub in commerce, with shining leaves silver on both sides, it is a beautiful sight when the foliage is stirred by winds. Even the fruit is silvery. The flowers are much like those of the preceding. It will tolerate seaside conditions.

Elaeagnus multiflora (Elaeagnus longipes): Cherry elaeagnus, gumi. Zone 5. To 6 feet.

With its scarlet edible fruit, this silvery-leaved plant is a good wild-bird-food shrub. It is also resistant to city smoke.

Escallonia montividensis: Peruvian honeysuckle. Zone 7. To 15 feet.

This tall shrub or small tree bearing fragrant white flowers in clusters in fall and winter makes an excellent background shrub with evergreen foliage.

Escallonia rubra: Red Peruvian honeysuckle. Zone 8. To 15 feet.

This is an erect, compact shrub, quite twiggy and dense, which bears bright red flowers in compact clusters.

Eugenia paniculata: Australian brush cherry. Zone 8. To 12 feet.

A popular shrub or small tree in California and Florida, it is often used for hedges. Its foliage is evergreen, deep green and glossy, but its young twigs are tinged with bronze. The fruit is a rich burgundy red or violet and edible. In Australia and New Zealand, it is used for making jelly. Another member of the family, *Eugenia aromatica,* produces the cloves of commerce.

Euonymus species:

This genus contains an amazing variety of forms and some of our most useful landscape plants. Unfortunately, practically all are susceptible to a serious scale insect, *Chionapis euonymi,* which often attacks so severely that they can check growth and even kill the entire plant. Only the following, in my experience, is troublefree enough to include in the present listing.

Euonymus alatus and its variety, *Euonymus alatus compactus:* Winged burning bush. Zone 3. To 8 feet, but seldom more than 5 feet in the variety compactus.

This tree has a corky bark formed in wings up and down the stems which is apparently thick enough to keep scale insects from causing serious damage. Of all the shrubs with autumn coloring, none is so gorgeous as this species. The foliage turns a glowing rosy red, and although it is not as garish as calling it a neon red would imply, it does glow like a neon sign. It is quite regular in habit and slow growing. A hedge of this plant is a real treasure.

Forsythia species:

Desirable for very early flowers, lemon yellow to golden yellow, these shrubs do require some attention because of their ready tendency to self-layer at the tips of drooping branches. Having just spent two hours pulling up volunteer layers, I can report that this is not a work-free species. In most nurseries the different species are so badly mixed up that listing them is of little help. Making a selection when they are in bloom is suggested. Hardiness of forsythias is doubtful north of Zone 5. The wood survives, but not flower buds.

Fremontia californica: Flannel bush, leatherwood. Zone 8. To 10 feet.

A striking shrub, the golden yellow flowers of this tree, blooming in early summer, contrast with the felted leaves and felt-covered branches. This plant needs a dry soil.

Fuchsia magellanica: Magellan fuchsia. Zone 8. To 20 feet, if not cut down by frost.

A relative of the florist's fuchsia with red and blue flowers, this shrub is particularly attractive to humming birds. It makes a magnificent hedge in areas where it is hardy. North of Zone 8, it survives but is only root-hardy. New shoots will reach a height of about three feet. Flowering on new growth is uncertain.

Hamamelis japonica: Japanese witch hazel. Zone 5. To 15 feet.

This is a tall shrub or small tree with bright lemon-yellow flowers that may open during January or February thaws. It needs full sun.

Hamamelis mollis: Chinese witch hazel. Zone 5. To 15 feet.

This is similar to the preceding, except that its flowers are larger and tinged with red. Both species need full sun in order to ripen branches.

Hamamelis vernalis: Spring witch hazel, spring gold. Zone 6. To 6 feet.

This one flowers from January to March. Its flowers are yellow with orange bases.

Hamamelis virginiana: Common witch hazel, autumn witch hazel. Zone 4. To 8 feet.

Blooming from September to November, this witch hazel has bright yellow flowers.

Hibiscus rosa-sinensis: Chinese hibiscus, shoeblack plant. Zone 9. To 20 feet.

Perhaps the most widely planted flowering shrub in southern Florida, it has many named varieties, including single, semidouble, and double, ranging in color from pure white to near black. Don't waste time on varieties with variegated foliage; these are weak growers and cause nothing but work.

Hibiscus syriacus: Rose of Sharon, shrub althea. Zone 4. To 10 feet.

This is the most glorious shrub for summer flowers that can be planted in the North. Typical hibiscus flowers are white, pink, purple, lavender, and crimson. To avoid unnecessary trimming, don't plant this where cold winter winds will hit it: this usually kills all branch tips.

Holodiscus discolor: Rock spirea, cream shrub, ocean spray cream bush. Zone 6. To 10 feet. A West Coast species, this shrub doesn't seem to like eastern conditions. It survives at Boston, but needs annual trimming. It thrives on sandy soils in the full sun and bears large drooping clusters of creamy white flowers in July.

Hydrangea arborescens grandiflora: A. G. hydrangea, snow-hill hydrangea. Zone 5. To 5 feet.

Huge flattish heads of creamy white flowers bloom in June on this shrub, which does require cutting back nearly to the soil each spring if these big heads of bloom are wanted.

Hydrangea macrophylla: Florist hydrangea, house hydrangea. Zone 6. To 8 feet.

This is the plant with the conspicuous ball-shaped heads of pink or vivid blue flowers seen up and down the East Coast in summer. To produce blue flowers, the soil must be treated with aluminum sulfate and iron each year; otherwise it requires little care.

Hydrangea paniculata grandiflora: P.G. hydrangea. Zone 4. To 20 feet (but see below).

Huge white balls of flowers that turn a rosy pink with age are produced by this tree. If allowed to grow to full height, though, most of the bloom will be on top, but if the wood is cut back severely each spring, a more attractive, lower plant will result.

Hypericum calycinum: Rose of Sharon (in England), Aaron's beard. Zone 6. To 12 inches.

An evergreen subshrub, this plant is useful for "facing" shrubbery borders. Flowering over a long period, from July to September, it bears clustered yellow flowers to 2 inches across. It tolerates light shade and sandy soils.

Hypericum densiflorum: Bush St. Johnswort. Zone 6. To 6 feet.

A native shrub that blooms so freely that the foliage is often hidden by its clusters of yellow flowers, it blooms from July to September.

Hypericum moserianum: Gold flower. Zone 8. To 2 feet.

With its lovely arching stems, its clusters of flowers like tiny golden single roses, and its habit of flowering in midsummer, this is an outstanding low-growing shrub.

Ilex aquifolium: English holly. Zone 7. To 35 feet, but usually grown as a shrub.

This is the traditional Christmas holly with its spiny leaves and bright red berries. Two limitations on its culture are (a) the need for a definitely acid soil, with a pH of 4.5 to 5.0, and (b) the need for including both male and female trees in the planting.

Ilex crenata convexa: Japanese holly, boxwood holly. Zone 5. To 8 feet.

A handsome evergreen shrub that does not resemble most other hollies, this is usually not grown more than 3 feet tall. It makes a handsome hedge, requiring a soil not as acid as other hollies. It is an excellent substitute for boxwood where the latter is not hardy. There are a number of varieties which have special qualities.

Ilex opaca: American holly. Zone 4. To 50 feet.

Although it is not as desirable as its British cousin, it is much hardier.

Itea virginica: Sweet spire. Zone 5. To 6 feet.

Fragrant, white spirelike flowers in July and a good red autumn color make this a useful shrub.

Kalmia angustifolia: Sheepkill, sheep laurel, dwarf laurel, lambkill. Zone 2. To 3 feet.

A delightful low-growing shrub for moist acid soils in the shade, its foliage is poisonous to sheep, cattle, horses, and goats. However, they will only eat *Kalmia* foliage when other vegetation is sparse.

Kalmia latifolia: Mountain laurel. Zone 5. To 30 feet.

A taller, but less hardy, species than the above, this plant bears striking rose-colored flowers in terminal clusters in June and July. Both species are beautiful when massed with *Rhododendrons.*

Kerria japonica: Japanese rose, globe flower. Zone 5. To 6 feet, but usually lower.

The five-petaled golden flowers on this shrub resemble yellow single or double roses. It flowers in early summer and tolerates light shade. The tendency of its twigs to kill at the end, necessitating annual shearing, is about its only fault.

Kolkwitzia amabilis: Beautybush. Zone 5. To 6 feet.

Although the shrub is graceful, with its arching branches smothered with flowers, I personally find the color effect weak—a pale pink but deeper in bud. This is, however, about as troublefree a flowering shrub as you will find.

Laburnum alpinum: Scotch laburnum, golden chain, bean tree. Zone 6. To 30 feet, but can be grown as a tall shrub.

With its long chains of golden pealike flowers, 15 inches in length, a specimen in full bloom is a spectacular sight. All parts of the tree are poisonous—the seed pods, which are sometimes eaten by children, can prove fatal.

Lagerstroemia indica: Crepe myrtle, crape myrtle, Florida lilac. Zone 7. To 20 feet.

See description under "Trees."

Laurocerasus caroliniana (Prunus laurocerasus): Carolina cherry laurel, laurel cherry, wild orange, mock orange, Laurier-amande. Zone 7. To 35 feet, but usually grown as a shrub.

With its glossy evergreen foliage and clean habit, this is a preferred hedge plant in areas where it is hardy, although its foliage is poisonous to cattle. It is often grown in tubs as topiary specimens and stored in frostfree cold storage for the winter in the North. Botanically this is usually classed as a prunus.

Laurus nobilis: True Laurel.

See description under "Trees."

Leucothoë catesbaei: Fetterbush, lily-of-the-valley shrub. Zone 5. To 6 feet.

This choice evergreen shrub is valuable in mixed plantings of broad-leaved evergreens. The leaves are beautiful in fall, turning to wine red and bronze.

Ligustrum species:

Although the most widely planted genus for hedge purposes, the ligustrums are not wholly troublefree. A disease, the cause of which is not fully known, called privet die-back may start anywhere in a hedge and run both ways, killing the plants to the ground. This, and the fact that privet is much overplanted and lacks quality, would suggest the selection of some more interesting species. There are, however, privets which make splended specimen plants and deserve planting individually.

Ligustrum amurense: Amur river privet. Zone 4. To 12 feet.

Introduced originally as a hardier substitute for California privet, it does not do too well as a hedge plant since it tends to get leggy. *Ligustrum vulgare* is more satisfactory.

Ligustrum lucidum: Glossy privet. Zone 7. To 30 feet.

Often grown as a handsome street tree in Florida, it is valuable farther north as an evergreen hedge. It is, perhaps, the best of the evergreen privets.

Ligustrum nepalense: Nepal privet. Zone 9. To 12 feet.

This evergreen shrub, which can be grown as a small tree, seems to do better as a hedge, in California, than does *Ligustrum lucidum.*

Ligustrum obtusifolium: Ibota privet. Zone 4. To 12 feet.

Perhaps the most disease-resistant of the privets, this shrub is valuable because of its variety Regal privet with its strongly horizontal branching and more compact growth. One weakness is its foliage color; unless given extra iron, it is somewhat yellowish.

Ligustrum vulgare: Polish privet, prim, common privet. Zone 4. To 15 feet.

This is an old, old species in commerce which somehow got lost when other species of privet were introduced, but which is too handsome as a specimen plant to ignore. It is extremely hardy, strongly upright in growth, and has nearly evergreen, deep green foliage.

Lonicera species:

One fault of the bush honeysuckles is that they can be abandoned without care and will survive, often growing into great ungainly masses of live and dead branches where children's toys, garden tools, and other trash accumulate and are lost. Yet no other group of shrubs is as valuable in "planting out" offending landscape features—the ugly junk yard, the badly designed house next door, the curving road that throws lights from passing cars into a bedroom window. The bush honeysuckles do have a misty charm when in flower and are not too bad when in fruit, but there *are* better shrubs.

Lonicera fragrantissima: Wintersweet, winter honeysuckle. Zone 5. To 9 feet.

After damning the genus with faint praise, I must wax enthusiastic about this particular honeysuckle. It is a choice shrub, which opens its intensely fragrant white flowers during thaws from January to early March. To come upon a specimen in bloom on a stroll on a winter afternoon is a delightful experience.

Lonicera ledebouri: California honeysuckle. Zone 9. To 9 feet.

This is a deciduous shrub bearing, in June and July, orange flowers tinged scarlet and then black fruits.

Lonicera maackii: Manchurian honeysuckle, amur honeysuckle. Zone 3. To 15 feet.

With its fragrant white flowers in May or June and its bright red fruits in September, this is one of the best tall shrubs for "planting out" offensive landscape features.

Lonicera morrowii: Morrow honeysuckle. Zone 4. To 8 feet.

This is one of the few honeysuckles whose fruits are attractive to birds. It has white flowers fading ivory in May or June and blood-red berries in July and August. There is also a yellow-fruited variety.

Lonicera nitida: Box honeysuckle. Zone 6. To 5 feet.

A semievergreen shrub with fragrant white flowers and blue-purple berries, this does not look like a honeysuckle. It is an excellent shrub.

Lonicera tatarica: Tatarian honeysuckle. Zone 4. To 10 feet.

Perhaps because it is the easiest of all shrubs to grow, this is found everywhere. It is too common to be interesting, but too useful to dismiss entirely. The white or pink flowers appear in pairs in May or June and the fruits, bright red in July and August, are attractive to birds.

Magnolia stellata: Star magnolia. Zone 4. To 12 feet.

See description under "Trees."

Mahonia aquifolium: Oregon holly grape. Zone 4. To 6 feet.

With foliage closely resembling that of true English holly, this is a handsome shrub, even though it is not truly evergreen at the northern limits of its hardiness. Shade-tolerant, it bears fragrant yellow flowers in clusters in late April or early May, followed by purple-black fruits that ripen in September.

Mahonia bealei: Leatherleaf holly grape. Zone 6. To 10 feet.

Its thick, leathery leaves and stiff upright habit lend this an appearance of an outstanding tropical shrub. Its long clusters of bright yellow flowers in spring are followed by blue-black fruits.

Malus sargentii: Sargent's crab apple. Zone 4. To 7 feet.

Although crab apples are supposed to be trees, this one insists on staying at shrub height and so is used as a shrub in landscaping. It forms a broad, oval bush, wider than it is high, which bears clear white flowers in late April or early May and dark red fruit, about half an inch in diameter, which is eaten by birds.

Melaleuca armillaris: Tea tree, bottle brush. Zone 9. To 20 feet.

Sometimes grown as a small tree, this tree bears creamy white flowers in cylindrical spikes about 3 inches long. It is an excellent hedge plant, thriving on poor sandy soils. There are species with lilac-colored and red flowers in addition to this species.

Chimonanthus praecox (Meratia praecox): Wintersweet, winterscent, Chinese allspice. Zone 7. To 10 feet.

Opening its intensely fragrant flowers during warm days in January, this is indeed a rare treat for the gardener. The outer petals are a pale lemon with a purple center.

Michelia fuscata (Michelia pensylvanica): Banana shrub, brownflower magnolia. Zone 9. To 15 feet.

Some find the banana odor of the flowers of this shrub offensive, but others think it delightful. The brownish yellow flowers are edged with light scarlet.

Myrica caroliniensis: Northern bayberry. Zone 4. To 8 feet.

A semievergreen shrub with strongly aromatic foliage, it thrives on dry, sterile, peat soils where few other shrubs will grow. The berries when boiled produce a wax used for bayberry candles. The southern form of this shrub, *Myrica cerifera,* is more treelike.

Myrica gale: Sweet gale, bay bush, bog myrtle, sweet willow, swamp myrtle. Zone 9. To 4 feet.

This plant is the emblem of the Scottish clan of Campbell and is used as a moth repellent and perfume. The odor is that of bay rum. This species must have moist soil.

Myrtus communis: True myrtle. Zone 9. To 10 feet.

The classic myrtle of history, this is everblooming in the far south and in July elsewhere. Grown principally for its glossy evergreen foliage, it is used in hedges, grown in tubs as specimen shrubs, and planted in borders. It is a highly useful shrub with an ancient history.

Nandina domestica: Heavenly bamboo, Chinese sacred bamboo. Zone 6. To 6 feet.

This is not a bamboo, but an evergreen shrub with reedlike stems topped with compound leaves which give the effect of a bamboo. The foliage turns red in fall and the edible fruit is reddish purple. This makes an excellent plant for patios when grown in tubs.

Nerium oleander: Oleander. Zone 9. To 20 feet.

Known to most northern gardeners only as a tubbed specimen, this is a popular hedge plant and landscape specimen in the South. Glossy evergreen foliage and bright pink or rosy red flowers in July make this a highly desirable species. All parts of the plant are poisonous, as is honey made from oleander flowers. Wild bee honey collected in oleander country should be avoided.

Osmanthus ilicifolius: Holly olive. Zone 7. To 20 feet.

Both of its common names are misnomers: it is neither an olive nor a holly. The foliage is quite hollylike—green and shining. Older plants produce the fragrant but inconspicuous white flowers. The shrub tolerates seaside conditions.

Parrotia persica: Iron tree. Zone 5. To 15 feet.

Except that it is much neater growing, this tree resembles the witch hazels. In March and April, the purple flowers are surrounded by brownish bracts. The most important feature of this shrub is its gorgeous autumn colors—gold and orange-scarlet. It can also be grown as a tree (to 30 feet in the North) trimmed to a single stem.

Philadelphus coronarius: Mock orange. Zone 4. To 10 feet.

Although there are dozens of species of mock oranges, this species contains varieties enough for any taste. Its white, intensely fragrant flowers have an orange-blossom scent in June. Its one fault is the lack of permanence in its wood: it requires annual pruning to cut out dead and weak branches.

Pieris floribunda: Andromeda, fetter bush, lily-of-the-valley shrub. Zone 5. To 3 feet.

This is one of the best of all shrubs for a mixed planting of broad-leaved evergreens. Its flower spikes are like drooping clusters of lily-of-the-valley, but it needs an acid soil to thrive. A Japanese species, *Pieris japonica,* is even finer, but less hardy.

Pittosporum tobira: Tobira. Zone 9. To 8 feet.

Those used to thinking of pittosporum as a tiny succulent pot plant are often astonished when they face a well-grown specimen of *P. tobira* growing in Florida or California, where it can be an 8-foot shrub. The flowers are fragrant, borne in clusters in winter, and greenish-white in color. The plants can be sheared at any height wanted.

Prunus species:

Several beautiful small peaches, plums, and cherries can be grown as shrubs, and although most are short-lived, are worth growing as accent or specimen plants. Borers, a definite hazard to treelike prunus species, are not as much of a problem in these multistemmed smaller specimens.

Prunus armeniaca: Apricot. Zone 6. To 20 feet.

If a young apricot is pruned low enough to form a shrub, it makes a lovely specimen because of its spectacular early spring bloom. The individual flowers are often an inch or more across and white, faintly tinged with pink. The apricot is supposed to be the "apple" that Eve gave Adam. Fruit can be produced by shrubby specimens, but in most areas, late frosts prevent this.

Prunus besseyi: Sand cherry, bush cherry. Zone 3. To 4 feet.

A heaven-sent shrub for the Great Plains where good flowering species are hard to come by, it is also useful near the sea, where it will grow on poor, sandy soils. White flowers in spring and black fruit in summer make it doubly useful. The fruit, while astringent, is edible and makes good jams and jellies.

Prunus cerasifera pissardi: Purpleleaf plum. Zone 4. To 10 feet.

The original species is used as an understock on which to graft fruiting trees, but this purple-leaved sort is grown as a shrub. In central Ohio and south, it can be grown to tree size if desired. While the color is not as purple as that of many shrubs with colored foliage, it does not darken as summer begins. It is perhaps the first shrub, other than the witch hazels, *Cornus mas*, and *Lonicera fragrantissima,* to flower. Although small, the blossoms are borne in such profusion that the effect is striking.

Prunus glandulosa: Flowering almond. Zone 4. To 5 feet.

This is not the true almond *(Prunus amygdalus),* but a hardy shrub that survives in spite of neglect. Sometimes grafted, it is susceptible to borers; try to buy it on its own roots. There are many horticultural varieties: the bright pink double form is by far the most popular. Perhaps no other flowering shrub creates as much questioning in flower shows as does the flowering almond because of the difficulty in classifying it.

Prunus tomentosa: Nanking cherry. Zone 3. To 5 feet.

In exhibits of cut branches of fruiting shrubs, those of the Nanking cherry are always outstanding. The brilliant red cherries, about half an inch in diameter, are edible. This shrub blooms at the end of April; pink buds tinged red open to white flowers. It is a choice species.

Prunus triloba: Double-flowered plum. Zone 3. To 5 feet.

Although often called a flowering almond, it is not. The two species are quite similar and are often confused, particularly the double pink varieties, but this one, although somewhat hardier, is not as long-lived as *Prunus glandulosa.*

Punica granatum: Pomegranate. Zone 7. To 20 feet.

This is a spiny shrub or small tree which is grown for its chambered fruit which has many seeds, each of which is surrounded by a sweetish pulp. Its flowers are striking—orange-red and about 1½ inches across. This makes a formidable hedge.

Pyracantha coccinea: Firethorn. Zone 5. To 8 feet.

There are a number of species of firethorn grown in the South and in California, but *P. coccinea* has been so highly developed by plant breeders that it is by far the most widely planted. If planted where it is out of winter sun and wind, it can be grown in Zone 4. The white flowers are unimportant; the glory of this shrub is its magnificent burst of orange to scarlet fruits in fall. A hedge of firethorn is a marvelous sight in fall, but the plants are rather expensive to use in this way unless propagated at home.

Rhaphiolepis indica: India hawthorn. Zone 9. To 5 feet.

A popular evergreen shrub in the South and on the Pacific Coast, it has pinkish white flowers that resemble those of our native hawthorn.

Rhaphiolepis umbellata: Yeddo hawthorn. Zone 9. To 12 feet.

This shrub is usually pruned much lower than its final height to form a broad, spreading specimen. Its hawthornlike flowers are intensely fragrant, white with a rusty red calyx.

Rhamnus cathartica: Common buckthorn, waythorn, hartshorn. Zone 1. To 12 feet.

Its black berries were an old-time folk remedy, a powerful purge. The seeds are poisonous. It is a rather untidy bush that can be kept neater by regular pruning, but this does take time.

Rhamnus frangula: Alder buckthorn, glossy buckthorn, berry alder, Persian berry, black dogwood (in England). Zone 1. To 12 feet.

This is a much neater, more disciplined shrub than the preceding. The Truehedge shrub (a copyrighted trade name), a more upright form, belongs here. The berries, which are red at first, turn black and are eaten eagerly by birds.

Rhododendron species:

The shrubs commonly called azaleas are botanically true rhododendrons. The one drawback to rhododendrons for the busy gardener is that they will only grow well in association with their own heathlike species—strongly acid soil, a mulching cover that should not be disturbed, constant attention to soil moisture in summer, and attention to spraying to control the many ills are a few of the limiting factors. Those in natural rhododendron country can get by with somewhat less

Azaleas and rhododendrons often require attention, but can be well worth the effort in a small patio garden.

attention, yet these are aristocrats which demand waiting-upon which the busy man cannot give them. Other heathlike plants help propagate a fungus that grows on roots of rhododendrons, essential to good growth.

Rhodotypos tetrapetala: Jetbead, white kerria. Zone 5. To 4 feet.

A troublefree shrub that has flowers like single white roses which bloom intermittently all summer long, that thrives on heavy clay, and that tolerates city smoke is hard to omit from this list. Its black fruits hang on all winter long.

Rhus aromatica: Fragrant sumac. Zone 3. To 3 feet.

This spreading shrub, usually wider than it is tall, is particularly useful as a "facing" shrub to tie in taller shrubs with flower borders or lawns. The leaves have a resinous-aromatic odor that most gardeners find pleasant. The fall color on this shrub is outstanding—a glowing ember red shot with brown, bronze, and gold. Birds eat the fruits. It is also a good city shrub that tolerates smoke and dust.

Rhus copallina: Shining sumac, dwarf sumac. Zone 5. To 20 feet.

This tall shrub or small tree with its greenish spikes of flowers, glossy leaves, and fruits which are hairy red spikes, also has good autumn color, but it is not as brilliant as some sumacs.

Rhus cotinoides: American smoke tree, purple fringe tree, Venetian sumac, wig tree, Chittamwood. Zone 5. To 20 feet.

Botanically, this is *Cotinus coggyria.* This is a striking tall shrub good for filling open spaces on a large property. Its gossamer flower spikes create an illusion of a shrub wreathed in smoke. The fall color is brilliant. There is a purple variety with distinctive foliage, but this does not develop as good fall color. The plants in commerce are sometimes mixed with *Cotinus americanus,* the American smoke tree, a species which has smaller and poorer "smoke" spikes, but whose autumn color is brilliant. It would be well to examine nursery stocks in bloom when making a selection.

Rhus glabra and *Rhus typhina:* Common sumac. Zone 4. To 15 feet.

The two species, confused in commerce, have botanical differences too slight to interest amateurs. Both are glorious in autumn color and both have cut-leaved varieties that are among the most striking of all fall shrubs. However they need to be cut back occasionally to keep them fairly compact.

Ribes alpinum: Alpine currant, mountain currant. Zone 4. To 8 feet, but usually grown as a hedge not over 4 feet.

Perhaps the most useful nonthorny hedge plant we have, this will tolerate shearing well and will grow in almost any situation. There is also a golden variety, which is a weak grower, and a form with cut foliage.

Ribes aureum: Flowering currant, buffalo currant, golden currant. Zone 2. To 6 feet.

In commerce, this species is mixed with *Ribes odoratum,* but the differences are unimportant. They both bear fragrant flowers, bright lemon yellow, in May and purple-brown fruit. If planted on poor dry soils, both develop beautiful gold and purple foliage in fall, making them some of the better shrubs for the Great Plains. On acid soils, autumn color is sometimes scarlet. All species of Ribes are prohibited by law in states where white pines are native. They are an alternate host of white pine blister rust.

Robinia hispida: Rose acacia, moss locust, pink locust. Zone 5. To 6 feet.

Although the wood is so brittle that branches snap off readily, and in spite of its suckering tendency, this shrub is so lovely when in bloom that it is worth a little trouble. The suckering habit is useful when large areas are to be planted.

Rosa species:

Although it will bring down on my head the wrath of my many friends who are members of the American Rose Society, I must warn the busy gardener against planting hybrid tea roses—they are perhaps the most time-consuming garden plants you can grow. There are, however, two roses which can be grown by the man with too little time to spend in spraying, pruning, and fertilizing the more-demanding garden roses.

Rosa multiflora: Japanese rose. Zone 4. To 15 feet.

Listing of this species must be preceded by a warning that the Japanese rose is an arboreal weed that can crowd out better shrubs and fill a small property with a tangle of brush that will leave little room for anything else to survive. At the same time, here is a no-care shrub that can be used on larger properties to fill space at low cost, with a reasonably attractive planting. Best of all, that planting will provide shelter for wild life—for nesting birds, for feeding quail, etc. Don't expect florist-type roses on this plant—the flowers are much like those of the wild blackberry and borne for only a short period in spring.

Rosa rugosa: Rugosa rose. Zone 3. To 10 feet.

The older varieties of this rose are amazing in their ability to survive. On my summer place in Maine, eighteen miles offshore on an island, they have self-seeded to form a solid thicket over an acre in extent, where they are constantly washed by salt air and exposed to the full force of north winds off the Atlantic. There are refined hybrids of this which are practically carefree, but which are still beautiful in bloom and excellent for cutting, even if they are not long-stemmed florist beauties.

Rubus odoratus: Flowering raspberry. Zone 3. To 5 feet.

This is another excellent shrub for wild places, suckering freely to cover ground rapidly and cheaply. Its maple-leaf foliage is distinctive and its flowers are a lovely purplish rose about 2 inches across. Its fruit is edible, but tasteless.

Sambucus canadensis: American elder, elderberry. Zone 3. To 10 feet.

The fragrance of elderberry flowers in June or early July is delightful. They are followed by black berries which can be eaten or used for making wine, if the birds don't eat them first. The flowers are sometimes coated with batter and made into fritters, but this is a bit exotic for my taste. A cut-leaved variety makes a handsome shrub. Elderberries should be cut back every two or three years to keep them compact if wanted as shrubbery border specimens.

Shepardia argentea: Buffalo berry, rabbit berry, beef suet tree, wild oleaster. Zone 1. To 15 feet.

With its silvery foliage and its bright red or golden fruits, this is an outstanding ornamental, but seldom carried by commercial nurseries because of lack of demand. It is one of the best for the northern Great Plains. The fruits are edible and are often used for making jelly.

Skimmia japonica: Skimmia. Zone 7. To 4 feet.

Grown principally for its bright red berries, the white fragrant flowers on this attractive evergreen shrub are borne in May. Both male and female plants must be grown if fruit is wanted.

Sorbaria sorbifolia: False spirea. Zone 2. To 5 feet.

This is another plant good for rough places where fine finish is not important. It suckers freely and is useful for its long perod of bloom—its spikes of white first bloom in June and appear intermittently to August. They do hang on, unfortunately, so a bit of snipping to remove faded spikes is needed when it is planted in more formal surroundings.

Spiraea species:

The spireas (note the difference in spelling between botanic and common names) are a mixed bag, containing species that bear their flowers in umbels, in flat clusters, in ball-like clusters, and in panicles. Unfortunately, one of the finest, *Spiraea vanhouttei,* has been so overplanted that it is almost banal in the spring landscape. Almost any landscape niche can be filled with some speces of spirea.

Spiraea bumalda: Anthony Waterer spirea, Froebeli spirea. Zone 4. To 2 feet.

The two varieties named here are among our most useful low-growing shrubs, producing flat heads of rosy crimson flowers in June and July.

Spiraea tomentosa: Hardhack, steeplebush. Zone 2. To 4 feet.

About the toughest shrub you can plant for wild places and along fence rows, it is not unattractive with its pinkish purple spikes of flowers blooming in July and August.

Spiraea vanhouttei: Bridal wreath spirea. Zone 4. To 5 feet.

In using the common name bridal wreath for this species, I am not forgetting that the original bridal wreath is *Spiraea prunifolia* but that genus is seldom in commerce. If only this species had not been so overplanted! Next to privet and Japanese barberry, it is the most common shrub in commerce. Even though spectacular in bloom, the season is so short that it should be judged for its landscape effect at other seasons. Although its arching branches are graceful and it requires little or no care, there are more shapely plants. Yet it cannot be omitted from any list of easy-to-grow shrubs.

Symphoricarpos chenaultii: Spotted Indian currant. Zone 4. To 5 feet.

This is a hybrid species with red currantlike fruits spotted white. The plants spread and are good for holding banks. It is much neater in habit than the common Indian currant.

Symphoricarpos albus (Symphoricarpos racemosus): Snowberry, waxberry. Zone 4. To 3 feet.

A sprawling, lax shrub that spreads rapidly, the snowberry is useful in holding banks and for planting in spots in light shade. It is often used in shrubbery borders, but it grows too loosely to give any feeling of mass. Its one distinctive feature is its white fruit that ripens in September, often hanging on until spring.

Symphoricarpos orbiculatis (Symphoricarpos vulgaris): Indian currant, coralberry, buckbush, snapberry, turkey berry. Zone 4. To 3 feet.

This shrub is much like the snowberry, except that its fruits are in purplish red clusters that ripen in October and cling to the branches until late winter. They are, however, eaten by birds (the berries of other species are not) when other food is scarce.

Syringa species:

If it were not for the fact that their omission would cause comment, I would be tempted to leave out lilacs entirely. True, abandoned specimens growing round old cellar holes in New England have been known to survive for a century or more without care, but the modern French hybrids refuse to be neglected. Faded flowers must be removed to prevent seed formation, regular pruning back is needed to keep the plant from growing out of bounds, borers are a problem, and fall mildew is disfiguring.

The French hybrids are legion: many nurseries list as many as twenty-five varieties. But don't trust to catalog descriptions—better buy them when they are in bloom and move with a ball of earth if you are fussy. I know of one major arboretum where nearly 20 percent of the varieties are mislabeled; nurseries are worse.

Syringa josikaea: Hungarian lilac. Zone 3. To 12 feet.

This shrub is valuable because it blooms later than other lilacs. The color of the blossom is a rosy pink and its odor is a haylike scent rather than a fragrance.

Syringa persica: Persian lilac. Zone 4. To 8 feet.

Although not as spectacular in bloom as the French hybrids, this species is lovely when in bloom with airy spikes of lavender, purple, or white flowers. Its stems are smaller than those of other lilacs and offer less attraction to borers. It is also not as subject to mildew. This is one of the best shrubs for tall hedges. Most of the plants in commerce are actually the Rouen lilac, *Syringa chinensis,* which blooms at an earlier age, is freer flowering, and grows to a height of 15 feet with broader leaves.

Tetrapanex papyriferus (Fatsia papyrifera): Rice-paper plant. Zone 7. To 12 feet tall.

This is a dependable plant for achieving tropical effects on a patio or sheltered location. Unsheltered, its large palmate leaves would be torn to shreds by the wind. It prefers shade.

Vaccinium corymbosum: Highbush blueberry. Zone 4. To 12 feet.

For soils that are constantly moist but not under water, there is no finer ornamental shrub than this species. It is beautiful in bloom, delightful when covered with half-ripe and ripe fruit, and just as beautiful in fall when its foliage turns red, gold, and orange. The improved horticultural varieties are just as fine as the wild species, but having the added advantage of bearing larger edible berries. It must have an acid soil to thrive.

Viburnum species:

One authority lists ten different uses for virburnums: certainly no more important group of shrubs is available. Some are evergreen. Many have good fall color. Never dust or spray viburnums with sulfur—it will take off all foliage.

Viburnum burkwoodii: Burkwood viburnum. Zone 4. To 8 feet.

Semievergreen in the South, this shrub is distinguished by the powerful fragrance of its white flowers, borne in clusters in May. It has no fall color.

Viburnum carlesii: Mayflower viburnum. Zone 4. To 8 feet.

Although this shrub is the parent of the preceding, it has flowers that closely resemble those of the true mayflower, *Epigaea repens,* in fragrance, in form, and in color. In April, it is one of the glories of the shrubbery border. Ask for it on its own roots: when it is grafted on *Viburnum lantana,* the roots often outgrow the top, killing it.

Virburnum dentatum: Arrowwood. Zone 3. To 12 feet.

This native shrub is vigorous, diseasefree, insectfree, and attractive to birds because of its blue-black fruits. It does well under seaside conditions. The autumn colors are lovely—soft rosy green to bronze, with purple shading. Although recommended for growing in the shade, my specimens in such a situation stretch for sun and are not at their best.

Viburnum lantana: Wayfaring tree. Zone 4. To 12 feet.

The white flowers of this shrub, which appear in clusters in May and June, are followed by berries that go through an interesting color cycle—green to near-white to red to black. As soon as they are ripe, birds strip the plant. It has hairy leaves. This is a really tough plant: on a neighboring property a row of it is crowded in a space not over 18 inches wide between the house foundation and the drive, on the north side of the house where the sun never shines.

Viburnum odoratissimum: Sweet viburnum. Zone 8. To 10 feet.

A dwarf variety of this shrub is sometimes grown in estate greenhouses as an ornamental. It is a choice species, if only it were hardier! Its white fragrant flowers appear in May and June.

Viburnum opulus: Highbush cranberry, cranberry bush. Zone 4. To 10 feet.

This is mentioned here only to warn against its extreme susceptibility to attack by the snowball aphid that curls its foliage every spring. The same holds true for *Viburnum trilobum* to a lesser degree. It is otherwise a useful shrub. The snowball aphid can be defeated by treating with a systemic insecticide in late August; this is absorbed and remains active until the aphids attack in spring. Spring treatment is useless. However, since treatment is expensive, there are other shrubs to fill the place of these two species.

Viburnum tomentosum: Doublefile viburnum. Zone 4. To 9 feet.

Perhaps the finest of all viburnums, this plant produces flat heads of white flowers, some sterile, some fertile, forming a halo around a greenish white center. The Japanese snowball, *Viburnum tomentosum* sterile, is a fully double form of this in which the flowers are all sterile and form a round ball, but it is much overplanted and less graceful than the single type.

Vitex angus-castus: Chaste tree, hemp tree, monk's pepper tree. Zone 7. To 10 feet.

This can be grown in Zone 5, but this means annual pruning back since the tops are killed by freezing. It flowers on new wood, however, so the bloom is not lost. It is one of the few summer- and autumn-flowering shrubs which has pale blue flowers, or sometimes white. They are fragrant.

Weigela hybrids: Zone 4. To 10 feet.

The true species are unimportant but there are many fine hybrids of this outstanding shrub. By cutting back the stronger branches from time to time, they can be kept flowering nearly all summer. Two varieties widely sold are Eva Rathke and Cardinal flower.

6

GROUND COVERS

ALTHOUGH MOST GARDENING BOOKS LIST the plants described below as perennials, they are being given a special classification here because of their importance as labor savers. Anyone who has tried to mow a steep slope covered with turf will appreciate a plant such as *Arenaria caespitosa,* a sandwort which is finer than the finest bent, covered with starlike white flowers in May, and so aggressive that only modern chemical weed-killers make it practical as a ground cover.

One of the most important factors preventing the use of more ground covers has been the attitude of the American gardener, who foolishly looks upon them as a confession of incompetence. Grass is easy to grow—why can't he grow it under maple trees or oaks? And so he keeps sowing seed year after year, only to see it die by August.

Far from being a sign of poor gardening, the use of ground covers is a mark of distinction, identifying the true plantsman who knows that no grasses will survive in areas where the total amount of sunshine is less than one-third of that in the open.

A fine planting of ground covers will draw more favorable comments than even a high-quality grassy turf. For example, I had an area under trees where grass was all but impossible to grow, but by using a special variety which actually thrived in 25 percent total sunshine, I was able to maintain a perfect grass cover. Just behind this area, I planted an English ivy, apparently *Hedera helix* baltica, sent to me by the late Eugene Boerner, who had developed it to survive in our rigorous climate. In seventeen years, I have never had one visitor comment on the grass, a really extraordinary planting under the conditions prevailing, but hundreds have "ohed" and "ahed" about the ivy.

The coming of chemical weed-killers has revolutionized the use of ground covers. Formerly, keeping them clean was a major task. Grasses in particular were difficult: I once gave up a planting of prostrate junipers, which had cost hundreds of dollars to plant, simply because quack grass could not be controlled between the plants. Today, a single spraying with Dalapon would remove the quack grass without injuring the evergreens.

One important fact to keep in mind when using ground covers is that they are not dug up regularly and replanted. This means that the initial planting and soil preparation should not be skimped on. Those that demand sharp drainage may need underground tiling or dry drains and wells to remove surplus moisture. Species that do best in rich soils should be given plenty of organic matter. Water lines may have to be run into wooded areas to provide the extra moisture many shade-loving species require.

Where a low, fairly uniform covering is wanted, a rotary type lawn mower (not a reel mower) can be set high and used to mow off the tops two or three times during the year. For example, I have mowed both wood violets and goutweed: both were improved by this rough treatment. When mowing is possible, it is mentioned in the following descriptions. Mowing does, however, reduce or eliminate flowering.

Achillea millefolium: Sweet maudlin, yarrow, milfoil. Zone 2. Foliage 3 inches, flowers 24 inches.

The pink variety is the one to grow because of its outstanding foliage. Its pink flowers are a bit tall, but this plant will stand mowing if they want to be removed. It needs full sun to do well, but it will thrive on any soil, even poor, sterile clays and sandy loams.

Achillea tomentosa: Woolly yarrow. Foliage 8-12 inches, flowers 18 inches.

This is like the above, except that it has yellow flowers and grayish woolly foliage. It is good when used between stepping stones.

Aegopodium podograria: Goutweed, bishop's-mitrewort, bishop's-weed, dwarf ash. Zone 3. Foliage 6 inches, flowers to 12 inches.

Once so weedy that good gardeners hesitated to plant it, this plant, if it becomes a pest, can be killed by using either Silvex (2,4,5-TP) or a mixture of Banvel-D and 2,4-D. In good soil in light shade, the variegated green-and-white variety is a real gem. Its leaves resemble those of the ash or highbush cranberry, green with a distinct white edge. It should be mowed two or three times a summer to keep it compact if a lower growth is wanted. For a tight cover that will smother all weeds, allow it to grow without mowing.

Ajuga reptans: Bugleweed, carpenter's herb, carpet weed. Zone 4. Foliage 3 inches, flowers to 10 inches.

In milder climates this is practically evergreen. It is an outstanding ground cover that thrives in shade, does well in full sun, and is not fussy about the type of soil. It roots by runners that spread rapidly. There are variegated, multicolor, and deep red varieties also available. To control, use either Silvex or a liquid mixture of Banvel-D with 2,4-D. This plant tolerates mowing.

Arabis alpina: Alpine rock cress. Zone 3. Foliage 3 inches, flowers 10 inches.

Good ground covers for full sun on dry soils are not common—this is one. It is smothered with fragrant white flowers in April and May, but should be cut back with a sickle or grass shears after flowering (not with a mower) to encourage next year's bloom. A pink form is sometimes cataloged.

Arabis albida: Wall rock cress. Zone 3. Foliage 4 inches, flowers 10 inches.

Another ground cover that tolerates or even demands a sunny location, it is sometimes mixed with *Alyssum saxatile compactum* (which see) forming a lovely white and yellow mosaic in April and May. The plants usually sold in American commerce are actually *Arabis caucasica,* which has gray feltlike foliage, all the more attractive for this feature. The true variety has green foliage—better inspect the plants before buying to see what you are getting.

Arctostaphylos uva-ursa: Bearberry. Zone 2. To 6 inches.

A charming native that demands special culture, this plant, when happy, will form great mats of green foliage (bronzy in winter) with bright red berries appearing from summer to early winter. They must be purchased as pot-grown plants—they are almost impossible to transplant otherwise. Demanding a strongly acid soil (a pH of 4.5 to 5.5 suits it), quite sandy, and well drained, it does poorly in the Middle West.

Arenaria montana: Mountain sandwort. Zone 4. To 4 inches.

Its mosslike foliage and great clouds of white flowers in May make this an outstanding plant to grow between slabs on stone terraces, in rock walls, and in pockets in rock formations. It needs an acid soil of a pH of close to 5.8 to 6.0.

Arenaria verna caespitosa: Mossy sandwort. Zone 2. To 2 inches.

Sometimes listed in catalogs as *Arenaria caespitosa,* this is a real gem, even though when it is at home, it tends to take over any spot in sun or shade that has good drainage. It burns badly if exposed to full sun during the winter: a covering of fluffy straw or excelsior will keep it evergreen.

Armeria maritima: Sea thrift, common thrift, cliff rose, lady's cushion, marsh daisy. Zone 2. Foliage 6 inches, flowers 12 inches.

A vigorous, healthy plant, it can be divided frequently to cover ground in a hurry. It tolerates seaside conditions so long as the soil is well drained. The flowers vary from deep pink to white.

Asperula odorata: Sweet woodruff, mugwet, sweet grass. Zone 4. To 7 inches.

Anyone who has drunk May wine or May bowl is familiar with the flavor of this herb. One of the few ground covers that will thrive under azaleas and rhododendrons, it is also at home in moist soils in other shady locations. It is grown primarily for its excellent deep green foliage.

Campanula carpatica: Carpathian harebell. Zone 3. To 9 inches.

With its compact foliage, nodding sky-blue bells, and vigorous habit, this makes a perfect ground cover for areas in the full sun. Since the plants do not spread rapidly, they need to be planted closely to cover the soil, usually about 10 inches apart each way if an immediate effect is wanted. *Campanula rotundifolia,* the bluebells of Scotland, often recommended as a ground cover, just does not spread enough to serve this purpose.

Cerastium tomentosum: Snow-in-summer, Jerusalem star, woolly-chickweed. Zone 3. To 6 inches.

A close relative of the mouse-ear chickweed, snow-in-summer has much of its vigor but less of its aggressive habits. Its silvery gray foliage and white flowers in June make it an excellent ground cover. A single plant spreads rapidly: planted 15 inches apart in spring, a bed will be solid by fall. If it gets out of hand, 2,4-D will easily control it. To make it more compact, shear after it flowers.

Ceratostigma plumbaginoides: Leadwort, plumbago. Zone 6. To 6 inches.

Bearing some of the most vivid of all blue flowers, with deep glossy green foliage that turns bronze in autumn, this is a favorite ground cover in milder climates. It tolerates light shade but prefers

A vigorous ground cover that grows well in sun and shade, the lily of the valley is also beautiful and fragrant.

full sun. It is practically evergreen, but does shed its foliage late in winter and does not leaf out until quite late in spring. If it becomes weedy, control with Silvex.

Convallaria majalis: Lily of the valley, mugget, conval lily, May lily. Zone 2. To 6 inches.

If anything, this plant is too vigorous: its need for digging up and dividing the bed every three years must be considered in relation to the amount of work you want to do. It grows anywhere, sun or shade, although half shade suits it best. No common garden flower is more fragrant—its bell-like blossoms on 6 inch spikes are in demand when it flowers in June for wedding bouquets.

Cornus canadensis: See under "Shrubs."

Coronilla varia: Crown vetch.

This is mentioned here only to warn against growing it except where complete domination of the area by this weedy plant can be tolerated.

It is harder to eradicate than quack grass once it invades an area. It is now being promoted under special trade names. It has value in the holding of steep sunny banks.

Dianthus arenarius: Sand pink. Zone 4. Foliage 3 inches, flowers 9 inches.

Although this has grasslike foliage, it is hardly dense enough to cover the soil well. It is valuable because of its ability to survive in full sun on sandy soils. It produces white fragrant single flowers in late June.

Dianthus deltoides: Maiden pink, carpet pink. Zone 2. Foliage 2 inches, flowers 5 inches.

Unlike the preceding, this pink forms a dense mat of grasslike foliage, and if planted not more than a foot each way, it will carpet an entire area. Formerly, quack grass invading large areas of maiden pink was a nuisance, but since this species is resistant to Dalapon, quack grass can be controlled without digging if directions are followed carefully.

Dichondra repens: Lawn leaf. Zone 7. To 3 inches.

This is used in California, in milder sections of the Gulf States, and on lower sections of the East Coast as a lawn substitute. It can be mowed. Grass that invades a dichondra lawn can be killed out with Dalapon. Its leaf is roundish; its flowers inconspicuous. It can become weedy, but can be killed with many common weed-killers. It is usually listed in catalogs under turfgrasses rather than as a ground cover.

Euonymus species:

Because of the nuisance and labor involved in keeping out euonymus scale, this group of fine ground covers is not recommended for the busy gardener.

Galax aphylla: Carpenter's leaf, white-wand plant, galax. Zone 4. To 5 inches.

This plant is stemless: its round, glossy evergreen leaves rise directly out of the soil, forming a continuous ground cover. In summer, tall spikes of white flowers, about 2 feet tall, arise from the carpet of stemless leaves. In fall, the foliage turns a delicate bronze. It is only for moist shade on slightly acid soil.

Gaultheria procumbens: Wintergreen, mountain tea, tea berry. Zone 3. To 3 inches.

This is another of the low-growing evergreen creeping plants of the acid soils in New England, which, like the preceding, thrives in light shade on moist, peaty soils.

Gypsophila repens rosea: Rosy creeping chalkplant. Zone 3. To 6 inches.

This is one of the few sun-loving plants that will thrive on limestone soils where moisture is not plentiful. Its generic name means "lime-loving" and it really is. Although strikingly beautiful when in bloom, its season is fairly short.

Hedera helix: English ivy, barren ivy, bindwood. Zone 5 in shade, Zone 6 in sun. Creeping vine.

If not exposed to winter sun, it is hardier: I have grown two strains in Zone 4 on the north side of a house. We think of English ivy as being beloved by the British (which it is by many), but I have heard old gardeners on the Tight Little Isle curse it as a pestiferous weed. However, it is one of the best ground covers for shady places in this country.

Iberis sempervirens: Evergreen candytuft. Zone 4. To 10 inches.

Don't use the improved, named varieties of this perennial: they are compact and do not spread. To produce a solid ground cover, shear (don't mow) the plants soon after its white flowers appear in late May or early June. If the plants are allowed to dry out, they tend to run to seed quickly; give them a moist situation in full sun.

Lamium galeobdolon: Golden archangel, yellow dead nettle. Zone 5. To 10 inches.

The interesting green leaves of this plant are blotched with grayish white. It is a vigorous-growing ground cover bearing yellow inconspicuous flowers and perferring a light limey soil in full sun.

Lamium maculatum: Spotted dead nettle. Zone 4. To 6 inches.

Similar to the above, it is hardier and has mauve-lilac flowers instead of yellow.

Liriope spicata: Creeping lily-turf. Zone 4. To 8 inches.

Once touted as a lawn substitute having miraculous properties, the foliage of this plant is grasslike and deep green. It might be called evergreen except that it turns a sickly yellowish green in winter. It is probably best planted only in Zone 5 and south, although it is hardy in the North. In the South, it is one of the best ground covers for shady spots.

Lysimachia nummularia: Creeping Charley, creeping Jenny, moneywort. Zone 3. To 2 inches.

The common names of this plant are shared with and confused with those of ground ivy. The leaves are somewhat alike, but this species has cup-shaped yellow flowers. It is an ideal ground cover for wet soil, and if it becomes weedy, it is easily controlled with 2,4-D.

Mazus reptans: Himalayan lavender. Zone 4. To 1 inch.

Small lavender-colored flowers appear on this prostrate plant which roots as it creeps. It cannot tolerate winter sun.

Mentha piperita: Peppermint. Zone 3. To 24 inches.

A plant for low, wet soils in the sun or shade, this is a weedy plant that can be kept under control by mowing with a scythe about once a year.

Mentha spicata: Spearmint. Zone 3. To 18 inches.

This plant is like the above but less rampant, needing mowing only once a year. Both these species can be killed out when necessary with chemical weed-killers.

Mitchella repens: Squaw berry, twin berry, partridge berry. Zone 3. Trailing.

For sandy, peaty soils in the shade, there is no better ground cover. It can be mowed. Its bright red berries remain all winter if not eaten by birds. Wants an acid soil.

Myosotis scorpioides: Forget-me-not. Zone 4. To 12 inches.

For moist soils in the shade, this is one of the best ground covers. It dies down completely in winter, but it soon clothes the ground in spring and is in bloom practically all summer long. The one to buy is semperflorens, a low-growing variety.

Glecoma hederacea (Nepeta hederacea): Ground ivy, Jill-o'er-the-ground, creeping Jenny. Zone 3. To 5 inches.

Whether this is a weed or a delightful ground cover depends on one's philosophy. No plant is more vigorous, aggressive, and trouble-free. It will invade lawns, borders, and any other area it can reach if not controlled, yet it is a lovely thing—creeping stems covered with round leaves with scalloped edges and tiny mintlike flowers, pale lavender-purple in color. It can be controlled chemically with a mixture of 2,4-D and Banvel-D (dicamba) if it gets out of hand.

Omphalodes verna: Marie Antoinette's forget-me-not, creeping navelseed, creeping forget-me-not. Zone 7. To 6 inches.

An evergreen creeper with striking blue or pale lavender flowers, this plant will grow in full sun or half shade.

Pachistima canbyi: Rat-stripper. Zone 5. To 12 inches.

If ever a plant deserved a pleasing common name, it is this one. It has delightful evergreen foliage, resembling that of a dwarf holly. Once established, it needs no care, but does need an acid soil with good drainage.

Pachysandra terminalis: Japanese spurge. Zone 4. To 6 inches.

Probably the most widely planted of all ground covers in America, this plant forms dense mats of evergreen foliage in which no weeds can grow. This is about the only plant that can survive under Norway maples, and even it should have an annual feeding to survive there.

It will not survive in full sun. Light shearing of the leaves is permissible, but don't cut the stems.

Phalaris arudinacea picta: Variegated ribbon grass, gardener's garters. Zone 3. To 3 feet.

This is the first plant I can recall from my youth; it formed great masses of green-and-white striped foliage in my grandfather's garden. It is an excellent ground cover for areas in full sun, although it will tolerate some shade. Its habit of sending out underground runners can make it a nuisance but the grass-killer Dalapon will readily control it. It is just the plant for that bank that can't be mowed.

Phlox divaricata: Wood phlox, wild sweet William. Zone 3. To 12 inches.

Although it is a bit tall for a good ground cover, in spring it will form great sheets of vivid cerulean blue along the margins of shaded woods. It needs some sun to do well, however, and rich, moist soil.

Phlox subulata: Ground phlox, moss pink, cushion phlox. Zone 2. To 5 inches.

In the past, the blatant magenta-pink flowers of this plant were so garish that anyone with a good sense of color would hesitate to plant it. Today, some truly beautiful shades of lavender blues, clear pinks, deep reds, and pure whites make this a highly desirable ground cover for hot, dry slopes, even in well-drained gravels. It needs frequent replanting as the older plants die out at the center of a clump, but it serves such a useful purpose that this one weakness can be overlooked.

Polygonum reynoutria: Carpet fleece flower. Zone 4. To 6 inches.

The head of one of the country's leading arboretums once said to me, "If you plant this d—— thing, be sure you have it surrounded by a cement curb and never let it get out." His advice was a bit harsh for a good low-growing ground cover, although this can be one of the most invasive and aggressive of weeds if it does escape. Fortunately, it can be killed out where not wanted by using a mixture of Silvex (2,4,5-TP) and 2,4-D. Its pink flowers are attractive in a situation in poor soil in full sun.

Potentilla cinerea: Rusty cinquefoil. Zone 3. To 4 inches.

Although it looks like a weed, its five-petaled pale yellow flowers are attractive in May and June.

Prunella vulgaris: Heal-all, self-heal. Zone 3. To 3 inches.

If allowed to grow, this can get 12 inches tall, but it should be mowed at least once in early summer to make it less aggressive. A weed that can escape into the lawn and cause trouble, it is still useful because it will grow in any moist soil in sun or shade. Control with 2,4-D plus Banvel-D (dicamba).

Pachysandra is extremely popular because it quickly forms a dense mat of evergreen foliage in shady locations.

Sagina subulata: Pearlwort. Zone 4. To 4 inches.

For planting between stepping stones on a shaded terrace or for producing masses of low green in other shaded areas, this is a gem. In summer, it produces tiny white flowers so profusely that the foliage is often hidden. The leaves are mosslike.

Saponaria ocymoides: Soapwort. Zone 2. To 6 inches.

Although a perennial, this is often short-lived, but since it self-sows freely, it needs no replanting. Its mats of bright pink flowers in late spring often last until August. It likes full sun and a rocky soil.

Sedum acre: Mossy stonecrop, carpet-of-gold. Zone 3. To 2 inches.

Many gardeners scorn the stonecrops because they grow so rapidly that no care is needed, but for the busy gardener, this is an asset, not a liability. If *Sedum acre* gets out of hand, it is easy to kill with most modern weed-killers. With its bright yellow flowers, this is one of the best ground covers for dry, sterile soils in full sun. It is too soft, however, to bear foot traffic.

Thymus serpyllum: Common thyme, mother-of-thyme, creeping thyme. Zone 3. To 2 inches.

Forming great carpets of grayish foliage with white, pink, lavender, and red flowers, no other ground cover can match it for covering rocks, cracks in flagstones, or dry sunny slopes of poor soil. It will tolerate some shade. Mow if it gets too rank: There are some interesting variegated varieties as well as some with distinctly colored foliage. Woolly thyme (*Thymus lanuginosus*) is usually classed as a variety of this: it differs only in the long white hairs that cover its stems and leaves.

Thymus vulgaris: Common thyme. Zone 4. To 8 inches.

This can be used as a taller ground cover, but is a subshrub, not a creeping, mat-forming ground cover. It may be ragged in appearance. Use a sickle to keep it neater.

Veronica filiformis: Professor's weed, creeping veronica, speedwell. Zone 4. To 3 inches.

With thousands of dollars being spent in research to find a chemical control for this humble blue flowering plant, to recommend it as a ground cover seems ridiculous. However, in spite of its aggressive, invasive nature, it is an outstanding ground cover, surviving in shade or sun, clothing the ground with its tiny oval leaves and forming clouds of blue flowers. It is certainly a no-care ground cover if there ever was one. If it does get out of hand, the only effective chemical control I have found for it is paraquat or diquat which, of course, kills everything growing with it. Avoid mowing it, since "stringers" caught in the mowing will spread it to every stretch of grass on which the mower is used later.

Veronica repens: Creeping speedwell, creeping veronica. Zone 5. To 4 inches.

Although not aggressive like the preceding, it still covers well. It prefers moist soil in full sun, but will survive on drier soils as well. There are rose-colored varieties as well as the typical veronica blue.

Vinca minor: Grave myrtle, periwinkle. Zone 4. To 6 inches.

Although more pachysardra or Japanese spurge is planted deliberately than is *Vinca minor,* the latter is perhaps more widely distributed, since it is spread by various natural agencies. It is a lovely thing, with glossy rich green foliage that forms solid mats in sun or shade. In my own garden, it is planted with Red Emperor tulips, which flower at the same time in spring. The color contrast between the scarlet of the tulips and the vivid blue of the periwinkle is spectacular. If used to keep soil of a bank from washing away, do not plant Bowles variety, which will not spread freely. It has, however, much more striking flowers, with individual blooms as large as a half dollar.

FOLIAGE COLOR

Although some ground covers flower so freely as to be worth planting for this feature alone, few do so in the shade. Here, the use of varieties of a single species with different foliage color can provide variety in a planting. One objection often raised against using ground covers is that they tend to be "monotonous." This seems a specious argument to anyone who has seen a sheet of *Vinca minor* covering a forest floor for an acre or more. Its simplicity is delightful, especially when dappled with sun and shade.

Those who prefer more color can easily have it by using the several varieties of *Ajuga reptans.* The rich green of the original species contrasts beautifully with the green-and-white variegated form and with its companion yellow-and-green type. In addition, there is a deep purplish maroon variety—a planting of this in Golden Gate Park, San Francisco, covers nearly an acre and is perhaps the most striking ground cover display in America.

To add further variety, there is a brown, gold, and green variety, difficult to find but beautiful when established.

Another example of a ground cover which has colored foliage

is *Thymus serpyllum*. In one European rock garden, there are the following forms: a woolly near-white, a variegated white and gray-green, a variegated yellow and green, a type with purplish stems and gray leaves, and a form with a purplish cast to the leaves. In addition, there were varieties with white, rose, pink, lavender, and purple flowers.

7

THE LAWN—WORK SAVER OR WORK MAKER?

ALL TOO OFTEN, the home owner looks upon the lawn as an essential feature of the home landscape, without once taking into account whether it *makes* work or *saves* it. Certainly, a house that is not surrounded by a stretch of green turf is unusual. Traditionally, any home that is not built directly on a cement sidewalk on a narrow city street is expected to support its quota of grass—grass that needs mowing at least once a week from early spring until late fall.

The question is whether the regular attention given to mowed turf adds up to, in the end, as much labor as would an equally large area planted to shrubbery, perennial borders, or other ornamentals. The answer is not simple since there are many *ifs* and *buts* to be solved.

Certainly, a well-established, nigh-perfect turf that is weedfree and untroubled by disease and insect pests can be mowed and swept in far less time than would be needed to care for an equal amount of space given over to almost any other form of gardening. In fact, the better the lawn, the less work it requires. This may sound strange, since few good things come easily, yet the lawn that really eats up hours of time, effort, and money is not the one that is uninfested by weeds, that shows no trace of turf diseases, and that has been kept free of insect pests. It is the poor lawn that calls for constant work.

No lawn absorbs more of the gardener's attention than does one which has been neglected on the mistaken theory that grass will survive in spite of such neglect. In spring, the neglected lawn will be found infested with snow mold and with large bare patches of grass dead or dying. In early summer, leaf-spot diseases may brown out bluegrasses; in summer and fall, weeds and grubs will take their toll.

WHY A LAWN?

A lawn can serve so many purposes that it is important to ask, "Why do I want a lawn?" The species of grass, how much money you want to spend on it, and many other such questions depend on what you want out of that grassed area.

Perhaps the most important aspect of a lawn is its ornamental value. No other landscape feature does as much to "pull together" all the elements of a design into a unified whole. At the same time, by allowing the eye to roam across longer sight lines, a lawn creates a feeling of spaciousness that makes a property look larger. Experienced real estate men have been known to raise the asking price of an average property by at least $1,000 if it has an almost perfect turf around it. As one explained it to me, "Not only does the grass itself look like more money, but your eye estimates the lot area as larger than it actually is."

Because of these considerations, a lawn may be worth considering, apart from the work it will require, if your property may have to be put on the market in the near future. The other alternative—limiting the grass area to a minimum and filling in the remaining space with trees and shrubs to save regular mowing and other lawn care details—may in the end call for more work than beginning a lawn.

Because an unbroken lawn both saves work and presents an appearance of spaciousness, the importance of avoiding cut-up areas, with dabs of shrubbery and badly placed trees, cannot be over emphasized.

One result of planting grass that the housewife will appreciate is that it helps to suppress dust and dirt, whereas even the best-cultivated flower border or vegetable garden will contribute something to her work load. Also of importance to the growing family is the availability of a grassy play area. Of course, unless the right

Just the right combination of lawn and paved area makes this appealing small garden.

species of grass is selected for this area, growing it can mean a great deal of work, since an active family can do more damage to a play lawn than a football team can in a quarter's play.

Even though initially we may not think of lawn areas as labor savers, when all the advantages are added up, they call for less work per square foot than any other form of planting. In spite of the attention needed to control their various ills, lawns require fewer hours of labor than do annuals, perennials, or bulbs.

CORRECT CONSTRUCTION SAVES WORK LATER

A fact to keep in mind is that a lawn can keep growing for a century; consequently, there are no opportunities for making major improvements of the soil underneath once the grass is planted. Drainage, humus content, "built-in" fertility, and other essentials are determined the day the lawn is seeded or sodded.

Although a great deal of nonsense is written about "ideal" lawn soils, some species of grass, or combinations of grasses, can be found that will produce a useable turf on almost any one of the over 200 soil types found in the United States. I have personally grown lawns on everything from pure dune sand to almost pure clay.

This does not mean that soil is unimportant, but it does mean, as explained in the chapter on soils, that this vital element can be modified before planting (and handled after the lawn is in active growth) so as to support healthy turf which will need less care. Four factors are important: (1) proper drainage; (2) built-in, or native, fertility; (3) proper soil modification of *texture* and *structure;* (4) a smooth, uniform surface.

Drainage should never be left to chance. Few lawn grasses like wet feet, although some bent grasses and *Poa trivialis* (so-called Danish bluegrass) will thrive on damp, rich soils. These, however, are special-purpose grasses which call for so much care as to be outside our purpose—that of saving effort wherever possible. For the gardener who wishes to avoid work, the only place that bents are desirable is in damp, foggy areas where they occur naturally and will even invade turf areas seeded to other species.

Check drainage as soon as the surface has been leveled. A good way to do this, if there is no chance to observe the lawn over a period of heavy rainfall, is to spill a barrel of water at the highest point and watch what happens to it. If it does not disappear within twenty minutes, make provisions for artificial drainage by means of tile drains. Also check whether it passes off by penetrating the soil or by running downhill. Some stiff clays on a slope will shed water so rapidly that most summer rainfall is lost: be sure to modify the soil as recommended in chapter 3 so that rain can actually penetrate to where the roots can absorb it.

Whenever possible drainage should flow *away* from house foundations. In grading, try to figure so that "cut" will equal "fill" to save work. This means taking away soil at the low end of the lawn and wheeling it to the top, which may seem like doing extra work; yet the amount of soil moved will be less than if the entire area were stripped and redistributed. This principle applies to either a small area to be worked by hand with a wheelbarrow or a large lawn to be graded with power machinery.

PREPLANTING FERTILIZERS

Perhaps the most neglected step in lawn construction is that of improving the native, or built-in, fertility of the soil. As already mentioned, once the grass is growing, all areas underneath are inaccessible. One element in particular must be worked deeply into lower layers—phosphorus. When applied as a fertilizer to the surface, phosphorus is quickly locked up in insoluble form almost at the point of application. Consequently, it moves hardly at all and cannot be reached by roots. The application of a heavy dose of superphosphate before planting, as much as sixty pounds of a 20 percent phosphorus to 1,000 square feet of surface, will provide enough of this vital element to last many years. It will become slowly available as roots reach it.

Although potash is more readily soluble than phosphorus, it is much less so than many other fertilizer elements. An application of twenty-five pounds of muriate of potash or sulfate or potash worked in to a depth of four inches will give any lawn a better start.

The ureaform high-nitrogen fertilizers mentioned in chapter 3 are also long-lasting when incorporated in soil. Because these supply only nitrogen, they should be used in trademarked products which also contain phosphorus and potash in addition to ureaform. I must emphasize that for each pound of nitrogen applied, at least half a pound of potash should also be used. This is a basic principle proved in agronomy by years of experience, yet one which is ignored by present-day fertilizer producers. Neglect of this principle will result in grass plants which have poor root structure and weak crowns, and are readily invaded by diseases, making the grass a source of more work for the home owner who is anxious to avoid extra effort.

I have already mentioned the use of the Hydrocare unit as a labor saver. Because it applies plant foods in liquid form, it cannot be used to build fertility into the soil in the manner just described. If, however, you live in an area where regular watering is necessary, say at least once a week, it can be used to supply light doses of plant foods at regular intervals. The advantage of this method of feeding is that it can be adjusted to the needs of the grass. If growth is slow during hot weather, feeding can be reduced. If the grass does not seem to be growing fast enough, feed oftener.

Note what is said about humus in chapter 3; this is the most important material available for building into soil fertility which will last for long periods of time.

SOIL TEXTURE AND STRUCTURE

We can modify the texture of soils, as described in chapter 3, to make the soil more permeable and better suited to grass growth. Structure (the arrangement of soil particles in various layers) is important only so far as it affects drainage. For grasses, it is not desirable to plow or rotary-till much deeper than four inches, except in unusual situations. The deeper you work the soil, the more it will have to settle afterwards; in settling, it will develop an uneven surface. Four inches of good friable soil, which is about as deep as roots will go to the first year after seeding or sodding, will provide all the food and moisture needed to get grass off to a good start. Deeper plowing will only mean more work having to be spent on achieving the next step—a level surface.

WHY IS LEVELING IMPORTANT?

Many irritating and time-consuming lawn problems arise as the result of an uneven surface. Take, for example, mowing. Both the reel mower and the rotary type will hit the high spots and skip the low. As a result, either the grass in the high spots is cut too short or, at the worst, the crowns of the grass plants will be actually injured. This weakens the turf, permitting crab grass and other weeds to take over. Low spots will be cut too high, not as serious a problem, yet this will result in an ununiform surface that hurts the appearance of the entire lawn.

Although producing a smooth, level surface does call for some work at first, it will be worth it in the end. Large areas may require power machinery, but any able-bodied man should be able to "drag" an area of up to 5,000 square feet and produce a uniform surface in less than one afternoon.

Leveling calls for a piece of homemade equipment which is simple to assemble. One section of a wooden extension ladder forms the drag. One end of a rope is tied to the top rung, and the other, to the bottom rung. When this device is dragged across the surface, dirt will be picked up between the ladder rails and dumped in low spots. Drag once from north to south and once from east to west.

Most lawn makers then make a serious error—they roll over the newly leveled ground with a water-loaded roller which is so heavy that the soil is pounded down. Rolling *is* needed but the roller used should be relatively light, with just enough water in it to firm the surface. After rolling, the surface should be dragged again in each direction. After the surface has been raked, it will be ready for seeding or sodding.

SODDING VERSUS SEEDING

Sodding done by professional labor is the ideal way to develop an instant lawn—if you can afford it. Not only will you save a long period of having to give it fussy care, but for at least a year, you will eliminate the expense and effort that otherwise would go into controlling weeds and insect pests, and if long-lasting fertilizers are used, of lawn feeding. This not-inconsiderable saving can go a long way toward offsetting the additional cost of sodding over seeding.

One drawback to sodding is that ordinarily sod is available only in a grass of a single variety. In the North, for example, perhaps 95 percent of all sod laid is Merion, or is at least claimed to be of that variety. Not that Merion is a poor grass; as the first garden writer to call it to the attention of the public, I have probably sung its praises louder than any other individual. But in the following section, I must warn against the dangers of monoculture—the growing of a single species or variety.

In the meanwhile, do check with the better sod nurseries in your vicinity and find out whether they are growing mixtures of various desirable permanent grasses for laying lawns which will in the end save time, effort, and money for you.

GRASS VARIETIES

Perhaps the best illustration of the dangers of monoculture is the widespread devastation which has been caused by Dutch elm disease. In the past, street after street was planted to the susceptible American elm, making the spread of this disease from tree to tree all but impossible to prevent. Had mixed populations been planted, spread by root grafts would have been avoided. In addition, flights of the elm beetle, which also carries the infectious fungus, would have been at least slowed down if not stopped entirely. The same spread from plant to plant can happen in a lawn.

At present, about the only grass we have which is practically 100 percent diseasefree is zoysia, a grass which cannot be said to be perfect, as desirable as it is. The perfect grass just does not exist. Some species and varieties resist certain diseases but are susceptible to others, resistance to which can be found in yet other grasses. Only by combining several named varieties or by using the mixed populations found in unselected pure species are we able to develop a turf which will present an attractive appearance at all times in spite of minor troubles.

NORTHERN GRASSES

ZOYSIA: Although there have been reports of minor diseases attacking some varieties of zoysia, this is the only grass that I would recommend planting in pure stands. Unfortunately, seed cannot be used, since it does not come true. The original *Zoysia japonica* is coarser than quack grass and forms ugly mats of thick stems. Its seedling variety, *Zoysia meyeri,* is quite another grass. It forms a thick, dense mat about the texture of Merion bluegrass but its blades are much tougher. Only a power mower of at least three horsepower will cut it.

Its one weakness (for the man who wants a green lawn for the longest possible period of time) is that it does not green up until about May in the North and it dies out with the first frost. To some, this is an advantage, since it shortens the period during which it must be mowed by at least two months. Also, the dead, brown grass can be dyed green with chemicals to reasonably resemble the appearance of a lawn which is still in active growth.

In the South, it would be foolish not to consider some variety of zoysia, particularly *Zoysia emerald* or *Z. matrella* (*Flawn* is the trade name for the latter).

Zoysias are established from plugs that are set in the soil at intervals of about twelve inches. In the North, spread is quite slow; for a filler between the plugs, sow annual ryegrass—zoysia will crowd it out about the second year. The ryegrass will, of course, have to be seeded each year in the spring until the turf is continuous.

MERION KENTUCKY BLUEGRASS: Luxury turf of Merion has become a status symbol in many suburban communities in the United States. Certainly, when it is at its best, no grass other than the professionally tended bent grass on a putting green can equal it. Merion forms a dense, deep green, vigorous sod that crowds out crabgrass and other weeds. From seed, though, it is a slow starter, not forming a solid turf until late fall from spring-sown seed. During this time weeds must be tolerated until the turf has been mowed at least twice. I would not recommend planting it south of a line stretching from the northern border of Kansas to the northern border of Delaware. Above that line, it should make up 40 percent to 50 percent of a good lawn mixture for any area that receives more than four to five hours of sun a day.

One weakness of Merion is the fact that it is in active growth at the time when wheat-rust spores are flying. Under humid eastern conditions, however, which necessitates frequent mowing of well-fed Merion lawns, this is no problem. Since wheat rust infests the tender growing tips of grasses, frequent mowing removes it. Too, well-fed Merion, with enough potash to balance the nitrogen, resists invasion by the spores.

In the wheat-growing areas of the West—Kansas, Nebraska, and eastern Colorado, however, Merion is slowed up in growth by summer heat so that it is mowed less frequently. Too, the presence of vast numbers of spores makes infection difficult to avoid. In these areas, Merion is not particularly desirable except as a small percentage of a mixture.

Unless Merion is well fed, however, it will be no better than common Kentucky bluegrass. It is not unusual to see a pure turf of this grass grow luxuriously for three or four years, then become thin and disease-ridden after it has exhausted the native soil fertility. It must have at least four pounds of actual nitrogen and two pounds of actual potash per 1,000 square feet, in addition to other essential elements. Quick-acting fertilizers require at least five applications during the growing season—this is a time-waster for the busy gardener. Only slow-acting, nonburning fertilizers that can be put on in a single application should be used. In some sections of the United States, a disease called stripped smut is badly injuring or killing Merion, which seems to be peculiarly susceptible to it.

Caution is advised in seeding or sodding Merion in pure stands. Check with your state experiment station for information on the advisability of using this variety.

ARBORETUM, DELTA, NEWPORT, WINDSOR, PRATO, AND FYLKING: All these are selections from the original Kentucky bluegrass, which were made because of certain advantages that have been observed by turf specialists. None, unfortunately, at this time, combines as many favorable qualities as does Merion. When, however, at least three of these named varieties are combined with Merion, high resistance to most turf troubles will result. Delta is a fast-germinating variety that helps fill in until slower-growing Merion can take over. Arboretum, which is more heat-resistant, is good for the area south of Merion's range. It also resists the root rot which occurs when Merion is starved for potash. Newport and Windsor have better color very early in spring and late in fall. Prato combines many of the resistances of Merion, but not to the same degree. Fylking is particularly valuable because it combines resistance to many diseases, makes low growth and a dense, tight sod.

FYLKING, a selection from Sweden, is perhaps the only grass which should be used as a single ingredient with Merion. It is so dwarf-growing that if it were planted with other bluegrasses, it would be crowded out. Since Merion can be mowed as short as one inch, with Fylking it forms an excellent turf where a close cut is wanted, as for a home putting green.

COMMON KENTUCKY BLUEGRASS: This agronomic mongrel is by no means obsolete. A pound of seed of common Kentucky bluegrass contains not one variety or subspecies, but a million or more. Since most seed of this grass is a blend of harvests from half a dozen different locations, opportunity for development of varieties within the batch of seed is great, each having a resistance to some condition which might occur in your lawn.

Including 15 to 20 percent common Kentucky bluegrass seed in a mixture is not a bad idea. Unfortunately, practically all plants resulting from a pure seeding of common Kentucky bluegrass alone will be susceptible to a condition known as summer dormancy in which the turf turns brown and makes no growth until cooler weather comes in late summer.

FINE-LEAVED FESCUE: In New England, along the Canadian border, and in the Pacific Northwest, where cooler nights are the rule, fine-leaved fescues can be seeded alone without creating conditions that will mean more work for the home owner. Here they thrive in either sun or shade. In warmer sections of the North, down to the Kansas–Delaware limit mentioned under Merion, they are among our better grasses for shade or for dry soils low in fertility.

They are by no means carefree, however, and must be planted with that in mind. They are susceptible to turf diseases which will wipe out most of a lawn in hot, muggy weather. Even so, I like to include at least a small percentage of Pennlawn fescue, the most resistant variety, in a turf mixture for any type of lawn. If some spot then happens to be dry and low in fertility, the Pennlawn will take over. If conditions, however, favor Merion, or other named bluegrasses, it will be crowded out, with no loss in turf quality.

Another reason for adding Pennlawn is that most home owners underestimate the amount of shade they actually have. Because they see the lawn at a time of day when the sun strikes it, they fail to note that it is in full shade at other times. In such a situation, the Pennlawn will make a satisfactory turf in spite of shade.

BENT GRASSES: Anyone who wishes to avoid extra lawn care should shun the bent grasses as he would the plague, unless, perhaps, it is to plant in cool, moist areas near the sea in a few parts of the country.

As wonderful as the bents look over a cocktail on the golf club veranda, they call for a prodigious amount of work to keep alive, let alone thriving. If you doubt this, ask your golf course superintendent: his greens represent a major portion of his labor load.

I must warn, too, against Highland bent, widely used to give an air of quality to cheap lawn mixtures. True, this is an upland bent that thrives in spite of neglect and relatively low fertility. Its weakness is a long, strawlike sheath which it has at the base of the blade. When the grass is mowed at lawn heights, the green portion of the blade is cut off, leaving this sheath as a brown disfiguring straw.

GROUND COVERS: If the area to be covered receives less than 25 percent of the total sunshine that falls on lawns in the open, don't waste any time trying to grow grass. The only grass I know that will survive so little direct sun is a special selection made by the Warren Turf Nurseries and is available only in sod. For seeded grasses, any spot that enjoys less than 33 percent sunshine during a June day will give nothing but trouble. To save work, plant a ground cover of one of the species described in chapter 6.

TALL FESCUES: Two grasses that need to be given special mention are Alta fescue and Kentucky 31 fescue. These are quite different from their fine-leaved relatives and need different treatment. They are clump-forming: nowadays I receive more complaints about them than I do about crab grass. If you see a lawn in which clumps of tall, coarse grass are scattered over an area which is otherwise covered by finer grasses, you can be almost certain that its owner sowed a mixture containing Kentucky 31 fescue.

This weedy grass is added to such mixtures to deceive the purchaser into believing it contains Kentucky bluegrass, an entirely different grass. Alta, incidentally, differs from Kentucky 31 only in a week's difference in seed maturity.

Although both of these grasses should be banned from all mixtures (federal laws now require that they be listed separately in the formulas on grass seed packages), they are not without their value for the work-conscious lawn maker. They can form a turf so tough that it can withstand the impact of an emergency landing of heavy aircraft or the abuse of a football play. In fact, many football fields are planted to these grasses.

They must not, however, be sown thinly. If too much space is allowed between plants, they will develop their normal clumping habit. When, however, they are seeded at a heavy rate—from six to ten pounds per 1,000 square feet—the plants are so crowded that they form a continuous sod. When mowed to a height of two inches, the effect is quite acceptable.

This is the only grass I know that can be used to form a lawn that will endure the abuse of play by active children. It will also require little care. Two pounds of actual nitrogen a year will feed it well. It is also the only grass I know that will grow on highly sandy soils (such as are found on certain areas of Long Island, for example), where it will send down roots for many feet to reach water that is completely out of the reach of finer-textured lawn grasses.

NURSE GRASSES: At one time, perhaps inspired by the fact that they were low in price, both so-called perennial ryegrass as well as annual or Italian ryegrass were included in even the best seed mixtures. They were dubbed nurse grasses, on the theory that they would provide shelter for the less-vigorous perennial seedlings during their critical first few months.

This theory has been so thoroughly exploded that you can be sure the only purpose in including them today in a supposedly good mixture is to lower the blending cost. Far from acting as protection, these are actually smother grasses which reduce the chances of survival for other grasses.

Ryegrasses do, however, have a place in modern turf culture. These are not the old-fashioned perennial ryes, though, which was far from perennial north of the Ohio River. Instead, they are two new selections of perennial rye put out by the Northrup King

Company, NK-100 and Pelo, which have been tested for several winters at temperatures lower than thirty below zero and have survived. In the East, Manhattan is a similar variety.

These really tough grasses are fast-growing, producing a solid turf the first year from seed. Ryegrasses are noted for their beautiful rich green color: these new varieties are no exception. In my own tests, NK-100 has combined beautifully with Merion; since it is so fast growing, it looks like an excellent variety with which to supplement the slower Merion the first year. In the East, Manhattan, released by Rutgers University is, if anything, better in quality.

Too new as yet to evaluate fully, these ryegrasses are worth watching.

SOUTHERN GRASSES

Although over forty years have passed since I saw my first southern "lawn," I can still remember it—it was an expanse of hard-baked red clay, leading up to what seemed to be fine Georgia homes, and there was not a blade of grass in sight.

Much has happened to lawn culture south of the Mason–Dixon line since that day. Many of our grasses for southern conditions can match the best the North can offer. Some of the better Bermudas have fooled many a Yankee into believing he was looking at a heat-tolerant bent grass.

One of the first facts that southern home owners had to learn when they did begin growing these better grasses was that lawns needed feeding as much as did their field crops. With a growing season that is three to four months longer than that of New York, the Mississippi garden enthusiast found that his grass could use twice as much nitrogen, phosphorus, and potash as could those of his friends in the North. One rule for lawn makers in warm climates that will assure success with these improved species and varieties is that for every month that frost does not occur, one pound of actual nitrogen per 1,000 square feet of lawn, properly balanced with the other nutrient elements, must be applied. Since the rapid breakdown of humus under southern conditions makes it difficult to build in reserve fertility, regular feeding becomes even more important.

At one time, insects were the most difficult problem to solve in the South, but the introduction of diazinon (sold under the trade name of Spectracide for lawn use) has given the lawn owner a highly effective weapon against these pests. Chinch bugs, which once made the growing of St. Augustine grass a risky proposition, are now a relatively minor pest when this insecticide is used routinely.

ST. AUGUSTINE: Often Northerners who move to Florida are surprised to learn that this is not a southern strain of quack grass, but a desirable lawn species. For many years, it was "the" luxury grass for warmer climates in spite of its flat, hard stems and wide, coarse leaves. It is still the most desirable grass for shady lawns which are less than 150 miles north of the Gulf of Mexico, south through Florida and Texas. Unfortunately, it is *not* a low-maintenance grass (see Centipede in next section) since it requires regular spraying with both insecticides and fungicides to keep it healthy.

CENTIPEDE: Normally, this grass would be mentioned last—it has little to recommend it for quality lawns—but since the purpose of this book is to reduce gardening labor to its lowest point, Centipede must be given closer attention. It is less shade-tolerant than Saint Augustine, is hard to establish, does not wear well under foot traffic, and is course in texture. The color is a dull gray-yellow-green, although if fed with chelated iron, it will color up well. It thrives on acid soils, but will kill out if limed.

Although seed is available, this is frightfully expensive and seeded lawns take ages to become established. It is best planted from sprigs. The resultant turf will win no prizes for quality, but it will survive.

CARPET GRASS: Often confused with St. Augustine, carpet grass makes less vigorous growth and lacks its deep, rich green color. It will grow in the damp, infertile soils, though, which occur so often in certain areas around the Gulf of Mexico. If it is not mowed regularly, it will produce ugly seed heads on short stalks. The seed will grow readily if sown in the spring when temperatures in the seventies occur.

BERMUDA GRASS: Once cursed by southern gardeners, Bermuda grass has become the darling of home owners since the introduction of some fine-leaved varieties which have better color. Too, the introduction of dalapon (sold under the trade name of Dowpon) has given them a chemical that will keep it within bounds when it attempts to invade perennial borders and other areas where it was once the South's worst weed. Since dalapon kills only grasses, it can be sprayed on other broad-leaved ornamentals without injury. Care must be used to avoid spraying monocotyledonous plants (those with narrow leaves with parallel veins), but otherwise, this chemical has tamed Bermuda grass.

Varieties to consider include Tiflawn, Tiffine, Tifway, Tifgreen, and Sunturf, mostly products of the USDA station at Tiffin, Georgia. All, unfortunately, must be planted as sprigs, since they do not come true from seed, or laid as sod.

All Bermudas are high-fertility grasses but do well without heavy watering. Their one weakness is a dislike for shade. Mow to a height of one inch. Because they brown out with cold weather, they are often overseeded with Italian ryegrass for winter green color, but a better grass for this is the Highland bent which I damned as a northern species. The seed is cheap enough when used at a rate of a pound to 1,000 square feet to compete with ryegrass, which must be seeded at a much higher rate even though it is cheaper by the pound. It kills out in Southern summers.

The strawy sheath which makes this grass offensive in the North does not show in the amount of growth Highland bent makes as a winter annual in the seedling stage.

Zoysia: See comments on this grass under "Northern Grasses." The South, however, has one advantage over the North in growing this grass: the varieties and species Matrella, Flawn, and Emerald are hardy and produce better turf here. In Florida and Southern California *Zoysia tenuifolia,* Mascarene grass, produces a turf finer than the finest bent, yet it is so tough that no weed can compete with it. It has been thirty-five years since I saw my first lawn planted to *Zoysia tenuifolia* on a Palm Beach estate, but I can see that lawn as vividly as though it were yesterday. No northern bent could match it. Unfortunately, it is completely subtropical in its requirements and cannot be grown where regular frosts occur.

MIXTURES IN THE SOUTH: Unlike the North, the South has not developed mixtures to combine multiple resistances to disease, insects, and other conditions. This is due perhaps to the fact that the appearances of the species available for lawn purposes differ so greatly that combining is not feasible. Overplanting, where one species occupies the area in summer and another in winter, is a different matter.

MOWING AS A LABOR SAVER

Proper mowing can save work for the home owner, just as improper mowing can cause trouble. The importance of having a flat, level surface to avoid skinning high spots has already been emphasized, but will bear repeating for those who are dealing with an existing lawn, rather than building one from the beginning. Half a day spent filling low spots and cutting down humps will in the end mean a saving of far more time in later care.

Here let me warn against the use of a heavy roller to mash down high spots—a favorite trick of some landscapers. This causes compaction and does a poor job of leveling. Instead, remove an area of sod, scrape away the excess soil, and replace the sod. A very light rolling will put the roots in firm contact with earth.

Low spots, unless really deep, are best treated by adding a little top soil at short intervals, allowing roots to fill the new soil before adding new. So long as most of the grass spears show above the light fill, all grasses used for permanent turf will soon produce new root growth in this way.

The *type* of mower used can contribute to lawn difficulties. The dull rotary mower plays an important role in encouraging lawn diseases. Even at best, rotaries do a poorer job of mowing than do reel units. If you will examine the tips of a lawn mowed with the former device, you will almost invariably find that grass blades will have horizontal bruises across them. A dull rotary breaks off grass rather than cutting it. A clean cut is much less likely to permit the entry of fungus spores.

Mowing patterns, too, can contribute to extra work. When the mower follows the same route each time, soil is pushed ahead of the roller a little, gradually building up bumps and hollows. Too, the grass develops a "set" in which the blades are slanted, making it difficult for the mower blades to cut cleanly. By changing the pattern—striking the blades from a different direction each time—a more uniform surface is developed, both in the soil surface and in the appearance of the blades.

A major cause of poor turf, on which hours of labor can be spent without improving matters (unless the right remedy is applied), is soil compaction. Even if you heed my warnings against heavy rolling, soil will gradually pack harder and harder: the pressure of mowing will result in compaction, particularly in spring and during wet periods. The use of a turf aerator (a device that punches cores of earth out of the sod), which can be rented from most good garden centers, will remedy this condition. Be sure to get instructions for use when renting—different types work differently.

In the North, a disease which makes work for the lawn owner at the season when time is most valuable is snow mold. When it invades a lawn, particularly one that is partially shaded, or where a mat or duff of organic matter has built up on the surface, spring will often find the lawn covered with patches of grayish white or pinkish gray dead spots. This condition is often called winterkill, but it is actually the result of a fungus disease which works only at low temperatures, even under snow.

Where snow mold has attacked, the grass will usually recover if the roots have not been killed, but often the dead spots must be cleaned out and reseeded. Chemical treatment—spraying with a turf fungicide as the lawn goes into winter but before it is covered with snow—will usually check the disease, but in areas that are infested year after year, a second application during a February thaw may be needed. Although spraying does call for some work, it will be far less than a serious invasion of snow mold would require in raking, spraying, and reseeding the resulting dead spots. These infections can be prevented by eliminating undecayed or partially rotted organic matter from the turf. Since they are unable to manufacture their own starches and sugars—energy foods vital to life—fungus organisms use those stored in organic matter.

The regular use of sewerage-sludge fertilizers on lawns which are severely attacked by snow mold is not advisable; use, instead, either pure chemical or mineral plant foods. Peat moss and peat humus have already been looted of their starches and sugars by centuries of decay and do not support disease organisms.

Fairy rings cause considerable consternation when they appear on lawns. Thousands of hours of labor have been wasted trying to eliminate these mysterious formations, which the Irish say the fairies cause when they dance by moonlight. In areas where Dutch elm disease is endemic, these green circles seem frequently to appear following the removal of a dead tree.

Often (but not always) fairy rings begin with the growth of mushrooms over some buried source of dead wood or other organic matter on which they can feed. The underground portion of this mushroom colony is called the *mycelium*—a threadlike structure that serves as a root. When the energy stored in the organic matter is exhausted, this mycelium grows outward, searching for more nourishment. Grass inside the ring dies. At the rim of the expanding mycelium, however, more food is released than can be used by the above-ground fungus growth. This excess food stimulates grass growth until it is a brilliant emerald green, much brighter than the surrounding turf; hence, the fairy ring which identifies this condition. If liberal amounts of buried organic matter are present, a ring can expand several feet in a single season, but growth is usually much slower than this.

The real problem of fairy rings develops inside the circle. The grass there becomes poor and thin, or may even die out completely. In an effort to correct the difficulty, the lawn owner may pour on fertilizer and water, only to see the condition worsen because the mycelium, which has formed a feltlike blanket about five to eight inches under the surface, has shut off all passages for water and food. Fertilizer may concentrate on the roots to a toxic degree. Fungicides do no good since the mycelium is already dead.

I have cured hundreds of cases of fairy ring by recommending the use of a tree root irrigator, the type of watering device that injects water deep in the ground to feed and water trees, to break up the felted mass. Most good garden centers sell tools of this type. Thrust the tip of this device into the ground inside the ring to a depth of about ten inches and turn on the water pressure. Keep it running until the surface inside the ring puffs up. In severe cases it may even pop open.

This treatment breaks up the mycelium and permits normal grass growth again.

CHEMICAL CONTROL OF WEEDS

The number of people who still try to control weeds by old-fashioned methods, or who allow them to take over an otherwise good lawn, is surprising when one considers how easily weeds can be controlled by chemicals. In half an hour's time, walking across the turf with a sprayer or a fertilizer distributor, any lawn owner can kill weeds (without injury to the grass) that would take weeks of work to eradicate by hand.

Since 1943, when Dr. Franklin D. Jones introduced his newly discovered weed-killer, 2,4-D, tremendous progress has been made in finding controls for thousands of different species. The search for new weed-control chemicals has followed two divergent paths. One has worked for greater selectivity—the ability to kill an undesirable grass, for instance, without destroying the desirable species and varieties which make up the permanent turf. This calls for some delicate manipulating of different "systems" within the plant to be killed which do not exist or are weakly organized in the plant to be saved. An important example of such a project is the control of crab grass in turf made up of bluegrasses, fescues, and similar permanent species. In this instance the weakness of crab grass is that it is an annual, but an annual whose seed is poorly supplied with phosphorus. By feeding with fertilizers low in that element and then treating with a crab grass killer which contains a poison—a poison which so closely resembles phosphorus that the seedling plant will absorb it—crab grass seedlings can be killed as they germinate.

Once the seedlings can make roots that will penetrate the layer of soil on the surface which was treated, however, the poison is no longer effective. This type of control, known as preemergence treatment, can be used effectively only in early spring. Several good materials are already available with some striking new ones almost ready for introduction.

Before purchasing a preemergence crab-grass control, however, decide whether grass reseeding must be done that spring, or not. If the lawn is thin and needs more seed, be sure to read carefully the cautions listed on the package. Some of these chemicals will not permit any seedling of the grass family to grow for several months after treatment. Others will permit seeding right on the sprayed lawn.

Postemergence treatment of older crab-grass plants (once the only way to control them) is much less successful, since new seed keeps germinating all summer long up to mid-August. Three or four sprayings will be needed for practical control, involving extra work, yet even so, this requires far less effort than do other methods of killing them.

Four chemicals are available that will control practically all the broad-leaved weeds that are likely to be troublesome in lawns. They are 2,4-D; 2,4,5-T; 2,4,5-TP (more widely known as Silvex); and dicamba (also known as Banvel-D). A mixture of Banvel-D and 2,4-D in *liquid* form is available which will destroy a longer list of lawn weeds than any other chemical combination I know. There is a *dry* formulation of these two chemicals, but in my experience, it is not as consistently effective as the type applied with a sprayer.

Perhaps the trickiest lawn problem of all is finding a way to kill winter annual weeds. Winter annuals are plants which produce seed in the spring or early summer which lies dormant until cool weather and then sprouts (usually about August 15 north of the Ohio River). The seedlings are not killed by freezing, making, instead, a little growth every time a thaw occurs in winter.

Common chickweed, knotweed, and annual bluegrass, *Poa annua*, are the three most important of these. The first two species are much less of a problem now that we have dicamba (Banvel-D). If the lawn is sprayed with a weed-killer containing this chemical during a warm day in mid-September, most of the seedlings will be killed and the rest weakened so that they will die during the winter.

Poa annua (annual bluegrass) is a much more difficult problem. This is the vivid green, low-growing grass that looks so beautiful in early spring, then goes to seed and dies during the first hot spell. Anything that will kill it when mature will also knock out desirable lawn grasses. A relatively new chemical called Betasan used in mid-September does a good job of control.

An alternative control is the application of calcium arsenate or lead arsenate in the fall: this is the remedy used by most golf courses because these will also control crab grass the following spring. The toxic nature of arsenic, however, has resulted in protests from conservationists because of the danger that birds encounter when they eat earthworms that have been killed by arsenate treatment.

RENOVATING OLD TURF

One way that a great deal of labor can be saved is to renovate old, worn-out turf rather than to start all over again. All too often, the advice of self-appointed experts is, "Plow it up and start from scratch."

This does little or nothing to solve the problem because in addition to the thin turf the owner once had, he will now be cursed with millions of weed seedlings which will appear as soon as the soil is disturbed. The vitality of buried weed seed must be seen to be believed. At what was once Michigan State College Dr. Beale buried weed seeds, digging them up at intervals over a forty-year period. At the end of the test, many species would still germinate, illustrating that when soil is disturbed, many species which need sunlight to sprout are stimulated and will produce strong seedlings—often as many as twenty to thirty to a square foot.

Thus, whenever possible, avoid disturbing the old turf if there is any chance to salvage some grass. The best procedure is to use a turf renovator, apply fertilizer, and reseed. Check on whether there is enough grass to save by looking down at the ground from an angle of forty-five degrees (if you are six feet tall, that means looking from the center of a twelve-foot circle). If at this angle, bare soil is visible all around you, the lawn is too thin to be worth saving.

Unless the soil is compacted severely, don't turn it over. Instead, kill off the old grass with Dowpon. A week after Dowpon has been applied, spray with a mixture of Banvel-D and 2,4-D to kill broad-leaved weeds. Six weeks after applying Dowpon, the soil should be free of all vegetation except for, perhaps, a few weak annual weeds. Pay no attention to these, but sow grass seed right in the old dead sod. The dead grass will act as a mulch and seed bed if kept moist and will ensure a good stand.

The best time to begin, if there is any choice, is about July 1, which will allow seeding to be done from about August 15 to 20, the best period for this operation in the North. In the South, early spring preparation is best, but be prepared for some weed infestation.

If the soil is so hard and compacted that it must be turned over and organic matter worked into it, be sure not to work deeper than four inches and then proceed as for a new lawn.

A frequent reason for complete renovation is bent-grass contamination of bluegrass turf. This is a complete reversal of former practices, when practically every luxury or deluxe mixture contained a percentage of bent. With the wider use of Merion Kentucky bluegrass, however, the visual effect of bent is to weaken its apparent texture. I have even had inexperienced lawn makers tell me that "moss" was invading their turf.

Since we have no really effective selective control for bent grasses, about the only remedy is killing out the old turf as described and reseeding. The most important fact to remember is that bent is persistent and hard to eradicate completely. If you leave so much as a single strand of it, the entire lawn will again be invaded. Thus, examine every inch of the surface to be sure you have destroyed this pest completely.

Two chemicals, both of which will remain active against new seed for a period of six to eight weeks, can be used to kill out bent grass. The most effective is dalapon. It will, however, kill only grasses, leaving dandelions, plantains, and other broad-leaved weeds as pests. While Silvex, used at the strength recommended for woody plants, will kill out most broad-leaved weeds, it is only partially effective against other grasses and won't do a thing to the worst of them all—quack grass.

Always figure on killing out bent grass two months before time to reseed, which, in most instances, means having an ugly lawn during the height of summer.

8

CHEMICAL CONTROL OF PLANT GROWTH

CHEMICAL CONTROL OF WEEDS in lawns has already been discussed in chapter 7. The entire subject of plant growth regulation is of such importance in reducing effort and time in gardening that a fuller coverage than that is necessary.

One of the most useful controls for unwanted plants, almost ignored by most gardeners but a tremendous labor saver, is "preemergence control" of annual grasses and broad-leaved weeds in flower beds and shrubbery borders. There are individuals who find pulling weeds by hand good therapy, but for most of us, this is the nastiest job in all horticulture. Not only is it tedious, but it puts undue pressure on the legs, arms, and back, creating a problem for even the physically fit, let alone those who have limited strength.

Preemergence controls affect only germinating seeds or seedlings that have yet to produce an adequate root system. This means that they must be on the soil in advance of a seed's germination. Once a plant has reached a height of three to five inches, they have little or no effect on growth. This makes them particularly valuable when setting out bedding plants. The soil can be treated before planting these or after they have been set in place. For as long as six weeks thereafter, seeds of any sort that germinate (even those of desirable plants) will be killed.

This poses a small problem for annuals which are to be seeded "in place." A solution for most species is to sow them in a seed bed and then transplant them into permanent beds when they are over three inches high and able to tolerate preemergence chemical controls. Annuals which do not tolerate transplanting well, such as annual poppies and sweet peas, can be allowed to reach a safe height, after which they can be hand weeded and the chemicals applied.

Three such preemergence chemicals are distributed widely: Amchem's Garden Weeder, Stauffer's Eptam, and Greenfield's Grass and Weed Control. Properly used, any one of these products can save literally hours of back-breaking stoop labor.

For some reason, no similar product has been distributed for use in *home* vegetable gardens, although Treflan, the active ingredient in Greenfield's Grass and Weed Control is sold for use on truck garden crops. The problem is perhaps the expense of getting official approval for their use by amateurs, which, since it is a relatively unknown market, may not justify the necessary price tag.

In general, I prefer to apply weed-control chemicals in liquid form rather than as dusts or granular products. In the case of 2,4-D and 2,4,5-T compounds, for example, the only practical dust form is in a sodium salt, which is perhaps less than half as effective as one of the ester formulations used in liquid sprays. Too, a liquid comes into much more intimate contact with leaf and stem surfaces.

Even if rains fall half an hour after application, an ester sprayed on a lawn for control of broad-leaved weeds will still give a satisfactory control. However, if rain falls within eight hours of application of a dust or granular product, it may fail to control. For this reason, the only satisfactory way to apply most products is in liquid form, using a first-class sprayer.

If at all possible, invest in one made of stainless steel. Such a unit is expensive but can be counted on to last for years. I have just gone through a painful experience with a cheap galvanized unit which cured me forever of relying on this type of equipment. With no source of supply at my summer home, I purchased a mail-order sprayer which, after being used once, dropped all its galvanizing which effectively plugged the outlet tube. This would have cost me an entire summer's work had not a cooperative friend at H. D. Hudson's flown in a stainless steel unit that worked like a charm and enabled me to spray a bed for a number of cultivated varieties of blueberries I had sitting around in pots.

The project in question, destroying all vegetation in a future garden, depended on another type of weed-killer—one which has unusual possibilities for killing all plants quickly and then disappearing from the soil so that it can be replanted almost at once. Discovered originally in England, paraquat is distributed in the United States by the Chevron Chemical Company. At this writing, it is available only under the name Dual Paraquat and only for professional use, but I am assured by the company that by the time these lines appear, it will be available as Spot Weed and Grass Killer.

Paraquat is unique in its immediate kill of a wide range of weeds and then its loss of toxic effect on all plants within a matter of hours. In the case of my blueberry patch, all quack grass and other deep-rooted weeds had been killed the previous year, but annual grasses, clover, and dozens of other unwanted species had produced a solid cover on this as yet unplanted plot. A single application of paraquat left nothing alive in the area, which was turned over and planted the following day. This is a chemical with great possibilities for a quick cleanup of weedy areas with no residual effects.

There are times when residual effects are needed, however. Along fence rows, on drives, along roads, and under hedges, there are areas which are better if left completely bare of all vegetation. Unfortunately, the only really effective chemical for this which is available in consumer-sized packages is sodium arsenite, a quite-toxic material which will render the soil sterile for a period as long as two years. Because of its poisonous nature, its sale is prohibited in some states. In spite of the danger connected with its use, I would still recommend it, but only to those willing to exercise the necessary precautions fully explained on the label.

The prospect of being able to spray a fence row and not having to repeat the operation for two years is well-worth the few minutes it will take to read that label—every word of it. I cannot overemphasize the importance of careful reading of all labels, even with the seemingly innocuous products now on the market. Someone has called the insecticide-fungicide-weedicide label the most expensive piece of literature in existence—a label four inches in area can cost as much as a quarter of a million dollars in research and testing before the government will give permission for its printing. In particular, always read warning notices: they are put there for your protection.

Unfortunately, a label offers little room for explanation of why certain recommendations are made. One of these deserves particular emphasis. Many products carry the phrase "apply with a coarse, breaking spray." This requires using a sprayer with a fairly large orifice in the nozzle so that instead of giving off a fine mist, it gives off drops that hit leaf surfaces directly and immediately spread out. The reason for this is that fine mists are likely to drift and, as a result, cause trouble. I have seen roses, for example, that grew 250 feet away from a lawn sprayed with 2,4-D which curled and died at the tips because fine mist drifted to them on a light breeze. In the South, cotton plants half a mile away from a field sprayed with a too-fine nozzle have been killed by a combination of 2,4-D and 2,4,5-T.

Poison ivy, an obnoxious weed in many suburban and rural areas, presents a special problem. Its existence in a bit of woodland or field makes the use of the infested area a hazardous proposition. This is not the place to discuss the complex nature of ivy poisoning, but I can say with authority that no such thing as immunity to the toxic principle exists, although build-up of sensitivity may take years to occur. Treat even the dead vines as highly toxic material which cannot be handled with bare hands. Above all, don't burn them—the smoke has been known to even kill sensitive individuals.

Fortunately, there is a specific control for this pest. Aminotriazol, sold under various trade names, will blacken it in a matter of days. I have had excellent results with Amchem's Weedazol, one of its trade names. If this chemical is not available, 2,4,5-TP (Silvex) is almost as effective, but since it is highly toxic to trees and shrubs, it cannot be used when poison ivy is growing on them. Another chemical, also toxic to woody plants, is the older 2,4,5-T. Aminotriazol, though, is highly selective in its action: many woody plants can be sprayed safely. At Valley Forge, a massive poison-ivy infestation festooned over flowering dogwood trees was controlled with Weedazol, leaving the dogwoods unharmed.

The control of winter annuals is discussed in chapter 7, but since they can also be pests in places other than the lawn, read this chapter for methods to control them. *Poa annua,* or annual bluegrass, is a particularly persistent grower in driveways and along hedge rows as well as in the garden.

OTHER CHEMICAL EFFECTS

Not all chemicals used for regulating plant growth have the death of the plant as their purpose. One gardener told me that his most important labor-saving device was the use of a maleic hydrazide product, MH-30, which he applied to the edges of his lawn to slow up growth of grass without killing it. Anyone who has spent hours with a lawn edger, only to have to repeat all the work a month later, will appreciate the simplicity of spraying a grass strip at the curb or sidewalk with a chemical that will check its growth for a month or two. Not all garden centers handle this type of product, but it is available if the dealer will check with his wholesale sources.

One of the most interesting chemicals of this type is called B-9. Sprayed on annual bedding plants when they are not too mature, it causes them to grow much more compact, with shorter internodes. Petunias, for example, which tend to sprawl and get leggy in about the third month after they are planted, are dwarfed and remain compact for their entire summer's life.

A similar product, Cyclocel, can be used on chrysanthemums, saving the labor of pinching them at regular intervals to keep them dwarfed. Consumer-sized packages of this chemical are available in most garden centers. A third product, Phosphoa, is also available.

One of the original uses of plant growth regulators was to stimulate plant roots by using such chemicals as napthalene acetic acid. When the base of a cutting is dipped in a powder containing one or more of these rooting "hormones," roots are formed much more rapidly and with greater certainty than if left untreated. Any gardener who propagates his own plants from cuttings should use such a product as a matter of routine. I once estimated that hormone treatment doubled the effectiveness of a propagating bench, both by speeding up rooting and by increasing the number of good cuttings in a given batch. On soft cuttings, I find Rootone highly effective, but for woody plants, Rootone #10 will produce more roots in a shorter period of time.

GIBBERELLINS

These are mentioned here only because their omission might cause comment. Gibberellic acid is a positive growth regulator, which has certain important scientific and commercial applications. Home gardeners, however, think of them almost entirely as a means of producing giant plants. When they were first announced, all scientific reports referred to the extreme elongation of the internodes which its use produced, which led me to suspect that the

A chemical pruning agent can save work and lead to fuller, denser small plants.

normal flow of growth regulators was being reversed and that the roots would be adversely affected.

I discussed this with Dr. Norbert Scully, who was, at that time, doing plant research at the Argonne National Laboratory for the Atomic Energy Commission. He then set up experiments to check this and did discover that gains in top growth were at the expense of the roots and that eventually this deprived the plant of so many nutrients that it fell over in the "lazy rice" disease which brought about the first investigations of these compounds.

Even though, in the hands of a plant scientist or trained worker, many of the effects of GA are highly desirable, they are not of importance to the home gardener, who would do better to devote his time and energy to other growth effects.

SYSTEMIC INSECTICIDES

Although most insecticides offer few or no advantages over conventional products for saving time and effort, systemic insecticides are a quite-different story. Instead of pumping up a pressure tank to apply liquid sprays or working the handle of a dust gun, home gardeners can now simply walk along under a favorite tree and dust the ground with some coarse granules that resemble bread crumbs.

These granules contain a powerful phosphate insecticide which has a peculiar affinity for roots and is rapidly absorbed by the entire plant. As a result, it becomes toxic to any insect which lives by sucking sap or by burrowing in trunks of trees and shrubs. It is, however, of little value as a control for free-flying insects, even those that may chew on leaves containing the insecticide, although there are differences in susceptibility among these insects.

Systemic insecticides have been highly successful in controlling such hard-to-reach pests as leaf miners, stem borers, and spider mites. I have had two dramatic instances of such control which are worth repeating as examples of what can be done with them. The highbush cranberry, *Viburnum opulus,* is regularly attacked by a particularly nasty aphid, or plant louse, which protects itself by injecting leaf buds with a toxic substance causing them to curl up and form tight cups, inside which the aphids thrive, safe from any ordinary spray. Because this stabbing of the leaf bud had taken place so early in spring that a systemic insecticide could not be translocated, I applied the control in mid-August, the time when woody plants begin storing food for the following spring's growth. As I suspected, the systemic insecticide (a phosphorus compound) was stored along with regular starches and sugars. The following spring, untreated highbush cranberries were severely infested, but not a leaf curled on those given the treatment.

The other dramatic instance of control involved a magnificent specimen of Almey crab, which stood close to the line between two properties. The house to the south of this line belonged to an ardent organic gardener who refused to permit any insecticides to be sprayed near her line. Uunfortunately, her grass and shrubs seemed destined to support the most enormous population of clover mites it has ever been my misfortune to see, all of which migrated *north* to hibernate on her neighbor's warm south wall.

Her neighbor to the north, as a result, was overrun every fall and spring by clover mites that swarmed over her Almey crab. When, however, she treated this tree and all surrounding shrubbery with a systemic insecticide, the mites disappeared, with no recurrence for six years. The organic-gardening neighbor, of course, claimed that her refusal to permit spraying (she did not know about the systemic insecticide) had solved the difficulty.

9

HERB GARDENS

Of all plant materials, herbs are among the least time-consuming to grow. They can also fit into a small space gracefully. A complete garden can be made of herbs in a space ten by ten feet without having it seem cramped or out of scale. Most herb plants are low growing.

Another advantage to growing herbs is that, as a rule, they do not require pampering. As I am writing I am looking out of the window of an old farmhouse from which I can see half an acre of caraway—self-sown from an original farm planting made more than fifty years ago. It has never been reseeded. Its only source of fertility is a poor sandy soil and a little nitrogen which is deposited in it by fogs and mists. In fact, many herbs flourish and spread so readily that they may require controls to prevent them from taking over a garden. This is often true of the various types of mint. I have found that either Banvel-D or Silvex weed-killers can keep them in check.

One of the joys of planting an herb garden can be designing it. Many of the most widely reproduced designs—for example, knot gardens—are copies of sixteenth-century herb gardens. However, there is a wide variety of different ideas to choose from. You might want to combine herbs that have blue flowers for an effective small garden. Or you might like the idea of a gray-green garden, since many herbs have foliage that has a grayish cast. If space is very limited herbs can be grown in a strawberry jar or between the spokes of an old wagon wheel. Herbs planted in handsome pots

Herb gardens are satisfying, handsome, and almost work-free.

and containers can add to the beauty of a small garden and allow the gardener to move herbs indoors for winter.

Most herbs demand full sun and develop their best flavor only when they are not growing too vigorously. The ideal herb garden would be planted on rather light soil, not too rich, which is exposed to full summer sunshine, but is shaded in winter by some solid obstruction to avoid damage from bright winter sun.

Herbs that will grow in shaded areas, if these must be planted, include several varieties of mint, chervil, tarragon, and parsley. Chives will do fairly well, but will lack the vigor (and flavor) of plants growing in full sun.

Flavor is of particular importance in herbs, since they are used, not as food directly, but as a means of adding interest to other foods. Because using the harvest is part of the fun of herb gardening, proper drying conditions for winter use should also be considered. All too often, leaves are gathered and dried in an oven.

This not only destroys much of the flavor (most herbs contain volatile oils that are lost by evaporation), but also changes the chlorophyll content so that green coloring is lost.

Most herbs are best harvested just before their flower buds open, at which time they contain the highest concentration of essential oils. Tie them in bunches of not more than ten stems each and suspend them, leaves down, in an airy, dry, and dark room. Darkness is necessary to prevent the chlorophyll from "wearing itself out" as it continues to try to manufacture food. Dried in the dark, the leaves will retain a good green color. An old-fashioned attic is the ideal spot for this operation; modern apartment dwellers can improvise a drying chamber out of plywood or use a corrugated cardboard carton with slots cut out for ventilation.

ANGELICA *(Angelica archangelica):* Biennial (but will survive as a perennial if not allowed to set seed). To 5 feet.

Because of its large size, this plant belongs in larger herb gardens, although it could be fitted into the background of a smaller one. Its seeds and bits of stems can be used for flavoring syrups, puddings, and candy. When its stems are candied, a tricky, slow process beyond the skill of most amateur herb gardeners, they are used in decorating pastry.

ANISE *(Pimpinella anisum):* Annual. To 2 feet.

The seeds of this plant are used to flavor cookies, cake, and bread, and its leaves are used in salads. Both seeds and leaves have a licorice flavor which is not enjoyed by everyone. Sow seed where it is to grow, since it is not easy to transplant.

BALM *(Melissa officinalis):* Perennial. To 2 feet.

Often called lemon balm because of the distinct lemon flavor of its leaves, this herb is usually planted by dividing old plants. It can become a pest from self-sown seeds. It's leaves are used to flavor tea, egg dishes, drinks, stews, soups, and salads.

BASIL *(Ocimum basilicum):* Annual. To 2 feet.

There are two species of this herb, bush basil (*O. minimum*) and sweet basil (*O. basilicum*), but both have about the same flavor. An ornamental purple variety has poor flavor—it belongs in the flower border, not the herb garden. A "must" in certain spaghetti sauces, basil seems to round out the flavor of tomatoes and adds a bay leaf flavor to stews. Use sparingly in salads. It will grow quickly from seed.

BEE BALM *(Monarda didyma):* Perennial. To 3 feet.

One of the more brilliant herbs, this one has vivid scarlet flowers.

There are also both white and pink varieties. Its leaves are dried for tea or can be used to perfume linens. It is begun from divisions of old plants.

BORAGE *(Borago officinalis):* Annual. To 2 feet.

Propagate this plant from seed. It is not a widely used herb, although its leaves add a pleasant taste to salads, and its flowers and tips of shoots may be added to iced tea, ades and other summer drinks. It is supposed to have a mild cucumber flavor.

BURNET *(Sanguisorba minor):* Treat as an annual. To 30 inches.

The leaves of this plant can be steeped in vinegar to add flavor to salad dressings or can be used directly in salads. They are sometimes also added to iced tea and ades. The seed is difficult to find in the United States but is available from English and French seed houses. Burnet was once thought to prevent drunkenness.

CARAWAY *(Carum carvi):* Biennial, but grown from seed as an annual. To 2 feet.

The young leaves of this plant are used to flavor salads. Its seeds are used in cheese, cake, bread, and, in German and Hungarian cooking, to flavor sauerkraut, soups and stews. The plant often self-sows.

CHERVIL *(Anthriscus cerefolium):* Annual. To 18 inches.

This herb adds an interesting mild parsleylike flavor to egg dishes, soups, and salads. Like parsley it is used for garnishing.

CHIVES *(Allium schoenoprasum):* Perennial. To 1 foot.

Widely used as an edging in herb gardens because of its neat compact growth, this plant is very ornamental when in flower. Flowers are a lavender-rose color. The leaves, with their mild onion flavor, can be used whenever onions are needed. Usually, chives are used in cold dishes, such as cottage or cream cheese, cold soups, and salads, but they add a delightful flavor to hot new potatoes and other vegetables. They are easy to grow from seed, but potted plants are often available.

CORIANDER *(Coriandrum sativum):* Annual. To 3 feet.

Sow the seeds of this plant either in late fall to germinate in spring or in early spring. Its seeds, often used in cookies, cakes and candies, also add a distinct flavor to curry. Add three or four seeds to a cup of espresso coffee. Whole seeds when candied make a delightful confection. The feathery leaves of coriander, called Chinese parsley, are much used in Chinese and Spanish cooking, but in the United States the leaves are rarely used and are even considered unpleasant-tasting by most people.

DILL *(Anethum graveolens):* Annual (biennial in mild climates). To 3 feet.

For a gourmet flavor, add dill to lamb stew or to sauce for boiled beef instead of using the usual horseradish. It is a must for dill pickles, but you may also add its leaves to salads and fish sauces. Potato salad and tomato juice take on a new character with the addition of dill leaves.

FENNEL *(Foeniculum vulgare):* Perennial, but grow as an annual. To 30 inches the first year.

Grown from spring-sown seed, the seeds of this plant are used for flavoring fish sauces, cakes, pickled beets, sauerkraut, and soft cheeses. Finnochio (Italian knob celery) is a vegetable, not an herb.

HOREHOUND *(Marrubium vulgare):* Perennial. To 3 feet.

Sometimes spelled hoarhound, this herb is of little use in the kitchen. The juice is used to flavor beer in England. A syrup made from it is a folk remedy for colds and a flavoring for candy.

HYSSOP *(Hyssopus officinalis):* Perennial. To 4 feet.

Propagate this plant either from seed or from cuttings. It is of limited use as a culinary herb, but an essential oil extracted from it is an ingredient in true eau de cologne.

LAVENDER *(Lavandula spica):* Perennial, but not hardy in the North. To 3 feet.

Protect this plant with straw in the winter. Its dried flowers are used for perfuming linens and an extract of it is used in perfumery. Lavender is also a country woman's name for *Chrysanthemum balsamita,* a perennial more properly called Costmary or, with equal inaccuracy, mint geranium and used in salads and flavorings.

LEMON VERBENA *(Lippia citriodora):* Perennial. To 12 inches.

Also called citronalis, this plant does form seeds, but these are never fertile—I have sown them dozens of times under varying conditions without ever getting a single sprout. Consequently, it must be propagated from cuttings. Since it is not a hardy plant, it must also be grown as a pot plant in the North. Dried leaves are used for tea; fresh, for flavoring drinks and fruit cups.

MARJORAM, POT AND SWEET *(Marjorana hortensis and M. onites):* Both are perennials, but can be grown as annuals. To 18 inches the first year if grown from seed.

Fresh marjoram leaves are used in salads; fresh or dried leaves, for flavoring meats, cheese, or salads. They are also an essential element in poultry seasoning. For a special winternight treat, try poaching eggs in olive oil and tomato sauce flavored with sweet marjoram.

MINT *(Mentha* species*):* There are a dozen or more mints, each of which has its own, special fragrance implied in its name, such as apple mint, lemon mint, peppermint, etc. Mint tea can be made with the dried leaves of most of these. They are slow to grow from seed: grow from divisions.

NASTURTIUM *(Tropaeolum majus):* Annual. Dwarf varieties to 6 inches but vining types to 6 feet.

The green seeds of this plant are sometimes pickled and used as a substitute for capers or added to salads for a piquant flavor. Its green leaves are a substitute for water cress. It is readily grown from seeds.

OLD WOMAN *(Artemisia stelleriana):* Perennial. To 30 inches.

The dense, woolly, silver-gray foliage of this plant is distinctive. Except that it has aromatic foliage and is used as a magic charm by the Chinese, it has little herbal value.

OREGANO *(Origanum vulgare):* Perennial. To 30 inches.

This herb may be grown from seed or divisions. Unless you are an enthusiast of true Italian spaghetti or pizza, sweet marjoram serves the same purpose. It is simply a stronger-flavored marjoram, and when combined with rosemary, basil, and thyme, will produce the same flavor in most Italian spaghetti sauces.

PARSLEY *(Petroselinum crispum):* Biennial. To 12 inches.

The most widely planted of all herbs, this is also one of the most useful. Be sure to plant the plain Italian variety if you want strong flavor; the curly types are better for garnishing. A much-overlooked gourmet's treat is cream-of-parsley soup. Thriving in richer soil than most herbs, the seed takes ten days to sprout.

POT MARIGOLD *(Calendula officinalis):* Annual. To 2 feet.

The petals of the common marigold can be used to add yellow color to soups and stews. It is also used in custards to give them a rich yellow color and is a substitute for saffron in hot cross buns.

ROSE GERANIUM *(Pelargonium graveolens):* Perennial. To 30 inches.

The most popular of a number of geraniums, this tender plant has intensely fragrant foliage. A single leaf in the bottom of a glass of apple jelly will flavor the entire contents. I can never think of this lovely old-fashioned plant without also thinking of Aunt Marian Young sitting in church on the island of Matinicus with a leaf held between her fingers. Dried leaves are used for perfuming linens. Cuttings propagate readily.

ROSEMARY *(Rosemarinus officinalis):* Perennial subshrub. To 6 feet in warm climates, but a pot plant in the North.

Propagate this herb either from seed or from cuttings. With oregano, thyme, and sweet basil, it becomes an essential ingredient in many Italian tomato sauces. It is also used to flavor rosemary butter, jams, sweet pickles, soups, meats, and poultry.

SAGE *(Salvia officinalis):* Perennial. To 18 inches.

The basic flavoring in pork and poultry stuffing, it is also used to flavor meats and cheese. The leaves can be dried for making sage tea. It is seldom used fresh. It is easily grown from cuttings, although seed is available.

SUMMER SAVORY *(Satureja hortensis):* Annual. To 18 inches.

Growing readily from seed, this is the *bonenkraut* of the Germans, a popular flavoring for green beans or fresh peas. It is also added to boiled rice, to soups, and to salads. The perennial winter savory is harder to grow and adds nothing to the flavor of the annual species.

SWEET WOODRUFF *(Asperula odorata):* Perennial. To 8 inches.

This is used largely to flavor white Rhine wine: two bottles of this flavored wine plus one bottle of champagne and fresh strawberries make up the May Bowl, one of the great treats of spring. We make it with *wild* strawberries—pure ambrosia.

TARRAGON *(Artemisia dracunculus):* Perennial. To 3 feet.

This plant prefers a location in the light shade, where the plants will grow hardier. It is the flavoring ingredient in tarragon vinegar and in tartar sauce for fish. A healthy stand of tarragon is a status symbol among herb gardeners. Must be grown from French tarragon roots. Seeds of tarragon are Russian tarragon, a tasteless variety.

THYME *(Thymus vulgaris):* Perennial. Prostrate to 8 inches.

There are many varieties and species of thyme, but for flavor, most people prefer this species. Some, however, feel that lemon thyme, *Thymus serpyllum citriodorus,* has more character. The enthusiast will grow both, or even all the varieties.

A sprig each of thyme, bay leaf, and parsley make up the flavor bouquet which French chefs add to lamb, pork, and other meat dishes. Fresh thyme leaves are also used to flavor soups, salads, soft cheeses, stuffings, and are mixed with sour milk to give a distinctive flavor to cottage cheese.

DESIGN HERB GARDENS

Although herb gardens are usually small and may not seem to require a great deal of work, many gardeners take on more than they should by copying the traditional knot gardens and other elaborate designs. These require constant attention, such as snipping and shearing, to keep them looking neat.

For the busy gardener, there is a solution to this difficulty—one which will be even more traditional. By copying the pattern of the medieval monastic garden, with its simple, rectangular, raised beds, he can be true to the past without taking on extra work.

In 1947, at the Chicago Flower Show, I designed such a garden for the exhibit by the Men's Garden Clubs of America. In front of a monastery façade, the herbs (both culinary and medicinal) were planted in raised beds formed by charred wooden sides about six inches high. Although simple in design, this garden won several awards and was photographed by hundreds of show visitors.

One interesting feature of the garden was a statue of Saint Fiacre, the true patron saint of gardeners, rather than Saint Francis. Saint Fiacre seemed most appropriate for a garden sponsored by a male organization since he was a misogynist and barred women from all the chapels and gardens he made.

HERBS IN WINTER

One advantage to a herb garden is that it can be enjoyed in the winter, both in the form of dried leaves and seeds collected earlier and from living plants growing in a sunny window. Not all herbs do well indoors, however—the modern house and apartment are too hot, dry, and airless.

Annuals, which have a short life span at best, will probably provide pleasure all winter long if young seedlings are started in pots in September. In my experience, glazed pots that do not dry out quickly are more satisfactory than the ordinary red clay pot. A good potting soil, with about a teaspoonful of ground limestone added for each pot, does nicely.

Sow the seeds on the surface without a covering of soil, moisten well, and then cover each pot with a pane of glass. Set the planted pots in a light but sunless place until the seeds germinate; then remove the glass and keep the soil moist. When frost threatens, bring in the pots to a sunny window.

Basil, dill, and fennel do well indoors when grown in this way. Although parsley is usually treated as an annual, it is hardy and will survive winter if protected slightly. For winter use indoors, pot up old parsley plants and cut them back to force new growth. Parsley does not like a room where air temperatures go much above sixty degrees. Mint makes a good house plant, but needs a fairly large pot: a six-inch bulb pan (shallower than the conventional pot) is just right.

I had bad luck with thyme until I learned to grow it in a hanging basket: perhaps the fact that this made it hard to water, thus not getting too much moisture, had something to do with its success. It, too, resents too much heat.

Sweet marjoram and rosemary are other good house plants; the latter cannot stand overwatering, but if grown fairly dry, it is delightful. Incidentally, it is a traditional Christmas plant all over Europe; rooted cuttings make excellent gifts for the holiday.

IO

SMALL VACATION GARDENS

WHEN MOST PEOPLE BUY summer homes, they do so to escape routine and to enjoy the out of doors with no responsibilities for doing regular chores. For the average home owner who maintains plantings around his permanent residence, the best summer gardening is none at all.

At the same time, some of the most ardent gardeners are those who reserve all their horticultural energies for maintaining a tiny plot near a summer home at the seashore, on an abandoned farm, or in the mountains. Many city apartment dwellers who live conveniently near to their vacation retreats do not take conventional vacations, but use weekends in the country to renew their contacts with the soil. To a considerable extent, these weekend gardeners are concentrated in two areas in the Northeast—New York City and Boston, with a somewhat smaller group in the Philadelphia area. As opportunities for gardening around the home increase, as has happened in the less crowded cities west of the Alleghenies, fewer and fewer individuals look upon gardening as a part of the summer's recreational program.

Perhaps this appreciation for gardening in the East is an expression of the older cultural traditions of that area. As Dr. Harold Tukey, Sr., prominent horticulturist, once pointed out, gardening is the ultimate flowering of a culture—the refinement of an existence no longer dependent upon agriculture for survival, yet tied to the soil by some primitive instinct satisfied only by contact with the soil.

Although summer home gardens tend to be small, this is not always the case. Recently, I helped a friend plant 300 hills of potatoes on his summer "farm" in Michigan—enough at the average rate of yield for this section to produce fifty to seventy-five bushels of spuds. Living as he does in a high-rise apartment on Chicago's Lake Shore Drive, I doubt that he will have enough room to store his crop! The urge to produce far more than can be used by the grower is a common tendency—not only do summer home gardeners enjoy growing vegetables for themselves, but they get added pleasure from being able to give gifts to citybound friends.

Perhaps my own attitude toward vacation gardening is more typical. Every spring we agree that it is high time we do some planting. Perhaps this is the year to plant those hybrid blueberries and show our summer neighbors what a real blueberry tastes like. Or those dwarf apple trees certainly should be set out to replace those tired old specimens in our ancient orchard. And wouldn't it be wonderful to have fresh zucchini this summer instead of the wilted specimens otherwise available.

Unfortunately for such plans, our summer home is on an island 25 miles by ferry to sea, 1,300 miles from our winter front door. In spring the ferry runs only twice a week, and fogs that may hang on for weeks make our landing strip, only 500 yards from our door, worthless. With no convenient transportation, we must forego the planting of a vegetable garden.

With twenty acres of wild blueberries, with raspberries and blackberries as pesky brambles along every road, and with an old meadow red with wild strawberries, any time spent planting small fruits would be wasted. Spruce forests and wild flowers so thick that both are a nuisance obviate any need for attention to ornamental plantings. Even the lawn, mowed twice a year, fills in with wild bent grass that any golf course superintendent would envy. It is even fed by the nitrous oxide dropped from fogs that blanket the island about one-fourth of the year.

PROBLEMS OF SUMMER GARDENING

Our problem, that of lack of opportunity for early spring preparation, is shared by those who garden at their country, seashore, or mountain second homes. Even those who are able to get away for long weekends to nearby areas may find the weather turning nasty or the farmer who promised faithfully to do spring plowing "mudding in" his oats instead.

Nothing is more frustrating than having to pass up tempting invitations to brunches, cocktail parties, and other city pleasures, only to spend the entire weekend in the country or at the seashore huddled around a fitful blaze that barely warms the nose as outside sleet and rain make garden work impossible.

Chances for favorable weather after summer is over is one reason that fall rather than spring preparation of the vegetable garden is a "must." At that season, not only is good weather more likely to occur, but local workmen are available and more willing to cooperate. If a perennial border is to be planted (surely the mark of true horticultural devotion), it should be dug deeply after the heat of summer is over but before frost comes and the plants moved into place as soon as the fall perennial planting season begins in your particular part of the world.

The problem of large-sized woody plants is not as easy to handle. For one thing, they usually need to feel a touch of frost before they can be moved safely. In seashore locations, particularly, frost often holds off until late in the year, by which time the cottage owner is deeply involved in winter activities and is unwilling to make a long trek back for the purpose of planting trees and shrubs. A good solution for this problem is to use container-grown stock—fairly large specimens can be grown in pots, tin cans, or baskets, which will be ready to pop into place before dormancy begins.

A good local nurseryman will often carry enough different varieties and species, in various sizes, to plant quite a respectable landscape scheme. Even though they will be smaller than similar trees and shrubs planted bare root, don't scorn a six-foot pin oak grown in a five-gallon tin—once planted, that six-foot tree will probably be twenty feet tall before a twelve-foot specimen moved bare root will be. Whenever canned stock is available, don't delay planting, but get it into the ground as soon as possible, at any time of year you can dig a hole in the earth.

Another solution, if the local nurseryman seems to be reliable, and if his rows in the field contain specimen plants of what you want, is to make selections while plants are in active growth, tag them for later moving, and identify them with a number or letter. Then select a spot for each tagged specimen and mark the location with the same number or letter. Your nurseryman can then do the moving at the proper time.

Because pleasant autumn weather provides a more favorable climate for outdoor work, plan to do sowing of both annuals and perennials as late in the fall as possible; just before a freeze-up is best, but otherwise after soil temperatures have cooled to forty degrees and are likely to stay there. There is no question of hardiness involved in the case of perennials: you can be certain that if the mature plant is hardy in your area, the seed will be also. Sown in fall, just before winter sets in, they will lie dormant until favorable growing conditions occur in spring, at which time they will germinate strongly. Such fall-sown perennials are usually stronger, healthier plants than those sown in late spring.

Not all annuals are as accommodating. Many of the plants we list as annuals are actually tender perennials which are able to flower the first year from seed, but because of their tropical origin, are not adapted to survive freezing as seeds. If, however, the summer cottage gardener will confine his sowing to the so-called hardy group of annuals, a wide range of floral material can be seeded in fall. Many will actually do better than will those sown later in spring. For example, by the time we in the Middle West are able to turn over garden soil, an operation often delayed into late May or early June by excessive rains, our soil temperatures are too high for satisfactory germination of Shirley poppies and annual larkspur. If, however, these are seeded in the fall, a magnificent show of color can be had in late June and early July.

Here is a list of annuals, for the busy cottager, which can be seeded in fall when the work can be done leisurely, a little at a time, first preparing the soil after a light frost or two, then seeding just before the soil freezes for the winter:

Alyssum
Candytuft
Bachelor's-buttons *(Centaurea)*
Spider flower *(Cleome)*
Coreopsis
Cosmos
California poppy *(Escholtzia californica)*
Flowering tobacco *(Nicotiana)*
Iceland and Shirley poppies *(Papaver)*
Petunia (only small, flowered)
Annual phlox *(Phlox drummondi)*
Pinks
Rose-moss *(Portulaca grandiflora)*
Sweet William (annual)

Garden balsam *(Impatiens balsamina)*
Larkspur
Marigold (a bit chancy, but worth trying)
Sweet peas
Scotch viola and Johnny-jump-ups *(Viola)*

The simplest way to handle them is to prepare the soil well, then broadcast the seed, and cover immediately with a tangle of branches or excelsior to discourage birds. Once the soil has frozen, this covering can be removed—a strand or two may stick to the frozen surface, but this will do no real harm.

Perennial seeds are sown in the same way, but are better for the protection of a cold frame since many of them may not be moved until the following fall from the seed bed. Do, however, space them out so they can develop fully either by transplanting excess seedlings or cutting them off at the soil line.

The vegetable garden can be dug and worked over in fall, but not too many crops can be seeded at that time. Perennial onions—the so-called tree or top onion—can be planted then, using small bulblets that form on top of stalks of the current year's crop. Old bulbs are too rank to eat, but in spring, these top bulblets will produce scallions that will be quite acceptable. An even better way to ensure a crop of early onions is to pick out dry onions in the fall that have failed to "size up." Those between 1 and 1½ inches in diameter can be planted and will be edible in spring even before the soil can be worked. If left too long, they will quickly shoot to seed (one reason that in spring no large sets should be planted), but for early use, these are better flavored than top onions.

Any Swiss chard plants left in the garden can be cut back and mulched lightly with straw or leaves. I have had these survive for two years and produce edible crops in early spring. Parsley, too, is relatively hardy.

Spinach can be seeded in fall and will sprout about two years out of three. If you miss, you are out only the price of a packet of seed. New Zealand spinach seed is fully hardy, even though the mature plant cannot tolerate the slightest touch of frost. Lettuce is "iffy," but worth trying.

LAWNS FOR THE SUMMER GARDENER

For years, I inveighed against zoysia lawns for the North because of their short growing season. To prove my point, I used my own test patch of Meyer zoysia—the first turf of this variety used outside the Beltsville test plots. Up to May 15, this would lie dormant —a dead-tan color resembling a cocoa fiber doormat. Gradually, tiny blades of green would appear until finally by June 1, the entire area would be as green as the bluegrass around it, which had resumed growth at least two months before. And with the first hard autumn frost, about October 10, zoysia would again go dormant, turning its cocoa-tan color it had lost in May.

But what I overlooked in considering Meyer zoysia as a grass for the summer cottage was that few owners of such properties care how their lawns look in May and October, so long as they are green during the summer months. Actually most of them would prefer a grass that made no growth in spring and late fall, since that would eliminate mowing during those seasons. Consequently, today, when someone asks for a recommendation for a carefree lawn for a summer cottage, my one recommendation, North or South, is zoysia. It forms a turf so tough and so tight that no weed can find root room, and the texture is wonderful—a tight, springy mat which one friend finds so pleasant that he removes his shoes to walk on it.

There are two possible objections to zoysia. The first is its tough, wiry texture. Not that it feels unpleasant to walk on, but let's face it—zoysia is hard to cut. I would hate to have to mow it with an ordinary hand mower. It will stop most two-horsepower gasoline mowers unless they are revved up to high speed, so if you do plant zoysia, be sure to buy a mower with at least a three-horsepower motor. The second objection (which is not serious if the grass is mowed once after it goes dormant) is that the dead blades are quite inflammable if left long.

Fertilize zoysia in spring if possible, or use a long-feeding fertilizer applied as early in the fall as possible so the plants can get some benefit from the feeding before they go dormant for the winter.

THE WOODED PROPERTY

Perhaps the easiest of all summer homes to "garden" is one located in a wooded area. In such a location the trees supply all the garden plant material necessary, and there is no need for intensive cultivation. There are problems to be solved, however, the most important of which is that of providing light and air around the house itself. There is nothing drearier in rainy weather than a house standing in deep woods with dripping foliage and dark shadows all around. True, it takes a bold, almost heartless, individual to put an ax to beautiful trees, yet unless this is done, a home in the woods can be anything but pleasant.

The moment brush and trees are cut away to permit air and light to surround a home in the woods, an area of soil is exposed which will need attention. This creates our second problem—how to garden in this area. Fortunately, when forest soil is exposed in this way, noxious weeds are seldom a problem, although a wide range of woody plants is almost certain to appear as soon as overhead shade is removed. Most of these will be tall-growing species which should not be kept. An application of Silvex (2,4,5-trichloropropionic acid) will save hours of digging out these unwanted arboreal weeds. (For application procedure and precautions to observe with Silvex, see the chapter on chemical weed control later in the book.)

The most satisfactory way to treat such newly opened areas is to plant them with a ground cover rather than with grass. In planning for such a planting, remember that Silvex will remain toxic to plants for six weeks after application. If the area is sprayed in mid-August, for example, ground covers cannot be planted until quite late in fall, which is sometimes risky when snow cover is unreliable for protecting the poorly rooted plants.

Because the surrounding forest provides all the landscaping necessary, tree or shrub planting seems unnecessary, although a single outstanding shrub or small tree will often lend distinction to an otherwise uninteresting property. For this purpose, the period during which the summer home is used should be considered. For example, a lovely shadblow would waste its fragrance on the desert air if the family does not occupy the cottage until July. In this case, a *Philadelphus virginalis* or a rose of Sharon would be a far more desirable choice, flowering in summer as these shrubs do.

When underplanting the native forest with wild flowers is attempted, the same thought should be given to their flowering season. When the cottage is used in spring, the problem is simple since hundreds of woodland species are available that flower in late March, April, and May. The difficulty is in locating those that flower in summer and early fall. Most of these prefer open glades, where the sun filters onto them during the day, with occasional bursts of pure sunshine. In such a situation, the blue woods aster, *Aster cordifolius* will bloom freely toward autumn. Red and white baneberries are not very conspicuous when in bloom, but in fall their brilliant fruits are delightful. Those of the white species, *Actaea alba* (doll's eyes or white cohosh), are particularly interesting because of the dark spots on a white ground which do resemble the eyes of old-fashioned dolls. These thrive in light-filtered shade.

Aaron's rod, *Thermopsis caroliniana* is a good subject for dry woods, but since it is a legume it will not tolerate the acid soil found under oaks. It flowers in summer. The golden yellow pea-like flowers will light up a forest glade.

Several native orchids thrive in open woods. I have a colony of over 2,000 plants of the long-spurred fringed orchid *(Habenaria macrophylla)* that covers nearly half an acre in the open area between spruces where they are shaded more than half the day. They flower in July and early August. Orchids are notoriously hard to move: if they can be located already growing in an area similar to the one to be planted, the best procedure is to lift them with a ball of earth and replant them at once.

Most lilies will do well in light woods if they can get two or three hours of direct sunshine at some time during the day. *Lilium candidum,* the Madonna lily, is an exception; it must have full sun. *Lilium philadelphicum* and *L. superbum* are two species with which I have had good luck.

Each section of the country has its particular favorites among wild flowers. A particularly thorough coverage of U.S. wild flowers can be found in *Wild Flowers for Your Garden,* by Helen S. Hull (M. Barrows & Company). Do not, however, pass up the possibility of using plants in commerce just because they are not labeled

Using native wildflowers as a ground cover makes an effective garden along the drive of this vacation cottage.

as wild flowers. After all, every species in existence was a wild flower somewhere: to date man has not created a single species. Japanese spurge, *Pachysandra terminalis,* looks as American as apple pie when given a chance to cover the soil under a woodland in the Middle West. Allow the bugleweed, *Ajuga reptans,* to run wild under the trees, and this European native will look as though it had been there for ages.

Perhaps the most difficult problem of all to solve is that of bringing in plant material not available from local sources. Summer cottagers cannot depend on mail shipments. Parcels addressed to city addresses on regular mail routes may be weeks on the way. Add to that the fate of a plant shipment addressed to a small post office without carrier delivery and you will see that its chances of survival are minimal.

About the only way this can be handled is to purchase plants at home and take them along. This usually means buying pot-grown stock, although flats of annuals can usually survive a ride of a day or less. A dry-cleaner's plastic bag drawn over a well-watered flat of bedding plants can make a world of difference in their condition on arrival.

Within your own state, transportation of live plants should not present a problem, except where local quarantines against such movement exist to avoid introduction of potentially dangerous pests. When such quarantines against insects, such as the Japanese beetle or Mediterranean fruit fly, are involved, it is sheer folly to try to evade them. If in doubt, call your county farm adviser or agricultural agent. Incidentally, this same government agent is a good man to know in your summer home area. He is familiar with local soils, insect pests, diseases, sources of supplies, and other important phases of gardening.

WATER—A LIMITING FACTOR

Most summer gardeners give less attention to supplying moisture to plants than they do to any other major element of plant growth. Since most of them are city dwellers, they take water supplies for granted. Suddenly they discover that a whole summer's gardening pleasure is being ruined for lack of this vital element.

Pressure from shallow well water systems is often too weak to permit the use of a hose for irrigation. A partial solution (for the strong and vigorous) is to drive a well near the garden area, using a pipe and wellpoint, topped with an old-fashioned pitcher pump. A few strokes will provide enough water to save newly transplanted seedlings or to keep tomato fruits from cracking. If a force pump is installed, and if a stout boy can be recruited to do the pumping, a hose can be attached for more effective application of water.

STARTING PLANTS

One way to gain time in the short growing season that may be available is to start seedlings of both annual plants and vegetables in the city and bring them to the summer garden ready to begin producing. Modern containers for growing seedlings have greatly simplified this operation. Nowadays, anything that will grow in a small pot can be started indoors. I know of several summer gardeners who start sweet corn in this way so they can beat their neighbors to the first roasting ears of the season. There is nothing more satisfying than to be able to invite friends to a barbecue at which they are served sweet corn when their plants have not even begun to tassel!

I was once enthusiastic about the peat-fiber pots being commonly sold nowadays, but have become disenchanted with them after having observed them in use. A common experience is to dig up a stunted plant only to find that its roots have not penetrated the pot as promised. This is due to failure to bury the entire pot. When the rim projects above the surface, it acts as a wick that pulls moisture out of the soil so that it evaporates instead. When using these peat-fiber pots, either bury them deeply or break off the rim so that the top can be completely covered with soil. Personally, I have better luck with plants grown in plastic containers.

In transporting seedlings I have found the thin plastic bags used by cleaners, as already mentioned, a great help. On arrival, if planting cannot be done at once, the well-watered flats or pots covered with one of these bags and set under a tree will survive for days. To cover smaller flats or individual pots, I have used Baggies, the commercial plastic bags that are torn off a roll as needed.

FERTILIZERS

Summer homes are seldom chosen because they are on good soil: fertilizers are almost essential. But fertilizers alone cannot supply everything needed. A compost heap solves two problems—what to do with most table wastes and what to do to build up the organic content of poor soils.

Because the summer gardener has little or no time for succession feedings, the most convenient plant foods are those which have some mechanism for slow release built into them. Modern plant foods can be had that will spread out the rate at which they feed so that a single application in spring will continue to feed until fall. The best-known slow-acting fertilizer is ureaform—actually a soft plastic that dissolves at a rate which satisfies the demands made on it by plants. Several firms make such a product. Since it supplies only nitrogen, it should be purchased only in mixed fertilizers in which ureaform is combined with other essential nutrients. Read the formula on the bag to be sure that phosphorus and potash are also in the product you buy.

Often, local farms are willing to give away manure, which is low in actual fertility, but does help build the humus content of the soil. If enough of it is used, it can supply all the nutrient needs of plants, but be sure to stockpile it at least a year in advance and allow it to rot down before using. Manures are low in phosphorus: an application of superphosphate should be made when they are applied to the garden. Save wood ashes; they are a valuable source of potash and lime.

Completely soluble fertilizers applied through a hose-end sprayer are convenient and effective. They are too costly for the larger garden, but if you have a small summer garden, they are worth considering because they are concentrated and are thus easy to take along in a car.

SEASHORE PROBLEMS

It is difficult to say whether persons who choose to garden at the seashore or near sandy lake beaches should be commended for their courage or condemned for their rashness. This is not easy gardening by any means: those who maintain a seaside cabin as a place to rest should never attempt it. Now that you have been warned, what *can* be done?

In the chapter on soils, a method for building a true soil out of sand is described: the work involved will probably discourage most gardeners from trying it. It calls for moving some tons of soil—a really hard job if the work must be done by hand, less so if mechanical equipment is available.

When this program is followed, no limit need be placed on the variety of trees, shrubs, and herbaceous plants that can be grown. There is one exception: where the garden is subject to salt spray or salt-laden air, the number of species which can be grown will be severely limited.

The real problem arises when time, physical effort, or money is not available to carry out the removal of sand, the installation of a water barrier, and the replacement of part of the sand with soil-building materials. I have personally worked on two such projects, one in Florida and the other in the Indiana–Michigan dunes area, and can testify that moving tons of sand in the hot sun may be good for one's figure but is far from the sort of work one would do for pleasure.

Fortunately, our native flora and the list of plants introduced from other parts of the world are rich in species that will survive both sandy conditions and salt spray. Since covering all those available would be outside the limits of this book, you whose homes have severe exposure to the sea are advised to refer to *Seaside Plants of the World,* by America's leading authority on the subject, Edwin A. Menninger, published by Hearthside Press.

Here, however, is a partial list of old reliables which can be found blooming on sandy wastes stretching from the New Jersey coasts well into Maine. Some are native to the bogs that form on the lee side of a dune, just over the hump from the actual shore. Others thrive in the forests that approach the sea on dry headlands. Others survive on the dunes just above the shore. All survive in spite of the buffeting of gale winds and an occasional dose of salt-laden rain or wind.

SHRUBS

Shrubs are particularly important for beach planting since they can be used to break the force of gale winds which not only cause damage by their force, but also bring in salt-laden spray. They serve this purpose best when planted just to the lee of dune crests: few species will survive on the seaward slope. (For descriptions, see chapter 6, "Plant Materials.")

Amelanchier canadensis	Shadblow
Aronia arbutifolia	Red chokeberry
Buddleia davidi	Butterfly bush
Caryopteris incana	Blue spirea
Clethra alnifolia	Summersweet
Cornus amomum	Silky dogwood
Cornus baileyi	Red dogwood
Cotoneaster horizontalis	Rock spray
Cytisus praecox	Warminster broom
Cytisus scoparius	Scotch broom
Elaeagnus angustifolia	Russian olive
Hydrangea macrophylla	House hydrangea
*Hydrangea petiolaris**	Climbing hydrangea
Hypericum calycinum	Aaron's-beard
Ilex aquifolium	English holly
Ilex opaca	American holly
Juniperus horizontalis	Creeping juniper
Juniperus sabina	Savin juniper
Ligustrum amurense	Amur privet
Ligustrum vulgare	Common privet
Myrica gale	Sweet gale
Prunus maritima	Beach plum
Rosa rugosa	Rugosa rose
Sambucus canadensis	American elder
Taxus cuspidata	Japanese yew
Vaccinium corymbosum	High bush blueberry
Vaccinium macrocarpon	American cranberry

*Grown as a sprawling shrub; as a vine, upper branches are readily killed.

TREES

Abies homolepis	Nikko fir
Abies veitchii	Veitch fir
Acer pseudoplatanus	Sycamore maple
Albizzia julibrissin rosea	Silk tree
Alnus glutinosa	Black alder
Caragana arborescens	Siberian peatree
Elaeagnus angustifolia	Russian olive
Fagus sylvatica	European beech
Gleditsia triacanthos	Honey locust
Ilex aquifolium	English holly
Juniperus chinensis	Keteleeri bottle-green juniper
Maclura pomifera	Osage orange
Nyssa sylvatica	Sour gum
Picea abies	Norway spruce
Picea glauca	White spruce
Pinus mugo	Swiss mountain pine
Pinus nigra	Austrian pine
Pinus sylvestris	Scotch pine
Pinus thunbergii	Japanese black pine*
Platanus acerifolia	London plane tree
Populus alba	White poplar
Populus tremuloides	Quaking aspen
Salix caprea	Goat willow

ANNUALS

Under "Shrubs" a recommendation was made for planting a barrier against wind and spray. Once such a barrier is established, the area behind it becomes a microclimate, an area where plants which otherwise might perish are able to survive. Here, almost any annual can be grown if the problem of sandy soil can be solved. The following list contains plants which have been known to

*The Japanese black pine, while not the handsomest of its genus, is by far the most satisfactory evergreen for areas exposed to salt spray. It will survive nearly 100 feet closer to high tide mark than will the next most resistant evergreen *Picea glauca*.

survive an occasional dousing with salt spray and are recommended for planting where protection is difficult to provide.

Abronia umbellata	Sand verbena
Ageratum houstonianum	Ageratum
Alyssum maritimum (*Lobularia maritimum*)	Sweet alyssum
Arctotis stoechadifolia	African daisy
Mesembryanthemum (various)	Ice plants
Petunia hybrida	Petunia
Phlox drummondi	Annual phlox
Portulaca grandiflora	Rose-moss
Salvia splendens	Scarlet sage
Tagetes (various)	Marigolds
Vinca rosea	Periwinkle

PERENNIALS

Provide shrub shelter for these perennials as for annuals. Some of the species recommended may not be highly ornamental, yet when seen against the blue of the sea, they can be lovely.

Aletris farinosa	Colicroot
*Artemisia canadensis**	Sea wormwood
*Artemisia stelleriana**	Old woman
*Asclepias tuberosa**	Butterfly weed
*Baptisia australis**	False indigo
*Baptisia tinctoria**	Clover bloom
Campanula rotundifolia	Bluebells of Scotland
Chrysanthemum maximum	Shasta daisy
Chrysopsis falcata	Golden aster
Coreopsis grandiflora	
Coreopsis lanceolata	
Coreopsis maritima	Sea dahlia
Echinops ritro	Globe thistle
Epetrum nigrum	Crowberry
*Eryngium maritimum**	Sea holly
Eupatorium purpureum	Joe Pye weed
Euphorbia corollata	Flowering spurge
*Gaillardia aristata**	Blanket-flower
*Glaucium flavum**	Sea poppy
Hemerocallis (various)*	Day lilies

*Hibiscus moscheutos**	Sea mallow
Iberis sempervirens	Perennial candytuft
*Lantana camara**	Red sage
Lathyrus maritimus	Beach pea
*Limonium sinuatum**	Sea lavender
Oenothera biennis	Evening primrose
Oenothera missouriensis	Missouri primrose
*Rosmarinus officinalis**	Rosemary
*Silene maritima**	Sea campion
Solidago sempervirens	Beach goldenrod
*Thermopsis caroliniana**	Aaron's rod
Thymus serpyllum	Mother-of-thyme
Thymus vulgaris	Common thyme
*Yucca filamentosa**	Adam's-needle

Many of the above, in addition to surviving well on exposed seacoasts and lake shores in the North, are equally suitable for planting in warmer sections of the country. Those marked * should do well wherever light frosts occur. The following plant material enriches the list available to warmer climates.

SHRUBS FOR WARMER CLIMATES

Acacia (various)	Mimosa
Atriplex halimus	Tree purslane
Aucuba japonica variegata	Gold-dust plant
Berberis darwinii	Darwin barberry
Callistemon rigidus	Stiff bottlebrush
Carissa grandiflora	Natal plum
Coccolobis uvifera	Sea grape
Coprosma baueri	Mirror plant
Elaeagnus pungens	Silverleaf
Escallonia rosea	Peruvian honeysuckle
Euonymus japonicus	Evergreen burning bush
Eugenia myrtoides	Spanish stopper
Fuchsia magellanica	Chile fuchsia
Genista monosperma	African broom
Hakea laurina	Sea urchin
Hakea suaveolens	Sweet hakea
Lavandula stoechas	Maderia lavender
Lavatera assurgentiflora	California tree mallow

Lonicera nitida	Box honeysuckle
Lycium halimifolium	Matrimony vine
Medicago arborea	Tree alfalfa
Myroporum laetum	Bastard sandalwood
Nerium oleander	Oleander
Olearia albida	Daisy bush
Phlomis fruticosa	Jerusalem sage
Pittosporum crassifolium	Karo
Rhus laurina	Laurel sumac
Rosa rugosa	Rugosa rose
Rosmarinus officinalis	Rosemary
Ruscus aculeatus	Butcher's broom
Spartium junceum	Spanish broom

GRASSES FOR SEASIDE LAWNS

About the only grasses that have much chance of surviving on the sandy soils around beach homes are the tall fescues such as Alta fescue and Kentucky 31 fescue (not to be confused with Kentucky bluegrass).

Where the soil contains a moderate amount of humus, seaside bent will survive and produce a luxury lawn.

MOUNTAIN COTTAGES

Gardens in the mountains generally suggest rock gardens, except that often summer vacation houses in such areas are built on the most level ground available—usually on an alpine meadow. In the eastern United States, this presents no unusual problems since rainfall and other factors are favorable to normal plant growth.

In the Rockies and other western ranges, however, rainfall may average less than ten to fifteen inches a year. At higher altitudes, dew and other sources of humidity make lack of rainfall less of a problem than it is on the lower slopes.

Shrubs that will tolerate quite low moisture conditions are few and far between. One of the best is from Siberia—*Caragana arborescens,* the Siberian peatree. It can be grown as a shrub or a small tree, but will become coarse and ungainly unless cut back occasionally. *Caragana pygmaea,* a close relative, is almost as tolerant and is lower-growing: it is excellent for low hedges in cold, dry country.

Surprisingly enough, lilacs also tolerate much lower moisture conditions than would seem possible. The hybrids developed in Canada are particularly useful. The Persian lilac is an excellent substitute for privet as a hedge in dry areas—they both belong to the same family. When trimmed back, Persian lilacs will form a dense, tight barrier. Another substitute for privet is the Peking rock spray, *Cotoneaster acutifolia,* which survives with relatively little soil moisture. In such areas, it is not subject to the disease which may kill it off in sections with more rainfall.

As a shrub, *Tamarix hispida* is a poor substitute for the real thing, although where nothing else will grow because of strongly alkaline or salty soils, it is acceptable. It needs to be cut back severely every so often to give it some semblance of form. Even hardier, but

This vacation garden in the Adirondacks was planned for beauty and easy maintenance.

difficult to find in commerce, is the salt cedar, *Tamarix gallica.* I have seen it trained in tree form growing in highly alkaline soils where air temperatures stayed as low as twenty degrees below zero for days on end.

The sumacs are worth planting, if only for their fall color, particularly the staghorn sumac, *Rhus typhina,* which is also desirable for its conspicuous red fruits. The variety *laciniata,* with its finely cut leaves, is a choice shrub or small tree worthy of a place, even in landscape plantings in less rigorous climates. A third species, *Rhus glabra* is an excellent low plant, seldom growing more than three feet high. It is difficult to find in catalogs, however. It is also difficult to dig from the wild because of its deep roots, but it can be grown from seed gathered as soon as ripe.

Three species of wild currants are both interesting and easy to grow. The first is *Ribes alpinum,* the alpine currant, one of our most desirable low-growing hedge plants. In drier areas it is not subject to the die-back which causes so much trouble in many moister sections. *Ribes aureum*—the golden currant is taller-growing with lovely fragrant yellow flowers, followed by blackish fruits. Although these are edible, many persons find them disappointing compared with the common garden currant.

Both of the above are quite hardy. For warmer climates, the buffalo currant, *Ribes odoratum* is a finer plant.

Another fruiting plant worth growing is the thimbleberry, *Rubus occidentalis.* It is attractive both in bloom, when its tiny white flowers are produced in a perfect cloud, and in fruit. The berries are edible, similar to those of the black raspberry.

Although the sand cherry, *Prunus besseyi,* makes a rather open bush and is not too good as a specimen plant, it does fruit and flower. It is one of the few fruiting plants hardy in northern Canada. Where a trickle of moisture can be given them, bushes of the beach plum, *Prunus maritima,* are also worth trying.

Perhaps the most satisfactory ornamental plant for such dry areas is Adam's-needle, *Yucca filamentosa.* If protected from winter wetness, it will stand cold weather.

Among the evergreens, only *Juniperus scopulorum,* the Western red cedar, has much of a chance to survive. It can be had in many varieties and is a choice landscape subject.

LANDSCAPING IN DRY REGIONS

Newcomers to semidesert areas often make the mistake of trying to imitate landscape techniques of more humid regions. Heavy-mass foundation plantings are not only out of keeping with tradition, but draw heavily on the limited moisture resources of the soil. By keeping plantings simple and allowing space around individual specimens so that they can be seen from all sides, a planting more in harmony with the natural appearance of the local landscape will be produced. As a pleasant side benefit, costs of plant materials will be reduced.

In no part of the United States is it more important to consider siting, or actual placement of individual specimens, than in these arid regions. Each must fill its space well and look well from all sides. For valuable trees it will pay to use water to get them started, but any species that cannot go it alone once established will be too much trouble to be worth planting for a vacation gardener. Planting less tolerant species in sheltered spots is a "must."

One idea that is worth considering: water from wash basins and baths can be diverted to a special cistern through a sand filter and used for watering ornamentals. Waste water from the kitchen sink, if also run through a sand filter, should be equally useful.

All watering for semidesert species should be quite deep, even if root irrigators, such as are recommended for trees in more humid regions, must be used to apply moisture. Survival is often a matter of deep rooting—shallow watering prevents this.

In moving species which are only marginally tolerant of dry conditions, the use of antidesiccant sprays to retard water loss through foliage is particularly important. Although successful collecting of native species from the wild is difficult with dry-land plants because of their deep rooting, the use of such sprays will often make the difference between success and failure.

ROCK GARDENS AT HIGHER ALTITUDES

Although moisture is usually adequate at higher altitudes, practically all the plants with conspicuous flowers bloom so early in spring that by the time summer vacationers arrive, nothing but foliage can be seen. For this reason, it is important to make selections in summer when plants are out of flower. With such wide variations in possible growing conditions—granite scree, limestone moraines, sunny slopes, shaded cliffs, etc., recommendations are of little use: consult local nurserymen or experienced gardeners for specific information.

One solution for the gardener who wants some form of plant life around a mountain home but lacks the strength or determination to make a true rock garden is making a stone-sink. This is an art we have inherited from the British—one of their practices which could be imported to the United States with profit.

In America, we cannot find the primitive stone sinks which were once used in British farm kitchens, but simple stone basins can be laid up out of flat rocks near entrance doors or other convenient locations. These should be made some time in advance of planting so the cement used as mortar can be aged and washed.

Once constructed, a "sink" can be filled with almost any soil you wish—alkaline for such alpines as the various pinks or with granite acidic soil for those that prefer a pH below 7.0. One such "sink" I remember in the Blue Ridge was made of a soft, pinkish gray granite planted with lovely cheddar pinks, *Dianthus gratianopolitanus* (the awkward name now attached to the former *D. caesius*). The blue-gray foliage formed perfect mounds above which floated the delightfully fragrant pink blossoms. No other planting was needed to make the cottage it decorated a real garden picture.

II

SMALL GARDENS FOR THE HANDICAPPED GARDENER

IN THE PAST, gardening for the handicapped has been looked upon largely as a type of therapy. Certainly, the therapeutic value of working with plants cannot be overestimated. In fact, I have had a keen interest in this type of therapy for many years. When I was president of the Chicago Horticultural Society, we developed a program for the physically handicapped that included an outstanding garden for the blind, horticultural education in the three Chicago public schools for handicapped children, and a therapeutic program in several old people's homes. The garden for the blind was designed to familiarize the newly blinded with the feel and smell of plants, as an aid in training them for a world without sight.

However, gardening can also be an excellent hobby and source of pleasure for those who are not badly handicapped but who must limit their activities because of some physical disability. For example, heart patients, under a physician's guidance, can enjoy a leisurely form of gardening and achieve satisfying results without taxing their strength. A sensible program is all that is required.

Each handicapped person needs to develop his own program, keeping in mind his own limitations and capacities. A good example of a handicapped gardener who took his limitations into consideration is Richardson Wright, for many years the brilliant editor of *House and Garden*. Dick Wright was compelled to retire from active work (and from active gardening) by a severe attack of arthritis. When the pain eased up somewhat, he asked his physician whether he could try to do something with plants and was assured that only his own discomfort would stop him. Since his greatest problem was a severe back pain, he decided to build a raised garden which could be worked in a standing position.

Beds of stone, laid up by a friendly mason, that were artistic as well as convenient were built. A raised propagating frame enabled him to continue raising his own plants, for many years one of his hobbies. The last time I saw him, he was extolling the virtues of a two-wheeled garden cart made with rubber-tired bicycle wheels which he found much easier to push than a wheelbarrow.

His experiences, at least in principle, might well serve as a model for anyone with physical handicaps. Fit your activities to your

Containers and raised beds are a perfect solution for the handicapped gardener who has difficulty bending.

capacities and enjoy gardening is as good a rule as can be laid down. First you must know when to quit. You should never push yourself. The time to quit is not when you are exhausted, but when you feel you can still go on.

The second rule is to take advantage of every physical help you can. It may be tough on the ego to admit you are unable to do hoeing, but once you admit that it is too much for you, you will probably enjoy experimenting with various mulches to see which controls weeds best. Also, there are small electric tools that can make that job a pleasure and give a sense of accomplishment.

After a back injury hospitalized me for several weeks, I found leaning over to work in a propagating frame all but impossible. Following Dick Wright's example, I built a propagating frame on legs which enabled me to reach every inch of it without bending. I have continued to use it ever since, even after the reason for building it was no longer valid. When I think of the lost years of physical effort—bending over cold frames, hotbeds, propagating frames, and similar structures that could just as well have been mounted on legs—I am chagrined that the idea of raised benches never occurred to me before.

Of all the devices a handicapped gardener should consider, a small greenhouse is the first. Not only does it put all operations on a no-bending level, but it protects him from working in unseasonable weather, far more of a strain than is often realized. Such a greenhouse need not be elaborate—a simple wooden frame (treated with a copper napthanate wood preservative) which is covered with sheets of fiberglas can be built for less than $100, if professional labor is not required. I would avoid using flexible sheet plastics as a covering, even though this might save a few dollars, because they have to be replaced every year. Thus, you do not really save money and you increase your work load. Furthermore, fiberglas distributes light better than sheet plastic or conventional glass. Any man handy with tools should be able to throw together a frame to be covered with fiberglas in a day or less. Write to your state agricultural experiment station for directions and plans. These can be used by a carpenter if your handicap does not permit you to do the job.

Another effective and satisfying method of gardening for the handicapped gardener is container gardening. Large areas of stone or other paving are used to replace lawns and mass plantings. Plants are grown in pots, urns, boxes and large planters. By limiting the area that needs attention, this type of culture (often used in courtyards and terraces), taking care of a fairly large-size garden becomes manageable for the handicapped gardener. One great advantage to this kind of gardening is that the best plant materials available can be used because fewer plants are needed. In addition, each plant can be given special attention. The result will be a group of quality plants that will be far more impressive than a larger display of ordinary plants.

Container gardening calls for quality containers. Because so much of the attention is concentrated on a small area, the observer can take in all elements of a planting. Ordinary clay pots are not things of beauty, but English, Italian, and Spanish pots are now being imported that have definite character. Use them whenever possible.

Large planters call for special care in design and in construction. Proportions are critical—if you lack an artistic eye, ask someone with training in design to sketch your idea in exact dimensions on paper, where you want to place it on a terrace, patio, or driveway. While such planters should be bold and have an impact on the eye of the observer, it is easier to overdo this effect than you think.

Place your planter at the eye level of the average person. Most planters are too tall and so look unnatural; they should give the effect of a natural raised ledge rather than of a box.

Handsome containers can be made from wooden shipping kegs and barrels of various types. For years, I used all the chop suey kegs a Chinese importer discarded. For tree tubs, I purchased large barrels in which sherry had been imported by a Chicago wine dealer. The hexagonal and octagonal redwood tubs now available in a wide range of sizes are excellent.

All except the redwood containers should be washed thoroughly with a strong detergent, rinsed well, and allowed to dry. Then treat with Cuprinol (copper napthanate) as a preservative. Never use creosote on any wood that will come in contact with plants. The most commonly available wood preservative is pentachlorophenol, but this must be weathered for three or four weeks before the container can be used for plants: otherwise it is an excellent preservative.

Window boxes are easy to care for and offer the gardener satisfaction and challenge in planning an effective combination of plants.

Conventional window boxes may have to serve for the city dweller anxious to see something growing. Here, the area available for holding the box will determine its dimensions. Formerly, I used metal liners, but today, the sheet plastics, such as polyethylene, are not only cheaper, but just as good. Since they can be discarded each year, they do not need to be cleaned before planting. Punch holes in the bottom of the plastic liners to permit excess water to drain away.

Since soil is heavy, the handicapped gardener may prefer to leave plants growing in individual pots which are easier to handle. In either case, lay down a layer of pea gravel on the plastic to allow for drainage.

One of the most difficult problems in caring for container-grown plants is watering. The amount of soil available is so limited that regular attention is necessary to avoid drying out or over watering.

A program that saves a great deal of fussing and work is to use an artificial soil mixture, which will drain quickly yet hold moisture, with some porous, inert ceramic or mineral material. A mixture that I developed, which does unusually well with a wide variety of plants, consists of two ingredients. The one is imported peat moss (German, Swedish, or Canadian), which is sphagnum peat, not the sedge peat which is the basis of so many domestic peats. The other is a calcined ceramic material normally used as a kitten litter or pet-box material. When half fresh litter and half imported peat moss are mixed, artificial soil is produced that will hold moisture, yet will drain and is difficult to waterlog.

Since such a soil mixture contains practically no nutrients, each time it is watered, the water should contain a liquid fertilizer. A regular commercial house-plant liquid fertilizer, used at one-half the recommended rate in water, can be used safely, even if the plants need watering every day.

One problem the handicapped gardener will have, unless he is the fortunate owner of a small greenhouse, is that of plant replacement. As a rule, his facilities for carrying over perennial plants will be limited. And because they are in raised containers, they are more subject to winterkill in severe climates than are those growing at ground level. Shrubs (and even trees) can be grown in containers, but in making your selection choose species and varieties from the list in chapter 5 that are recommended for one zone north of your location.

Never attempt to protect plants in raised beds or containers by covering them with clear plastic. This is poor insulation, at best, since heat moves rather freely through clear materials. As a result, sunlight can build up high temperatures which disappear as soon as the sun goes down. Cold then moves in as quickly. Such heat fluctuations are deadly to plants.

The purpose of protection is not to keep out cold, but to keep it in, so plants will stay dormant. The ideal protection would be made from an aluminized plastic (such materials are available but are expensive) covering a mulch of some loose, airy material, such as pine needles or excelsior. Tarred papers, being black, absorb heat and so are almost as bad as clear plastic. One of the best coverings I have used was a wooden frame covered on the inside with black tarred felt and painted on the outside with a white exterior latex paint. Its one defect—lack of ventilation—was solved by punching a few holes.

Lacking an ideal material, keep in mind that any white, opaque fabric that will slow up wind movement over the plants will help. Moving the plants to a winter storage room or cellar not only involves extra work, but is often beyond the physical capacity of the handicapped gardener.

Most aches and pains resulting from gardening affect the back. Often these are due to the use of a tool that forces you to work in an awkward position because the handle is too short. Roy Hay, the well-known British authority on gardening, showed me how he advises a gardener to select a hoe, rake, or long-handled spade. With the bottom of the blade of the spade set on the ground, the tip of the handle should just reach the shoulder. In the case of hoes and rakes, handles should be long enough to reach your ear.

GARDEN CALENDAR

GARDEN CALENDAR

Do not feel that just because an operation is listed in the following calendar that it is recommended for every gardener.

Fortunately, gardening is a personal matter which need involve only those operations which fit your time, finances, and physical strength.

The purpose in listing them here is only to give a general idea of when each needs to be done.

If it becomes a part of your gardening program, this calendar will enable you to plan ahead for each operation, always a conserver of time and energy.

No schedule can pinpoint the whims of weather to exact man-made dates. Read chapter 3 on "Climate": it will at least console you when you guess wrong.

THE IMPORTANCE OF PLANNING ahead as a means of saving work in the garden cannot be overemphasized. In order to deal effectively with the vagaries of climate, materials must be on hand before they are needed and a schedule of operations set up in advance.

Although the processes of growth begin, rise, fall, and finally cease in an orderly sequence, they do not follow man-made calendars with any degree of consistency. From year to year, they advance or retreat, whichever the case may be, in a manner difficult to anticipate. We say that spring is "late" when the first crocuses do not appear by an early Easter, or that it is "early" if snowdrops and aconites display their gold and yellow amid February snows.

Unless accurate records are kept, differences in plant growth between one year and another are difficult to appreciate. The first year of World War II, my garden diary showed no frost in the Middle West after March 16. Tyro gardeners planting their first victory gardens rushed out to plant snap beans, tomatoes, and other tender crops amid the jeers of old-timers. These same old hands were red-faced when such early crops not only grew, but matured weeks ahead of their own "safe" plantings.

In that same diary, another year saw killing frosts as late as June 4. Here in a single weather factor was a variation of as much as two months. Certainly, such variations, which determine success or failure in a garden, pose a problem for orderly gardeners who try to plan ahead.

Mother Nature (to fall back on that scorned anthropomorphic figure) has a calendar of her own, however, which is exactly in step with the amount of heat accumulation from the sun. A dormant anemone beneath a blanket of snow cannot respond to a square on the calendar that says it is April 15, but it can be stirred by the accumulated energy from the sun as that snow blanket melts.

In the month-by-month schedules which follow, there are certain operations which are listed according to the dates on man's calendar, particularly in the spring and fall, but these have been modified by additional references to certain natural signs which are more reliable guides.

JANUARY

Who looks on winter sees a fragile thing
Embroidered on the living tapestry of trees.

James B. Follinsbee

Down with the rosemary and so,
Down with the baies and mistletoe,
Down with the holy, ivie, all
Wherewith you drest the Christmas hall.

Robert Herrick (1591–1674)

Except that January is a month for reading garden books and catalogs and for placing advance orders for seeds, bulbs, and garden supplies, this would seem an illogical time to open the garden year. Even in the far South, except for specially favored places in Florida, Texas, and California, most outdoor work is confined to cleanup operations.

NORTH

While boughs are bare and lifeless, study trees and shrubs for possibilities of "cosmetic" pruning—shaping them into more pleasing silhouettes. Now is the time to mark branches for removal that are weak or badly placed. Do not prune, however, while wood is frozen—it is brittle and may break in wrong places. Check its condition by shaking small twigs. Although these operations can be delayed until later, there is usually more spare time for them in January than at any other time of year.

Study winter color in landscape masses. If it is dull and uninteresting, make a note to plant species with colored bark next March or April—such striking species as *Cornus stolonifera,* kerria, or the various birches.

Whenever the soil is bare, check the amount of moisture it contains, particularly near house foundations, where it dries out most rapidly. Evergreens in particular are apt to be harmed by drying out because their foliage gives off water all year around. During the winter is no exception. If necessary, irrigate during a January thaw.

Spraying trees, while they are still dormant, is often done during January thaws, but only if air temperatures can be relied upon to stay above the freezing mark well into the night following application. Otherwise, freezing will cause the oil to separate from the emulsion which can kill the bark.

Salvage discarded Christmas trees for mulching. Branches make an ideal supplemental covering for roses which have been hilled with soil for winter protection. Set up cut trees around rhododendrons which are in exposed positions to shield them from sun and wind. These same set-up trees can serve as a temporary grove to shelter birds. To feed them, tie suet and cut fruit, such as oranges and apples, to branches. Evergreen needles which have been shed form a perfect mulch for azaleas and rhododendrons.

If it has not been done earlier, and if the wood is not frozen, make hardwood cuttings of deciduous shrubs. Six-inch-long pieces of last summer's growth are best. Tie them in bundles of ten to twenty, with lower ends all pointing the same way, and with the lower ends *up,* bury them in damp sawdust, sand, or peat moss. Temperature within the covering should be near freezing, but not quite. In spring, these can be planted in the garden, burying the lower two-thirds of the cutting. They should root in several weeks.

Bring in branches of forsythia, Japanese quince, flowering almond, and other early-blooming shrubs for forcing. They will not force as easily as they would in late February, but if plenty of material is available, they will be even more welcome. Either dampen the branches with warm water or soak them overnight in a bathtub. Often, forced branches will root in water and can be potted up to produce new shrubs later. This is particularly true of pussy willows.

Brush snow from evergreens before it can freeze to the needles. It it does freeze before this can be done, don't shake the branches. If evergreens were not treated with an antidesiccant earlier, those in positions which are exposed to snow can be sprayed during a thaw.

After each snow, tramp down the accumulated snow around trunks of trees (young fruit trees in particular) so that mice cannot tunnel underneath and girdle trunks.

Winter winds are apt to whip vines badly: examine them for loose ends and tie them securely. Climbing roses will need protection if unusually cold weather occurs.

Examine broad-leaved evergreens, such as holly, leucothoe, and rhododendrons. If they do not have winter protection and their leaves are curling, wrap them in straw or burlap at once. Or wait until a warm spell occurs and then spray with an antidesiccant before wrapping. Never use either clear or black plastic for covering: it is deadly. If it can be had, aluminized plastic is excellent because it reflects sun heat.

LAWNS: If snow mold was bad last spring, apply a suitable turf fungicide during a January thaw, even if an application was made in fall. Thawing weather may have washed away the earlier application.

Avoid the practice of applying manure or other organic fertilizers to lawns in winter: the organic matter often feeds snow-mold fungi better than it does the grass. During thaws, check the lawn for low spots where water accumulates and mark them for leveling later. Never cover a lawn with plastic and then flood it for use as a skating rink—this has killed many a fine lawn.

FRUITS AND VEGETABLES: Roots of witloof chicory (sometimes called French endive) as well as clumps of asparagus and rhubarb dug last fall and allowed to freeze can now be brought into a cellar for forcing.

Examine vegetables in storage for signs of rotting or shriveling. The former cannot be redeemed so throw out the rotten specimens. Those that have shriveled can often be salvaged by sprinkling with water or covering with a damp cloth.

Make scions of fruit trees for grafting later, using tip growth of last summer's wood. Store in the same way as described for hardwood cuttings. This can be done at the same time as pruning.

FLOWERS AND HOUSE PLANTS: Now is the time to start seeds of slowgrowing annuals. Most of these are actually tender perennials which can be made to flower the first year if they are seeded early enough to produce a mature plant. These include ageratum, *Asparagus sprengeri, Asparagus plumosus,* fibrous-rooted begonia, tuberous-rooted begonia, annual carnations, *Centaurea candidissima* (the all-important dusty miller), annual chrysanthemums, coleus, unwin dahlia, impatiens, lobelia, neirembergia, pansies, double and large-flowered petunia, verbena, and *Vinca rosea.*

At this time, most house plants are resting. Water them only enough to keep the leaves plump, but don't allow them to dry out. Give them all the light possible (adding artificial light through the use of fluorescent tubes will help). Keep temperatures as low as human comfort permits. Do *not* fertilize at this time. Watch for mealy bugs and other insect pests.

On cold nights, place clear plastic between window glass and the plants. In subzero weather, several layers of newspapers may be needed in addition to supply some insulation.

Force lily-of-the-valley pips (these come from florists and are preconditioned for early bloom). They should flower in three weeks after planting. Continue planting paper-white narcissus as long as sound bulbs can be had. Lily-of-the-valley pips will flower in a sunny window, but paper-white bulbs need storage in the dark for four weeks first.

Amaryllis bulbs about to flower should be given all the light available and adequate water into which has been dissolved a good house-plant fertilizer. As they go out of bloom, apply only enough water to keep them from shriveling, but keep in active growth so that the leaves can form to feed next year's blossom.

The earliest tulips (Single Early, Double Early, Mendel, and Triumph types) can be brought in for forcing now. Darwins, etc., need to be kept in storage until next month. Bring in hyacinths now, but cover each shoot with an inverted pot to draw up the leaves and flower spike.

The day length is too short yet for good bloom on African violets but they can be given several hours of additional light from fluorescent tubes.

Most Christmas plants are not worth saving after their flowers fade because they require skillful handling to keep healthy and may need special treatment to make them flower again.

Check summer-flowering bulbs which are in storage. Any showing signs of rotting should be thrown away before they damage the rest. If shriveled, pack in moist peat moss or sawdust for a while and then reexamine.

Order achimenes, gloxinias, and tuberous begonias now. For earliest flowers, start these into growth, toward the end of this month, in a mixture of sand and peat which should be kept damp and at seventy-five to eighty degrees.

To enjoy flowers on the Christmas rose *(Helleborus niger)* out of doors, cover the plants with a bottomless box covered with a pane of glass. Even if the flowers freeze solid, they will still thaw for use in flower arrangements. This amazing flower is sure to draw ohs and ahs in midwinter.

Next December's flowers on Christmas cactus plants will depend on how they are handled after flowering. Don't overwater—apply just enough water to keep them from shriveling. Keep plants as close to a window or greenhouse glass as possible.

Go over the perennial border during thaws and press back any plants that have heaved out of the soil. Stepping on them is usually sufficient. Replace any mulch which has been blown away by winter winds.

Odd Jobs: Start a garden diary. As a record of what happens from year to year, it is invaluable. Human memory is fallible. Try to remember and record when various flowers bloomed last year, but if you can't, content yourself to record these data this year.

If you burn wood in your fireplace, save the ashes. Store dry until needed. They are a good source of potash, plus lime.

Read a good book or two on some specialized aspect of gardening.

Feed the birds, but once you start, don't fail them. Once they become dependent on artificial feeding, they will rely on finding food at that spot until spring. Be sure they have access to unfrozen water, often more important than food. An electrically heated poultry fountain will ensure this.

To melt snow, use ammonium sulfate or muriate of potash instead of salt: these won't injure the grass when the melted snow runs off walks and drives. One caution: don't use any chemical for snow melting if the concrete underneath is less than a year old. Salts will cause cement to crumble until completely cured.

Clean and repair garden tools. Make flats for starting seedlings; repair and paint garden furniture and equipment.

Place orders at once for garden seeds, bulbs, nursery stock, and supplies. Orders are filled in rotation as they are received and the earliest get the best service, as well as the items in short supply.

Although mowing time is months away, send in your mower for repairs and sharpening right away. Workmen do a more thorough job when there is no pressure on them for immediate action.

Build a basement greenhouse or plant-growing unit. For seedlings, use the standard Gro-Lux tube: it concentrates all its energy in the plant-growing parts of the spectrum. For growing seedlings once seeds have germinated, use one wide-spectrum Gro-Lux to two standard Gro-Lux tubes. An efficient basement plant-growing unit will cost less than $25 to $50 and should save far more than its cost in producing bedding plants at a fraction of their retail cost.

Kill an unwanted tree during the winter by cutting a frilled collar around it about two feet from the ground and soaking it with 2,4,5-T or with Silvex.

SOUTH AND WEST COAST

Where the soil seldom freezes, garden work should never stop, even though occasional frosts nip tender foliage. Elsewhere, chilly weather may make working outdoors uncomfortable, yet the dedicated gardener will keep busy.

FLOWERS: Annuals to sow this month include annual larkspur, lupine, Phlox, poppy, bachelor's-button, pot marigold, California poppy, candytuft, clarkia, cottage pink, godetia, helipterum, flax, love-in-a-mist, snapdragon, sweet alyssum, sweet pea, and sweet sultan.

Perennials to sow now are columbine, delphinium, and sweet William. Where soil temperatures stay below forty-two degrees, they may lie dormant until warmer temperatures occur, but they are better for this early seeding.

Bulbs to start now are belladonna lilies *(Amaryllis belladonna),* ginger lilies, gladiolus, single and double tuberoses, gold band lilies *(Lilium auratum),* Easter lilies *(Lilium longiflorum), Lilium speciosum,* and tuberous begonia. In cooler climates, start indoors in peat-fiber pots.

VEGETABLES: Sow at once: asparagus (to produce plants for transplanting later), beets, broccoli, Brussels sprouts, Chinese cabbage, onion sets and seeds, squash, and turnips. Indoors, start seeds of tomatoes, eggplant, peppers, and okra in individual pots.

Spray fruit trees (particularly peaches) while they are dormant. Where they will survive, set out figs, guavas, loquats, and pomegranates. Trim, spray, and fertilize ornamental trees and shrubs.

Feed broad-leaved evergreens if the soil is not frozen.

PACIFIC NORTHWEST

All the recommendations made for the North apply here, but in addition, preemergence crab-grass controls can be applied to lawns. Also plant nursery stock as soon as possible. Dealers should have dormant stock available at any time.

Sow seeds of pansies, violas, and Iceland poppies.

FEBRUARY

The year ahead—
what will it bring?
At least we may be sure
of Spring.

Anonymous

NORTH

In the North, February is largely a repetition of January, except that if a spray for snow mold has been applied in that month, there is no need to repeat it now. In addition, the following operations need attention:

TREES AND SHRUBS: This is a favorite month for nurserymen to move big trees because by this time, the balls of earth which are attached to them are frozen solid.

By now, evergreens in cities have accumulated a coating of soot and oil from furnace fumes. This coating can be removed by adding a dish-washing detergent to a quart of water in the container of a hose-end sprayer and using this to wash off the grime.

Snow sliding off a roof can ruin evergreens. Where this danger threatens, lay a section of an extension ladder or planks above the evergreens to break the force of falling snow.

Check dormant trees, shrubs, and evergreens for bagworms and for clusters of gypsy moth eggs. Burn them. White, woolly clumps found on white pine bark are probably pine bark aphids: spray with double-strength malathion to control.

FLOWERS AND HOUSE PLANTS: Annuals to start indoors this month, in addition to the January list, are annual asters, *Cobaea scandens,* fibrous-rooted begonia, candytuft, annual Canterbury bells, annual foxglove, snapdragons, ten weeks stocks, and gaillardia. Perennials to sow include delphinium and Shasta daisy, to flower late in the summer when other perennials are scarce. Keep inspecting the perennial border during thaws to press back any plants heaved out by frost action.

Bulbs to start now are tuberous begonia, gloxinia, and fancy-leaved caladium. Press them into a mixture of damp peat and sand and hold at seventy-five to eighty degrees.

Pots of Darwin tulips can be brought in for forcing from now on.

Toward the end of February, repot foliage plants and ferns and give them more water, food, and light. Do the same to stock plants of geraniums, lanata, fuchsia, etc., so as to force young growth from which cuttings can be made during March.

FRUITS AND VEGETABLES: If it wasn't done soon after fruiting last summer, cut out all old hard canes of blackberries and raspberries. This should be done before any signs of new growth appear. These clippings may harbor disease—burn them. If the wood in grapevines is not frozen, prune the vines at once. They may bleed a little later, but this does no harm.

A sowing of lettuce, radishes, and onions (either sets or seed) in the hotbed will provide early vegetables long before outdoor crops will be ready.

LAWNS: Winter annual weeds, such as *Poa annua* and common chickweed, are now vivid green and easy to see against the more-or-less dormant lawn grasses. Nothing can be done at this time, but make a note to apply a preemergence control in late August or early September when their seeds germinate.

ODD JOBS: It is now time to start up the hotbeds so they will be ready in March. This is easy nowadays with electric cables to supply the heat.

SOUTH AND WEST COAST

LAWNS: Where ryegrass is used for winter color, don't neglect mowing. If it is allowed to grow too long, it can smother permanent grasses. In warmer sections where Bermuda grass is the main lawn species, delay turf work until next month. In cooler sections where bluegrass does well, reseed old lawns and sow new whenever the weather is favorable. Apply fertilizer to lawns in both areas. In warmer sections, preemergence crab-grass controls must go on this month.

TREES AND SHRUBS: Feed fig trees this month, using a high-nitrogen fertilizer. This is the time to move trees, shrubs, and roses.

Fertilize holly, azaleas, rhododendrons, and other broad-leaved evergreens now. Feed camellias as soon as they finish flowering.

All shrubs that flower in the summer can be pruned early this month, but don't touch those that flower early, such as forsythia, deutzia, bridal wreath, and weigela.

FLOWERS: It's time to divide perennials before they make too much new growth, but do it after this new growth has just started so that the point at which to divide them can be seen.

Plant seeds of ageratum, sweet alyssum, amaranthus, fibrous-rooted begonia, candytuft, calendula, coreopsis, annual Canterbury bells, *celosia*, *centaurea*, clarkia, cleome, cynoglossum, unwin dahlia, cape marigold, feverfew, gaillardia, godetia, lantana, larkspur, linaria, lobelia, annual lupine, nasturtium, nicotiana, nierembergia, penstemon, petunia, annual phlox, salpiglossis, salvia, scabiosa, schizanthus, verbena, and wallflower.

As new shoots of peonies break through the soil, spray them with Phaltan, or with Bordeaux mixture, to kill the botrytis fungus which causes flower buds to blast and turn brown.

Make cuttings of coleus, fibrous-rooted begonia, impatiens, geranium, heliotrope, and other bedding plants for setting out as soon as the danger of frost is over.

Perennial seeds to start now are delphinium, Canterbury bells, foxglove, coreopsis, lupines, Shasta daisies, and sweet William.

Prune roses this month, removing any dead wood killed by winter.

Where frost seldom occurs, start these bulbs in the open (farther north, do so inside in pots and set out later): achimenes, agapanthus, allium, *Amaryllis belladonna*, *belamcanda*, fancy-leaved caladium, calla, crinum, gladiolus, *kniphofia, Hymenocallis, Tritonia*, oxalis, scilla, sprekelia, tigridia, and zephyranthes.

Hardy chrysanthemums should be dug up and old clumps divided into single-stem divisions. Plant out these divisions twelve inches by twelve inches. When these have made five true leaves, remove the tip and upper three leaves to make a top-cutting, to root in damp sand. Both division and cutting will flower next spring.

In warmer sections, aphids may attack day lilies: spray them as soon as detected.

PACIFIC NORTHWEST

FLOWERS: In warmer sections, rose pruning can be done at any time from now on, but in cooler sections, delay until next month.

Seeds of sweet alyssum, clarkia, calendula, and annual larkspur can be sown out of doors at this time. Sweet peas must be planted in this month for best results.

Start summer-flowering bulbs as directed for the South and West Coast.

Divide chrysanthemums as directed for the South and West Coast.

TREES AND SHRUBS: Prune summer-flowering shrubs, such as butterfly bush and French-type hydrangeas.

Complete planting of all nursery stock by March 1.

Cut back the vines of large-flowering clematis to within a foot of the ground.

MARCH

There are winter days so full
of sudden sunshine that they
will cheat the wise crocus
into squandering its gold
before its time.

Oscar Wilde (1854–1900)

NORTH

If the season is early in the North, March can be the busiest month of the year. If late, it can be a frustrating time for the gardener. Watch for these natural signs of spring—flowers on maple trees and the first snowdrops and aconites in bloom. When these appear, perform any operations marked (M) as soon as the soil is workable. For proof of workability, use the mud pie test. Pick up a handful of soil and press it into a "mud pie," or ball. If it is really to work, the ball will crumble under slight pressure into friable loam. If it is too wet and sticks together, to work it would mean a soil ruined for an entire season. If it falls into dust without pressure, it is too dry and should be watered before digging. (The latter condition seldom occurs except when a winter drought has exhausted all soil moisture.)

TREES AND SHRUBS: (M) The earlier that dormant trees and shrubs can be moved, the better. This is the only time of year to transplant woody species with a "slip bark" on their roots, such as magnolias, cherries, and plums. It pays to wrap the trunks of all newly planted trees with a crinkled kraft-paper tree wrap to prevent excess loss of moisture through the bark. Birches, maples, and dogwoods must be moved before sap starts flowing to avoid "bleeding." This is not harmful but may be disfiguring. Don't cut back magnolias or prune them, and don't prune those shrubs that flower in early spring, such as forsythia, daphne, pussy willows, etc. Instead, prune them after they are through flowering.

Remove winter protection from broad-leaved evergreens cautiously. Scrape away hilling-up soil from around roses a little at a time. Be ready to cover again if late frosts threaten. With the new polystyrene rose cones, you can uncover them entirely on sunny days and recover them at night until settled weather occurs.

Hydrangea paniculata needs annual pruning it if is to flower well. Cut away at least one third of the old wood—the upper third of the branches.

(M) Plant out the hardwood cuttings made last fall which have been stored in sawdust.

FLOWERS: (M) Transplant pansies, forget-me-nots, and English daisies from cold frames to wherever they are needed to provide spring color. Be ready, however, with straw or excelsior to cover them if unseasonable late frosts occur.

Fill flats with a mixture of half peat moss and half sand (by volume) and dampen the mixture well. Set bulbs of fancy-leaved caladiums, gloxinia, and tuberous begonia on the mixture and spray over them with warm water. Keep damp and warm (above seventy-five degrees) until sprouts and roots form. Then pot up and grow until warm, settled weather arrives for planting them outside.

(M) If using old-fashioned Spencer varieties, sow sweet peas. The newer hot-weather-resistant varieties, such as the Multiflora and Cuthbertson, can either be sown now or later. Sow all hardy annuals out of doors.

(M) Uncover perennial beds gradually. Keep mulching materials handy in case unexpected frosts occur.

Annuals to seed indoors include all those on the February list, plus *Salvia splendens* and *Cobaea scandens* (the latter in four-inch pots). *Vinca rosea* sown in March may not flower until August.

Start tubers of dahlias into growth in the same way that was recommended for tuberous begonia. Use the new shoots as cuttings. Continue making cuttings of geraniums and other bedding plants.

For a breath of spring, dig a clump of hardy violets, pot them, and set them in a sunny window. Handle trailing arbutus in the same way.

Feed perennial borders with a good mixed fertilizer as soon as mulch and trash have been raked off. Apply a preemergence weed-killer sold for use on garden plants.

Spray the soil over peony clumps with Phaltan or Bordeaux mixture to stop bud-blast caused by a botrytis fungus.

(M) As soon as hardy chrysanthemums start growth, separate into single-stem divisions and replant these about a foot apart. Hardy phlox will also benefit from being divided at this time.

Increase watering and feeding of house plants and give them all the sun possible from now on. Repot as needed.

FRUITS AND VEGETABLES: (M) Sow all hardy vegetables as soon as possible where they are to grow, including Brussels sprouts, beets, cabbage, carrots, lettuce, parsley, peas, radishes, salsify, and spinach. Despite its heat-resistant characteristic, New Zealand spinach must be seeded when it is cool, as it does not germinate in hot weather.

(M) Plant onion sets now, using only those that are less than one inch through. Larger sets will not bulb up, producing only scallions.

Fertilize the asparagus bed and apply a garden weed-killer.

Any parsnips and salsify left in the ground over the winter should be dug at once for immediate use. They are still good but will not keep too well. Multiplier onions planted last fall should be ready for use. Leave a few plants to produce bulbils for replanting.

(M) Plant bush and tree fruits as soon as possible. All fruit-tree pruning should be completed before leaves are half an inch long. On gooseberries and currants, cut out all branches older than three years. Pruning of grapes should not be delayed beyond this month.

Remove straw mulch from strawberries and press back any plants heaved out of the soil by frost action. (M) Plant new strawberry beds as soon as weather permits.

If grafts are to made on fruit trees, do so now, before buds swell, using scions cut last fall and stored in sawdust.

Now is the time to start seedlings of tomatoes, peppers, and eggplant to be set out about Memorial Day. Although cabbage, cauliflower, broccoli, and Brussels sprouts started earlier can be set out at this time, they will make little growth and become tough, so nothing is gained by too-early planting. They will make additional growth if kept indoors and will produce more tender vegetables.

LAWNS: March is the most critical month of the year for lawns. If snow mold has killed out patches of turf, rake away the browned-out grass, treat with a good turf fungicide, and reseed.

More lawns are ruined by rolling than are helped from this operation, but if any rolling is to be done, be sure the soil is not soggy. Compaction is a much worse enemy of turf than are a few rough spots.

Spring is definitely not the best time to start a new lawn, but waiting until next August will merely cheat you out of a season's growth. Spring-seeded lawns will need watering two to three times a day when rain does not fall. (M) Do not sow seed atop snow, a practice that is often recommended, because the seed will be washed into clumps when the snow melts.

(M) If a feeding program based on the new lightweight fertilizers is being followed, make the first application now, but remember—it will have to be followed by four additional feedings to supply enough plant food for top growth. Better yet, use one of the season-long fertilizers that can be applied in a single application. Always rake out dead grass before feeding.

Don't waste time trying to grow grass in the shade under trees where it dies out year after year. Instead, plant a good ground cover which has some chance of surviving.

(M) Preemergence crab grass killers must be applied before

any seed germinates. But don't apply on frozen ground or over snow: when this is done, the chemical often concentrates by washing and will kill grass crowns. Do apply, though, before the saucer magnolia is in flower or before apple blossoms show pink. Otherwise crab grass seedlings may germinate and survive.

ODD JOBS: If your soil is too acid, spread ground limestone at once so it can get to work before growth starts.

Before soils warm up, apply a sprinkling of a good mixed chemical fertilizer to mulches and dig them under to rot.

Watch hotbeds and cold frames on sunny days: If they are not ventilated, the inside temperature will run too high.

SOUTH AND WEST COAST

FLOWERS: Roots of dormant cannas can be planted out now in open ground. In cooler sections, they should be mulched if freezes are expected.

Bulbs to plant out include those on the February list, but tender species, such as dahlia, can be planted outdoors in cooler sections if well mulched. These will produce earlier flowers, but for the better late bloom delay planting until May or June.

In warmer sections, set out bedding plants. Do so in cooler areas only if the season is well advanced. Be ready with protection in case of late, unseasonal frosts.

Finish planting dormant roses as soon as possible. Plant out daisies, forget-me-nots, and pansies.

TREES AND SHRUBS: Feed broad-leaved evergreens with an acid fertilizer. In areas with strongly alkaline soils, adding sulfur may be necessary to maintain acidity.

Cut back ground covers, such as English ivy, St.-John's-wort, dichondra, etc., to make them bushy. Clean out trash from between plants, then fertilize.

Hedges, such as laurel, privet, and boxwood, should be trimmed and fed this month. Prune early-flowering shrubs as soon as blossoms fade.

LAWNS: Sow seeds of Bermuda grass as soon as soil temperatures reach sixty degrees. Plant sprigs of vegetatively propagated grasses, such as zoysia, Saint Augustine, and Centipede.

First feeding of grasses with high fertility demands such as zoysia and Bermuda, should go on this month. If a ureaform nitrogen is used, apply half of the annual feeding (i.e., half a pound of actual nitrogen per 1,000 square feet for each month that the grass is in active growth) at this time. Apply the other half-pound after mid-July. If fast-acting temporary fertilizers are used, apply one pound of actual nitrogen per 1,000 square feet and repeat in two months.

As soon as air temperatures can be depended upon to stay above seventy degrees for at least eight hours, apply 2,4-D type weed-killers.

VEGETABLES AND FRUITS: As soon as warm weather is reasonably sure, transplant tomatoes, peppers, and eggplant outdoors. Plant seeds of bush beans, limas, okra, and other warm-season vegetables if soil temperatures are over sixty degrees. If still cool, plant cool-season crops and wait for tender sorts until later.

Plant strawberry plants and protect from the hot sun until well established.

Make succession plantings of gladiolus corms as long as sound stock is available.

ODD JOBS: Southern soils lose humus faster than do those farther north. A compost heap is an important aid to maintaining soil in good tilth. The sooner one is started, the better.

Insect pests and diseases are usually active by late March: be ready with pest control programs for roses, vegetables, and ornamentals.

Cotton nolls and peanut hulls are valuable southern mulching materials worth using. In California, low-grade Perlite can often be had at a low price.

PACIFIC NORTHWEST

As in the North, March is a fickle and unpredictable month in the Pacific Northwest. Be prepared for almost anything. In general, though, the schedule for the North applies.

TREES AND SHRUBS: The ever-increasing use of rhododendrons, azaleas, hollies, and other broad-leaved evergreens calls for careful feeding with acid-forming fertilizers. Renew mulches rather than cultivating.

In the interior, be ready with smudge pots to protect against unseasonal frosts. Prune roses as soon as buds begin to swell.

Divide perennials before they make too much growth.

APRIL

How many Aprils came
Before I knew
How white a cherry bough could be
A bed of squills, how blue!

Sara Teasdale (1884–1933)

Now 'tis spring and weeds are shallow-rooted:
Suffer them now and they'll o'ergrow the garden.

Sara Teasdale (1884–1933)

Lo, the winter is past, the rain is over; the flowers appear on the earth; the time of the singing of birds is come and the voice of the turtle is heard in the land.

Song of Solomon

NORTH

Many of the operations marked (M) in the March list are timely in April if spring is late, as it often is. By this time in normal springs, all winter mulches should have been removed, except along the Canadian border west of the Great Lakes. This is usually the month when half-hardy plants can be moved out of doors safely. All half-hardy annuals can be seeded out of doors regardless of the weather. As a guide to some operations, watch for these natural signs—star and saucer magnolias are in bloom, trumpet narcissus are fully open, buds on oak trees are swelling, and Dutch hyacinth blossoms are fading. In unusually late seasons, these natural signs might not appear until May, in which case those operations marked (X) should not be carried out until they do show up.

TREES AND SHRUBS: Unless leaf buds show a crack of green, it is still safe to apply dormant oil sprays. If applied after leaf bud coats begin to crack, they can cause serious injury.

Woody plants will benefit from an application of a completely soluble high-nitrogen fertilizer washed down into their roots before the soil warms up.

(X) As soon as birches leaf out, spray for control of leaf miners, using diazinon or malathion. Better yet—apply a granular systemic insecticide to the soil underneath the tree: it will be absorbed and kill both leaf miners and any borers that may attack it. This is also a good treatment for willow trees that are infested annually with sooty aphids.

Watch the new growth on yews for crescent-shaped bites—on needles, a sign that the black vine weevil is at work. Spraying with sevin diazinon will control them.

Whenever tent caterpillars are detected at work, spray their webs with a strong stream of water, then spray with diazinon or malathion.

Although spraying for control of Dutch elm disease is best left to professionals, if you must do your own, be sure to use a light misting spray, not one that produces heavy dripping. Cover bird baths and feeding stations before spraying. Follow the recommendations of your state entomologist (usually stationed at your state experiment station) as to timing and materials. Write for this information well in advance of April.

Lilacs do not flower well in acid soil. Check the pH reading (you can buy a simple kit for this purpose from most garden centers for a dollar or two). If the reading is lower than 6.8, apply ground limestone to the soil. Retest in a month, and if still low, add more ground limestone.

Although sometimes recommended, it is not safe to shear evergreens yet. Wait until the new growth at the tips of branches is two to three inches long, then shear off half this new growth. Exceptions to the rule are hemlocks and yews, which can be sheared almost any time; hedges of these two species can be pruned now.

Trees that have been girdled by mice during the winter can be saved if you can find a tree expert who knows how to bridge-graft. Shrubs that have been stripped of their bark should be cut off below the girdle areas on the chance that there are still live buds below which will sprout.

Examine red cedars *(Juniperus virginiana)* for cedar apples—rusty-red balls that produce horns, turn into a nasty jelly, and then dry up and blow away. These represent the winter stage of cedar apple rust which causes rusty spots on apples, crab apples, hawthorns, and related species. Cut off and burn whenever found and then spray all members of the rose family (apples, pears, hawthorns, quince, etc.) with Phaltan as soon as the leaves are an inch long, and again two weeks later.

If maple trees were infested with red galls on the leaves last summer, now is the time to kill the insect that causes the galls. Spray with malathion as soon as leaves unfold and again in two weeks.

FLOWERS: If hardy annuals were not seeded earlier, they must be sown as soon as possible since many species will not germinate in warm soil. Half-hardy species, on the contrary, prefer soil temperatures above sixty degrees. Both can be sown now with good chances for success.

As tulip shoots break through the soil, spray with Phaltan to kill the fungus that causes fire blight. A second spraying just before the petals open is good insurance. The same treatment should be given to peonies: both flowers are subject to attack by the botrytis fungus.

As soon as growth begins on bearded irises, spray near the ground line with diazinon to control the iris borer. Be sure to use a spreader-sticker, as the iris leaves are quite waxy. Repeat in two weeks, and again in May just before flowers open.

This is the most important time of the year for sowing seeds of perennials. Following the old British custom of sowing these in June is responsible for many failures in our warmer climate. April sowing is a "must."

Now is the time to divide old perennial plants and to set out new plants. Because perennial beds are not dug over every year, be sure to do a good job of soil preparation.

Many phlox plants lose their lower leaves in July and August, caused by a lack of both potash and phosphorus. To correct this, apply about a teaspoonful each of muriate of potash and superphosphate around each plant and work into the soil.

Divide old clumps of hardy water lilies now, and set out new ones. A handful of a good organic fertilizer or old rotted manure in the bottom of the planting box will help feed them.

As the sun rises higher and higher in the sky, be careful of African violets placed in south windows: they can't stand too much sunlight.

Plant roses as soon as the soil is workable. Hill up with soil for several inches around the plants until new leaves begin to show, then remove this covering. As soon as the winter covering is removed from established roses, cut back any dead canes to live wood. Always try to leave at least ten inches of old wood on each cane. Spray the trimmed plants at once with Phaltan; also spray the soil beneath the bush to catch any spores of black spot that have survived the winter. Begin a regular spray program as soon as there is any foliage to protect.

If ground covers are ragged and overgrown, cut them back with a sickle or hedge clipper, then fertilize to force new growth. To remove trash from between the plants, try using a vacuum cleaner of the type sold for home workshops.

(X) Plant sound gladiolus corms as long as they can be had.

As soon as they have finished flowering, potted Easter lilies can be set out in the open garden. They will often produce one more bloom in the fall, but are seldom strong enough to survive the winter, even where they are hardy. Most other Easter plants require too much specialized care to be worth saving.

Watch for new shoots on Regal lilies. They often start growth much too early in spring and are nipped by late frosts, which kills flower buds for that year. Cover with straw or other protection if late freezes threaten.

Sometimes tuberous begonias are planted upside down when starting. If they fail to sprout, turn them over and see if a pink bud is showing, in which case, plant with the pink bud up and try again.

Apply a good mixed fertilizer to all flower beds. Those which contain nitrogen in the form of ureaform will feed for a much longer period than those which do not contain this element.

(X) If they have been gradually exposed to cooler temperatures to harden them, most annuals and perennials started from seed indoors can be planted out, but be ready to protect them if late frosts are predicted. If indoor light is adequate and space is available, they are probably better off indoors until in mid-May or later.

FRUITS AND VEGETABLES: Examine peach trees for such signs of borers as sawdust around the base of the trunk and holes that exude gum. If they are present, treat with paradichlorobenzene (PDB, or painless death to borers) or with parascalicide. Your state experiment station can tell you how.

Be sure to have on hand the fruit-tree spray program recommended for your area before growth begins. Your state experiment station can supply this. Some states maintain a codling-moth warning program (codling moth larvae are the cause of wormy apples) and will notify you when to spray. Get on this list if you have apple trees.

Fertilize strawberries and set out new plants if this was not done in March.

Tree and bush fruits can still be planted, but time is running short.

(X) Set out plants of early cabbage, broccoli, cauliflower, and other hardy vegetables.

The earlier asparagus roots can be planted, the better. Don't follow the old rule of planting with the crowns six inches below the surface; this merely delays growth in spring. Set the plants with the crown one inch below the surface and enjoy asparagus a week or two earlier in spring.

Remove mulch from blueberries and fertilize with either ammonium sulfate or ammonium nitrate—blueberries utilize nitrogen best in ammonia form.

Sow hardy and half-hardy vegetable seeds now directly in the garden. Use of liquid fertilizer in the row will get them off to an early start. Use protective treatments sold to prevent fungus attacking seeds. They cost very little and pay big dividends. They are sold in most garden shops.

If the weather is too cool to sow cucumbers and melons in the open, start them indoors in four-inch pots in mid-April. When planting outside later, protect the tender plants with Hotkaps or other covering for a few days.

Most vegetable plants are started indoors at too early a date, which results in long, weak, stretchy plants. The first week in

April is plenty early enough to start tomatoes, eggplant, and peppers.

Start annual herbs from seed at once. Plants are usually available of the perennial species.

Even if transplanted seedlings are used for an early crop, try sowing seeds of tomatoes in the open in April. They will usually outproduce transplants in the fall. The seeds are perfectly hardy and can be sown at any time now.

LAWNS: In warm, early springs, watch grasses for the first signs of leaf-spot disease in bluegrass lawns. Merion is not affected, but Arboretum, Beaumont, common, C-1, Delta, Newport, and Windsor are all quite susceptible. Spray with a good turf fungicide to prevent the disease from getting any worse.

Don't neglect early mowing. Begin as soon as blades are two inches long. A well-fertilized lawn at this season of year may require mowing twice a week. Change the direction of the cut each time to prevent a "set" in the allover appearance of the lawn.

If the popular lightweight fertilizers analyzing 20-10-5 are being used, remember that these will only feed the lawn for a month or so. At least four additional feedings will be needed during the growing season if quality turf is wanted. If the grass does not respond after feeding, suspect that native potash in the soil is exhausted and apply ten pounds of muriate or sulfate of potash to 1,000 square feet of lawn, watered in as soon as it is put on. Don't expect results for about three months.

If the saucer magnolias or flowering crabs have not yet opened their flowers, there is still time to apply a preemergence crab grass control.

After air temperatures go above seventy during the day and can be expected to remain there for several hours, spray lawns for control of broad-leaved weeds, using mixtures of 2,4-D with 2,4,5-T. Even better are the liquid sprays containing both 2,4-D and Banvel-D. For really tough weeds, such as creeping Jenny *(Glecoma hederacea)* or hard knotweed, use Silvex (2,4,5-TP) followed by a spraying in two weeks with 2,4-D plus Banvel-D. This combination spray will even kill mature common chickweed.

This is a good time to install an underground sprinkling system, using plastic pipe laid in slits cut in the lawn. The cuts will heal quickly at this time and be invisible in a month's time.

ODD JOBS: Regular preventive spraying for insects and diseases on all susceptible plants should begin as soon as there is any foliage to protect.

On any plant over six weeks old, whether annual or perennial, there are preemergence weed-killers which can be used to simplify garden maintenance. For these, one just cultivates the soil and applies, following the directions carefully.

After transplantng or setting out, don't throw away surplus plants, set them in some corner to use for replacements when needed.

SOUTH AND WEST COAST

Except for the area just south of the Ohio River and west to the Great Plains, summer is in full swing.

FLOWERS: Keep up a full spray schedule on roses and on other ornamentals subject to disease. Diseases cannot be cured; they can only be prevented. Once black spot, mildew, or rust get started, they cannot be eradicated. Spray early enough in the day that the foliage can be dry toward evening because wet leaves favor the spread of many diseases.

If they are crowded, plan to divide tall bearded irises as soon as their flowers fade. They go semidormant at this time and can be moved without loss.

Continue planting warm-season bulbs. Gladiolus will need a spray schedule to control thrips.

Finish planting all annuals as soon as possible.

Lilies are often difficult to grow in warmer parts of the country unless the soil can be kept cool by shading. Plant them between clumps of perennials, or sow a shallow-rooted annual, such as alyssum or portulaca, over them or apply a deep mulch.

This is the best month for planting out dahlias in warmer sections of the South and Southwest. All summer-flowering bulbs should be in the ground by the first of this month at the latest. For summer bloom along the Gulf Coast, try Gloriosa lilies. In areas where tulips and narcissus are grown without exposure to freezing in winter, dig and store in a temperature between fifty degrees and seventy degrees. Chill to below forty degrees for six weeks before planting next fall.

Plant out tropical water lilies as soon as settled warm weather occurs.

It is time to move house plants out of doors into a lightly shaded spot under trees that have foliage light and airy enough that some sun is able to trickle through. Repot those that are root-bound.

LAWNS: Sprigged and sodded lawns can still be planted if they are watered regularly enough to give the new planting a good start.

Zoysias and Bermudas will need feeding every month from now until frost with enough fertilizer to supply one pound of actual nitrogen per 1,000 square feet. Less luxurious grasses should also be fed now, but only one or two more feedings will be needed for the rest of the year.

Always use a grass-catcher when mowing zoysias or Bermudas, clippings are quite difficult to pick up in the tight sod which these grasses form.

TREES AND SHRUBS: All early-spring-flowering shrubs should be pruned or trimmed as soon as blossoms fade. Needled evergreens (but not broad-leaved) can be sheared now. If done carelessly, the plant can be permanently injured, so follow directions carefully. Cut off only one-half of the new growth made this spring.

After small-flowered rambler roses have finished blooming, cut away the old canes that bore this year's flowers—they will not bloom again and will slow up the growth of new canes that will. These new canes will rise from the base of the old.

If not done last month, feed all woody plants now.

VEGETABLES AND FRUITS: Make successive plantings of all earlier crops to continue the harvest. In cooler parts of the South and West, sowing of cool-weather crops is still possible. Even in warmer areas, Wando peas will produce a crop if planted now.

In warm weather, even organic fertilizers are rapidly consumed. Keep feeding for maximum growth.

PACIFIC NORTHWEST

For cooler sections, recommendations for the North should be followed. Along the coast and in other warm areas, recommendations for cooler parts of the South are germane.

FLOWERS: Cut back and fertilize all heathers, whether winter or summer flowering.

Set out baits for moles that damage flowers and vegetables by burrowing around their roots. Slug bait should also be set out now.

LAWNS: April is the best time to start new lawns in the Pacific Northwest and to renovate old. Don't neglect feeding of established lawns; most soils have been leached by the winter rains.

There is still time to plant evergreens in most sections but not if new growth has started.

Although Peegee and paniculata hydrangeas must be cut back severely, those of the florist's type—with pink or blue flowers—form their buds the previous fall and should not be touched.

Now is the best time of year to transplant the magnificent western flowering dogwood, *Cornus nuttallii,* even if it is in full bloom. It is a touchy subject at best. Give it a sheltered location, wrap the trunk with crinkled kraft paper, and mulch heavily.

MAY

BEAUTEOUS MAY

Now the bright morning star, Day's harbinger,
Comes dancing from the East and leads with her
The flowry May, who from her green lap throws
The yellow cowslip and the pale primrose.
Hail, beauteous May, that dost inspire
Mirth and youth and warm desire.

John Milton (1609–1674)

FUMITORY

Fumiter is herbe, I say,
That springeth in April and in May,
In feld, in towne, in yerd and gate,
There land is fat and good in state.

Stockdale Medical Ms. (circa 1400)

NORTH

In the northeastern United States and in the Golden Triangle of Ontario, May is the month when gardens explode into bloom, a period which one Englishman describes as a "glorious, gaudy, chromatic riot." Most spring flowers are in bloom at least for part of the month, unless the season is unusually cool holding back tall late irises and Oriental poppies.

Weeds, insect pests, and plant diseases, too, make their appearance this month, piling programs of pest-control on top of more pleasant tasks. This is the month when time is much too short to do all the work necessary to do.

Allow the following signs to guide you for scheduling certain operations which may be advanced or slowed by weather conditions. Watch for the flowering of apple trees and crab apples, the fading of tall late tulips, or the first blooms on tall bearded irises. When these signs appear, jobs marked (S) in the following schedule of operations should be given first attention.

FLOWERS: Although perennial plants can still be set out, having them shipped to you by mail is unsafe because of delays. Either buy locally or transport your own. If plants arrive dry, plunge them in a pail of water overnight before planting, but do not leave them in water longer than this.

(S) All tender bedding plants and vegetable transplants should go out of doors at once. Select a cloudy day without much wind for this operation, or be prepared to shade them with newspapers or with shingles.

(S) Sow all tender annuals, even those that like tropical heat. It is usually too late to plant cool weather annuals, such as larkspur and annual poppy, but if a soil thermometer registers below sixty-two degrees, these can be seeded at once and kept cool with water until they germinate.

If peonies were not sprayed earlier, an application of Phaltan to the unopened buds can still prevent botrytis bud blast. Stake the plants and feed with a quickly available fertilizer to increase flower size. If top-sized blooms are wanted, pinch out all buds except the large center one on each branch.

Don't fertilize tulips; this merely encourages the splitting of the old bulbs.

Another application of diazinon to irises will catch late-hatching borers.

(S) Plant some gourds for next winter's decoration. Be prepared to fight aphids, however—they thrive on gourd vines.

(S) All summer-flowering bulbs should go into the ground at once. Do, however, save some gladiolus corms for planting later to prolong the flowering season, unless they are badly sprouted.

Keep up preventive spraying of roses and all other ornamentals that are attacked regularly by insects and plant diseases. A general-purpose spray that controls a wide range of pests is best for this, but when heavy invasions of specific insects occur en masse, better switch to chemicals designed specifically for their control.

Hardy water lilies can still be planted. Over the northeast quarter of the United States it is still too cool to set out tropicals; wait until after June 1 with these.

Provide support for sweet peas before the vines begin to climb. Brush is still the best support material. Don't use wire—it gets hot and burns the tendrils. You can still seed the hot-weather-resistant varieties, such as Cuthbertson and Multiflora.

If you want pansies and violas to continue flowering, keep the flowers picked off. If pansies go out of bloom for you in hot weather, switch to large-flowered Scotch violas which are as big as most pansies and much easier to grow.

Now is the time to plant material for next winter's dried arrangements. Bells of Ireland, gomphrena, acroclinium, and other everlastings are easy to dry for this purpose.

Now is the time to plant window boxes. Have the soil rich but well drained.

Never cut off foliage from tulips, narcissus, hyacinths, and other bulbs! It must ripen naturally so the bulb can store food for next year's growth and bloom.

When arabis, aubretia, and *Phlox subulata* go out of bloom in the rock garden, shear off the flowers about an inch or so below the dead flower head. So treated, they will sometimes produce a second crop of flowers in the fall.

(S) Most annual vines are warm-weather plants and should not be planted out too early. Try cardinal climber, scarlet runner beans, moonflowers, or Heavenly Blue morning glories on a fence. Incidentally, the beans of scarlet runners are edible; the British consider them the tastiest of all shell beans.

VEGETABLES AND FRUITS: All flowers that form on strawberry plants set out this spring should be removed as soon as they can be seen. Ever-bearing varieties, however, can be allowed to bloom and fruit after July 15.

(S) More tomatoes are injured by planting them out too soon than are helped by rushing the season. Memorial Day is about as early as they should be set out. If chilled, they will shuck off any flowers that have formed, requiring sixty days to replace them and produce a crop of fruit.

All vegetables can be direct-seeded now. Succession plantings of radishes, lettuce, onion sets, and other cool weather crops can be made.

A new asparagus bed should not be cut the first year, but an established bed should now be producing the peak asparagus of the year.

(S) Melon plants started indoors in April can be planted out of doors as soon as the weather warms up. Don't rush matters, however. If vines are chilled early in their growth, they will produce fruits low in sugar. If the weather turns cool after planting, protect plants with Hotkaps, sheet plastic, or similar devices to keep them as warm as possible.

(S) Cucumbers, squashes, and melons, as well as snap beans, produce seedlings that lift large cotyledons out of the ground. Since they have a hard time breaking through crusted soil, use horticultural vermiculite, sand, or sifted compost—materials which will not crust over—instead of covering the row with soil.

Plant witloof chicory now. Roots can be forced next winter for a true luxury salad.

Rhubarb does best in rich soil. Fertilize well and mulch with well-rotted manure (if this can be had) after the cutting season is over.

If the season remains cool, bush and tree fruits can still be planted, provided dormant stock from cold storage is available. Wrap trunks of late-planted fruit trees to keep them from drying out.

Use only rotenone or pyrethrum on gooseberries and currants

to control the currant worm. After the fruit has been gathered, methoxychlor can be used instead.

If borers make summer and winter squashes hard to grow, try butternut squash. This variety is borerproof. The immature fruits can be cooked like summer squash. Those left to mature will produce hard winter squashes that will keep until the following February, if hungry appetites spare them that long.

TREES AND SHRUBS: If dormant stock is no longer available, investigate "canned" stock grown in large containers. Even species of larger trees can now be purchased in five-gallon tin cans. Mulch all newly planted nursery stock as soon as planted.

Hawthorns, flowering crabs, and many other members of the rose family should be sprayed with Phaltan, if this was not done earlier, to prevent infestation with the cedar-apple-rust spores that are now flying.

Maples that were infested with red galls last year should be sprayed now with malathion and again in two weeks.

ODD JOBS: The best way to get rid of rabbits is to keep a cat. Cats find the hidden young and drive away old rabbits. Some protection from rabbits can be given plants by dusting them with wood ashes—until these get wet, the odor of fire will keep rabbits away. The best protection is a thirty-six-inch-high chicken-wire fence, or three electric fence wires spaced twelve inches apart.

As soon as cold frames have been emptied, remove all old soil and add it to the compost pile. Allow the wood in the frames to dry out and then treat with Cuprinol wood preservative. (Never use creosote.) When dry, fill with a 50-50 mixture (by volume) of peat moss and vermiculite for making softwood cuttings during the summer.

In the past, weed controls used for driveways were mainly sodium arsenite, a highly dangerous poison which makes weed-control experts shudder when they see it used by amateurs. Today, equally effective, relatively nontoxic, chemicals are available to do the job without risk to the user. Consult a good garden center.

Watering correctly—supplying just enough moisture but not too much—is an art. Since droughts are likely to occur anywhere in the United States and Canada, why not be prepared for them? Check your equipment for supplying water. Hoses should be ready, sprinklers checked for operating condition, and underground water lines laid (which is easy to do with today's plastic pipe).

A compost pile, never a thing of beauty, can be effectively screened by planting it with butternut squash or cucumbers. Perhaps the world's best-tasting cucumbers are English frame varieties grown out of doors on a compost pile. Simply stick seeds into the soil used to cover the pile.

Sawdust makes an excellent mulch for practically all plants if about half a pound of ammonium sulfate is added to each bushel, plus a sprinkling of lime after the sawdust has been in place for a few weeks. Don't, however, use lime under acid-loving plants, such as azaleas, blueberries, rhododendrons, and hollies.

SOUTH AND WEST COAST

FLOWERS: Three annuals that enjoy heat are arctotis, dimorphotheca, and sanvitalia. Sow them now for summer bloom. To germinate less-heat-tolerant annuals, soak seed overnight in cold water, then sow in soil misted during the day from time to time with cold water.

Pinch chrysanthemums to make them bushy. Take out the tip, leaving two or three leaves on the main stem. If more plants are needed, treat the tips with a rooting hormone and root them in damp sand.

In warmer sections where tulips must be dug and stored for the summer, remember that subjecting them to temperatures cooler than fifty degrees will stimulate root growth, ruining them for next year's planting. Instead, hold at a temperature somewhere between fifty and seventy-five. If this temperature is not available, then hold them *below* forty degrees, but above freezing. This will delay flowering somewhat in fall, but this will be less serious than had they been held between forty and fifty.

Feed roses this month and continue to spray.

For color in the shade, try fancy-leaved caladiums, alternanthera, coleus, and perillia, all of which depend on leaf color instead of flowers for display.

Water is the greatest need of most plants during this season. Roses in particular can be kept flowering only by liberal use of the hose. Never fertilize without also watering thoroughly: plant foods must be in solution before plants can absorb them.

LAWNS: Feed zoysia and Bermuda lawns. Careful spraying with

dalapon will control Bermuda should it persist in invading flower beds and shrubbery borders. Remember, however, that dalapon will kill *all* grasses; it is not selective. Even those tough clumps of Pampas grass will die if hit accidentally.

VEGETABLES: Plant seeds of chayotes where they are to grow. Toward the end of this month, make a second planting of summer squash and cucumbers—these will not be injured as badly when blight and borers attack earlier plantings.

Heat can retard germination of many seeds that will grow well once they are up. To start these vegetables, soak the soil with the coolest water available before planting. After sowing, cover the row with vermiculite instead of with soil: it will act as a partial insulator against heat. On row crops, lay boards, painted white, along the rows. These will not only slow up evaporation, but will keep out some heat. Watch carefully and remove them as soon as seedlings begin to break through the soil.

PACIFIC NORTHWEST

With Portland's famous Rose Festival staged in this month, it is obvious that this is the most important flower at this time.

FLOWERS: Keep spraying roses. Keep faded flowers picked. When applying water, avoid wetting the foliage: rose leaves that go into the night damp are particularly susceptible to disease. If roses look too leggy, plant the edges of your beds with *Campanula carpatica,* coral bells, pinks, violas, or similar low-growing perennials. Or use ageratum as a bedding plant: its bright violet-blue coloring is not found in any rose and contrasts beautifully with those colors that are common in roses.

Pick off faded flowers from perennials, but pass up the forget-me-nots until they have dropped seed from which next year's flowers will come.

After cutting off dead flowers from primroses, remove any ragged lower leaves and feed the plant with a good mixed fertilizer.

Unlike sections of the United States where summer nights are hot, there are many areas in the Pacific Northwest where May and June sowing of seeds of biennials and perennials is good practice. Now is the time, too, to start new plants of foxglove, Canterbury bells, hollyhock, and wallflower. Seeds will grow better, however, if given a little light-filtered shade at noon.

Have some bedding plants handy to plant over Oriental poppies and Madonna lilies when these flowers go dormant after flowering.

TREES AND SHRUBS: This is the beginning of the red spider mite season. To knock down these pests, spray underneath evergreens every time you water. In case of serious infestations, spray with dimite, aramite, malathion, or diazinon.

Shear needled evergreens as soon as they have made three to four inches of new growth. Cut off half the new growth made this spring.

If florists' hydrangeas *(Hydrangea macrophylla)* produce flowers that are a wishy-washy blue, you can deepen the color by feeding them with a 50-50 mixture of ferrous sulfate and aluminum sulfate—a small handful scattered under the bush and watered in thoroughly will suffice.

All vegetable plants started indoors can be set out now, even in cooler sections. Make succession sowings of radishes, lettuce, and rose-ribbed endive.

If the spring drop does not leave plums, peaches, and apricots will spaced on the branch, hand thinning will be necessary.

Cane fruits and strawberries in particular need careful weeding. The new garden-weeder preemergence sprays greatly lessen the work needed.

JUNE

Summer afternoon—summer afternoon: to me these have been the two most beautiful words in the English language.

Henry James (1843–1916)

TO AN OAK SEEDLING

Thou wast a bauble once: a cup and ball,
Which baes might play with: and the thieving jay
Seeking her food, with ease might purloin.
The auburn nut that held thee, swallowing down
Thy yet close-folded latitude of boughs
And all thy embryo vastness, at a gulp.

William Cowper (1731–1800)

NORTH

This is no month for arm-chair gardening: make every minute count. Although the spring rush of transplanting and seeding is largely over, regular maintenance—hoeing, watering, weeding, and fertilizing leaves very little time for relaxing.

FLOWERS: Early this month, if no temperatures lower than seventy degrees can be expected, plant out tropical water lilies. These are usually in bud and bloom when received from growers.

Move house plants out of doors to a slightly shaded spot under trees with thin foliage (a honey locust is ideal). Lacking such an area, make one with a lath shade or cheesecloth on a frame. Plunge pots in earth up to the rim. Repot any plants that need this care, then water and fertilize.

As soon as perennial candytuft, *Iberis,* is through flowering, give the plants a crew cut, shearing them back to half their height.

There is still time to plant quick-growing annuals, such as sweet alyssum, baby's breath, candytuft, and portulaca. Heavenly Blue morning glory seed planted now will sprout strongly, even where earlier plantings failed because of cool soil.

If more bedding plants are wanted, nip out the tops of any you happen to have, root them in sand, and use them wherever needed as soon as they are rooted. A shaded cold frame is ideal for this operation. This trick for increasing plants will also work with hardy chrysanthemums.

When cutting peony flowers, don't remove the entire stalk down to ground level. Leave a few leaves at the base to feed the root for next year's growth. If long stems are cut, take only one or two from each plant, preferably from the older, well-established clumps. Feed plants now with a completely soluble fertilizer in water to build up vigor for next year's growth.

Where masses of minor bulbs, such as grape hyacinths or blue squills, are wanted, allow them to set seed when through flowering: they will form large colonies if allowed to do so. Where space is at a premium, prevent seeding by cutting off flower stems as soon as they fade.

There is still time to plant gladiolus corms if healthy stock without long, weak sprouts can be had. Once the shoots appear above ground, a regular program of thrips control is essential if clean flowers are wanted.

Now is the time to cut faded flowers from rhododendrons, laurel, and lilacs. All these shrubs produce next year's bloom from buds that have already formed at the base of old flower spikes. If these are cut away, there will be no flowers next year. Nip out only the faded flowers and the faded, dried stalk on which they appeared.

Instant gardening is easy. To fill vacant spaces when no home-grown seedlings are available, buy annuals already in bloom from garden centers and pop into place to achieve instant glamour. The same treatment goes for spaces left by rose plants that failed to survive last winter: simply fill in with potted plants already in bloom.

Should tulips be lifted? Only if soil temperatures around the bulbs cannot be kept cool by overplanting them with shallow-rooted annuals. They keep much better in soil.

Sweet peas, now staging a revival because of the new heat-resistant strains, should be coming into bloom this month. They can be kept flowering all summer only if the faded flowers are kept picked, or if those newly opened are removed daily for indoor use. Once they ripen seed, the vines will start dying down. A deep mulch will help keep them green and growing, provided all mature flowers are removed.

Hollyhocks and delphinium are likely to develop both rust and mildew. The best fungicide (effective against both rust and mildew) is Phaltan, with Fermate as a second choice.

Irises, Madonna lilies, Oriental poppies, and mertensia all go dormant or partially dormant in July and August, the best time of the year to move them. To have them on hand at that time, orders must be placed in June. If catalogs from specialists have not arrived, write for them at once.

There is a difference of opinion among experts as to the best time to plant the so-called hardy amaryllis, *Lycoris squamigera.* Some dealers offer them in June. If so, they must be planted at once so they can start making new roots before July for flowering in late summer.

A reliable perennial for summer color is the day lily, hemerocallis. It can be lifted at any time, even when in full bloom, to provide summer color.

Early in June plant candytuft, calliopsis, annual gypsophila, annual scabiosa, and zinnia. They will flower in late summer and continue the show of annuals until cut down by frost. The last week in June, make a sowing of the new Pacific strain of calendula, which will produce flowers even after a few light frosts.

Make a final pinch on hardy chrysanthemums, barely nipping out the end bud on all branches. From now on, allow them to grow naturally. Dahlias should also be pinched, but in exactly the opposite way for mums: leave the fat central bud and take out any side buds near it.

Siberian and Japanese irises are often moved at the same time as the tall bearded type: this is definitely wrong. The former have fibrous roots and should be handled like most perennials, moving them in early spring or late fall.

LAWNS: Watch for sod web worms, leaf-spot diseases, and white grub injury in June and for the rest of the growing season. Sprays for sod web worms should remain on the foliage for at least three to four days to be effective, without being washed off. They have little or no effect on this pest when washed into the soil. Best control is diazinon or chlordane. Diazinon also stops chinch bugs which often invade lawns when nearby agricultural crops are infested. See May recommendations for leaf spot and grub control.

If lightweight 20-10-5 fertilizers are being used, it is time for another feeding the last week in June. If a mixed ureaform product was applied last fall at full rate, a half-rate feeding in late June should be applied if luxury growth is wanted.

If preemergence crab grass controls were not applied in time, postemergence sprays or granular dusts can be applied. Best controls are DSMA, Sodar, or AMA liquid. Remember that postemergence sprays have no carryover—they kill only crab grass in active growth. Repeat applications will be needed for good control.

If the grass is healthy but pale in color, suspect an iron deficiency, particularly in Merion, which has a high iron demand. To check whether iron is missing, treat a small patch with an iron chelate; if it turns dark green, treat the entire lawn.

Instead of trying to fill in bare spots by sowing seed, try borrowing patches of sod from along the edge of the lawn.

Daily watering often does more harm than good. Actually, unless rain misses you for a week, Merion Kentucky bluegrass is better off without artificial irrigation. When you do apply water, be sure it soaks in to a depth of three to four inches at least.

TREES AND SHRUBS: Old canes on rambler roses should be cut away at the base after they bloom: they will not produce flowers next year. Do save new canes forming at their base: next year's flowers will come from them. Be sure not to use this treatment on large-flowered modern climbers, however; all they need is for the old, hard wood that flowers poorly to be cut out.

Now is the time to prune needled evergreens. Notice that new growth at the ends of old branches is beginning to firm up. Cut off half this new growth, which will force two soft buds to grow where only one grew before. This thickens up the entire tree. Don't cut into old wood: evergreens do not retain live buds for more than a year back of the tips. Exceptions are yews and hemlocks, which can withstand a more severe shearing.

Locust leaf miner is a nasty pest now infesting honey locusts. The best way to control it is to apply a granular systemic insecticide to the soil now. It will be absorbed by the entire tree and make it toxic to insects feeding on it. This is about the only effective control for black locust borers.

Keep watering all newly planted trees and shrubs, but don't drown them. All too many amateurs overdo this operation. Suspect overwatering if leaves droop: even if standing in water, their roots cannot take it up unless there is air in the soil.

If Japanese quince must be pruned, do so as soon as the flowers fade. Since it does not recover too rapidly, do as little pruning as possible.

Broad-leaved evergreens need a feeding with cottonseed meal or with ammonium sulfate as soon as flowers fade. Be sure this is washed in well with water. Give hollies the same attention. In dry areas, such as the Middle West, all broad-leaved evergreens should be misted lightly every day to prevent wood from getting too hard and dry.

Either malathion or diazinon can be used for control of birch leaf miners, but a granular systemic insecticide applied to the roots does a more thorough job.

Green wood cuttings can be made from the current year's growth when tips of shrub branches snap clean. Cut tips from five to six inches long, stick the lower end in a rooting hormone powder, and then put in damp sand or vermiculite. When kept shaded and watered, they will soon root.

Now is the time to check elms for signs of Dutch elm disease. From now until August 1, look for branch tips that wilt suddenly. If these turn a caramel tan, or if the tree seems to be generally unhealthy and loses foliage at the tips, call a reliable tree man. Amateur diagnosis is as often wrong as it is right. Your city or village forester is a good man to consult.

FRUITS AND VEGETABLES: Only fair-weather gardeners stop planting vegetables in May. Succession crops sown in June mean summer-long crops for the table. Toward the end of the month, plant vegetables for storage for next winter, including carrots, beets, rutabagas, onions, and winter radishes. For greens and salads, plant curly endive, Chinese cabbage, escarole, cabbage, kale, and cauliflower. Set out plants of Brussels sprouts. A direct-seeding of tomatoes will produce vines that will bear fruit after earlier crops have been all but killed by late blight. Now is also the time to seed succession crops of cucumbers, snap beans, summer squash, and sweet corn.

To germinate lettuce seed in hot weather, mix with damp sand and store in the crisper pan of an electric refrigerator for two weeks: examine daily, and when germination starts, sow at once.

Stop cutting asparagus after mid-June. Allow the "fern" to grow from now on. Apply a weed-killer recommended for use on asparagus. Simazine is widely used by commercial growers. Fertilize to feed next year's crop.

LAWNS: This is the most critical month of the year for lawns, a time when disease often takes over. If leaf-spot disease and brown patch occur, go to work at once with a good turf fungicide.

A condition sometimes confused with turf disease is a delayed nitrogen burn, caused by overfeeding with organic fertilizers. This does not occur until soils warm up, releasing more nitrogen in a short period than the grass blades can handle. The usual symptom of this is a sudden wilting and collapse after a week or two of hot weather following a cold spring. The best remedy is heavy leaching with water.

ODD JOBS: When old-time directions (usually copied from English books on gardening) recommend applying liquid manure, substitute modern fish emulsion fertilizers or a solution of a complete chemical plant food on any flowers or vegetables that need a boost.

Time to kill poison ivy and other tough weeds. Aminotriazole is a specific for poison ivy, but a brush-killer, silvex (2,4,5-TP) or the older 2,4,5-T, will also do the job, although not as fast. One of the toughest of all lawn weeds to kill is nimble will (muhlenbergia). No satisfactory chemical control is available. Use a power rake to tear it out by the roots: it is shallow-rooted.

Don't neglect putting oil and grease on power equipment. More such equipment rusts out than wears out. Judicious use of brushes and rags to remove excess dirt, etc., will save repair bills.

SOUTH AND WEST COAST

TREES AND SHRUBS: It doesn't pay to try to force bloom on roses in hot weather. Stop feeding until late August or early September when the return of cooler nights will permit better growth. Keep spraying, however, as loss of foliage will weaken the plants for fall blooming.

Move azaleas and camellias this month: spray with Wilt-Pruf or Foligard to reduce water loss through the leaves. Lace bugs are active on azaleas and rhododendrons now: spray with diazinon or malathion: be sure to hit the underside of the leaves where they hide.

In warmer sections, figs, citrus, and guavas can be moved if the foliage is treated with an antidesiccant to reduce water loss.

FLOWERS: If tulips must be lifted, see calendar for May for instructions on handling them for the summer. Dutch, English, and Spanish irises should also be dug and stored for replanting in November.

After each period of bloom on lantana, cut off old flowers and allow them to produce new buds. Feed lightly after each such "haircut."

Usually, bulbs of autumn crocus, colchicum, and sternbergia are not available this early, but if they are, plant at once for fall bloom. Now is the time to move those already in the garden that need separating.

Warm climate soils lose fertility much faster than do those in cooler climates; regular feeding is a "must" if good growth is wanted.

LAWNS: Chinch bugs are perhaps the worst insect threat to southern lawns. Diazinon has proved to be a specific control for this pest.

Bermuda and zoysia lawns should be fed on a regular schedule, applying a pound of actual nitrogen for each month the lawn is in active growth. Both these grasses need mowing once a week: if they don't grow that fast, feed more.

Seeded Bermuda lawns can be started now if they are kept moist until the seedlings are well established.

FRUITS AND VEGETABLES: To sow now—beets, parsnips, velvet beans, soy beans and lima beans, mustard, peppers, salsify, cucumbers, and summer squash.

Keep up a regular spray schedule on fruits and vegetables.

FLOWERS: Annuals you can still sow—candytuft, African and French marigolds, nasturtium, *Phlox drummondi,* portulaca, and zinnia.

If bulbs are available, now is a good time to plant *Lycoris squamigera,* the so-called hardy amaryllis.

After they have flowered, cut back *delphinium* plants. If given a little liquid fertilizer, they should produce some new flower spikes next fall. Such cut-back plants are not as likely to survive the winter, however, as those which have not been cut back. In warmer sections the Pacific hybrids are reliable perennials, but in more northern areas, they are best treated as biennials.

Keep removing faded flowers on annuals. If they grow too tall, cut them back to force more compact growth.

Irises that need to be transplanted and separated should be dug up as soon as the last flowers fade. Place orders now for new plants for delivery next month.

ODD JOBS: Slugs are invading new territory each year and becoming serious pests. The best program of control calls for sanitation. Get rid of flat stones, bits of board, and debris under which they hide. Use metaldehyde baits to kill them.

PACIFIC NORTHWEST

About the only important job to be added to the May list is to cut back winter jasmine, *abelia,* and *photinia.*

JULY

The poetry of earth is never dead:
When all the birds are faint with the hot sun,
And hide in cooling trees, a voice will run
From hedge to hedge about the new-mown mead.

John Keats (1795–1821)

NORTH

LAWNS: Summer heat is hard on bluegrass and fescue lawns. Summer brownout is no longer thought of as summer dormancy—instead the true cause, leaf-spot disease, can be identified. While chemical sprays can help control this, a better solution is to plan to overseed next month with resistant varieties and strains, such as Merion and others.

Now is the time that undernourished turf begins to suffer, but care must be used in applying fertilizers in hot weather. At no other time is it so important to water in thoroughly.

If a lightweight fertilizer program is being followed, another application should go on in mid- to late July.

Treatment of lawns with heptachlor, chlordane, or dieldrin, for control of grubs and other soil insects is good practice, particularly if digging in patches of brown turf shows they are working there. If starlings and other birds dig into the turf regularly, it is a good sign grubs are at work. Applying chemicals will not only get rid of insects, but also of the moles that tunnel through lawns to find them.

Sod web worms may appear. Watch for tiny moths flying a zigzag course over the grass at dusk. Their larvae eat off grass at ground level, hiding in webs between the blades during the day. Spray the grass with any of the insecticides recommended for grub control. Be sure, however, to spray so the foliage is wetted, not the soil.

Now is the time to kill broad-leaved weeds and crab grass with postemergence chemicals. This should be done before the end of July, so their residual effects will have dissipated by the time grass-seed planting time is here in mid-August.

To control bent grass in bluegrass lawns, first go over the area with a power rake to tear out the shallow-rooted bents. Then spray with Silvex (2,4,5-TP). Since Silvex has a six-weeks' residual period, this should be done the first week in July, to permit reseeding after mid-August.

FLOWERS: Old-time recommendations (often copied uncritically from British books) called for sowing seed of *delphinium* in August as soon as seed was ripe. This will sometimes work if August is unusually cool, but not if the weather remains hot. Refrigerating them for spring sowing is better practice, unless a greenhouse is available for December seeding. If saving your own seed, keep it frozen in a glass vial in the refrigerator until spring.

Shear off annuals as soon as flowers fade. They have finished their life cycle if seed has formed and will then die. Cut-back plants will usually keep blooming until frost.

All summer-flowering bulbs should be kept moist. A mulch will prevent much soil evaporation, but only if moisture was adequate to begin with.

The "rust" that appears on phlox lower leaves is usually the result of a multiple deficiency of both potash and phosphorus. Once it appears, it is not possible to correct. Rust is only a secondary invader that moves in on leaves weakened by lack of these elements. Although they will do little good now, both potash and phosphorus will "fix" on the soil if applied now and be available to plants next year to correct this condition.

Although hollyhocks are listed as biennials, they are actually short-lived perennials that will flower next year if kept healthy. Clean off old leaves and spray the plants with Phaltan to control rust. Sow new seeds as soon as they are ripe.

Keep removing faded flowers from roses and maintain a regular spray program.

This is the big month for moving bearded irises. In resetting plants, discard the old, tough central rhizome and use only the younger ones with strong growing tips. Check for borer infestation when rhizomes are out of the ground.

Allow mums to grow from now on without further pinching. Stake tall-growing varieties, particularly those being grown to a single stem for big flowers. Give all plants a good feeding now.

Spray lower leaves with Phaltan to control fungus diseases that cause foliage loss.

As soon as old stalks on Madonna lilies die down, the bulbs can be lifted and replanted if they have formed crowded clumps. Never disturb them unnecessarily if they are happy where they are. Order new bulbs now, which usually arrive from France next month. Plant as soon as they are available since they must make a rosette of leaves yet this fall.

Unless the weather is unusually cool, pansies and violas will normally slow up growth about now. When this happens, cut back severely to force new young shoots for fall blooming. Fish emulsion fertilizers are a good substitute for the old-time manure water so often recommended for pansies. Order seed this month for sowing in August. At the same time, order seeds of forget-me-nots and English daisies.

TREES AND SHRUBS: Any shrub with long, drooping branches can be propagated by layering. Many species that produce branches which touch the soil may form natural layers without treatment. Otherwise any limber branch can be bent over and pinned to the soil and should root in a month or so. When cut away from the parent plant, use anywhere a new shrub is needed.

Make green wood cuttings of shrubs as soon as new growth snaps clean.

As soon as the plentiful soil moisture of spring is exhausted, evergreens will suffer unless this is restored by watering. Shearing the ends of branches to make them bushy should be completed by early July at the latest.

Red spiders thrive in hot, dry weather. Regular syringing with a steady stream of water from the hose discourages them. If they appear in abundance, apply a good miticide. Yews may be attacked by the black vine weevil: control with diazinon, chlordane, or heptachlor. Also effective is a mixture of malathion with methoxychlor. The same sprays will control lace bugs.

VEGETABLES AND FRUITS: There is still time to plant crops of beets and carrots the first week of July for winter use. Sow moss-curled endive after mid-July. The variety Rose-Ribbed is best for a summer with hot, dry weather since it does not turn bitter. Sow Chinese cabbage and escarole the first of the month for late fall and early winter salads.

A planting of rutabagas this month may not make big roots for winter storage, but those that do form will be tender and tasty for fall use. Winter turnips should not be planted until the end of July, unless they are wanted for greens. Seed spinach the last week in July.

Set out plants of late cabbage, broccoli, kale, and Brussels sprouts. There is also still time to sow a crop of Wando peas for a fall crop: this variety resists summer heat. Plant a succession crop of snap beans.

To germinate lettuce seed in hot weather, mix with damp sand and store in the crisper pan of an electric refrigerator. Sow as soon as the seed coat shows signs of cracking.

Plant a succession crop of summer squash, which will mature about the time older vines are dying from borer injury. Also plant cucumbers now to fruit when the first crop dies from wilt.

Allow plants of ever-bearing strawberries set out this spring to bear their first fruit from now on.

Birds that attack grapes can be foiled by covering the bunches with either brown paper or plastic bags. The latter should be punched with holes to permit hot air to escape.

When blueberries come into fruit, feed the plants with ammonium sulfate to increase berry size. Apply a mulch to conserve moisture. To keep away birds, use the new plastic "spider webs" made of fine hairlike threads that tangle their feet. They seldom try again once they struggle free.

If the June drop did not leave apples spaced about four inches apart on the branch, thin by hand to that spacing.

Keep up a regular spray program on fruits and vegetables.

ODD JOBS: When using a nonselective weed-killer on driveways and along fences, be careful that it is not so soluble that rain will cause it to flow into nearby trees and shrubs. Highly poisonous sodium arsenite, while highly effective, should never be used where children, pets, or birds will come in contact with sprayed areas. Use only if an effective, nontoxic weed-killer is unavailable, and *be careful.*

Now is the time to check the accuracy of the fertilizer spreader so it will be ready for use when lawn work begins next month. Spread sheet plastic or roofing paper over an area of the driveway. Place a single pound of fertilizer in the spreader and see exactly how much area it will cover. From this, calculate the rate per 1,000 square feet and compare with markings on the spreader. Many severe cases of turf injury result from inaccurate application of potent chemicals.

Turn the compost heap at regular intervals. Add a sprinkling of a good mixed fertilizer to speed decay.

SOUTH AND WEST COAST

FLOWERS: Move Oriental poppies, irises, and Madonna lilies now.

Keep spraying roses, but don't fertilize until toward the end of August. Keep the soil moist at all times.

Transplant annuals into the perennial border to fill any vacant spots. Or use clumps of hemerocallis, which can be moved at any time, even when they are in full bloom.

It is time to sow quick-flowering annuals, such as California poppy, annual phlox, African daisies, sweet alyssum, and others, for fall bloom.

When mildew attacks tuberous begonia plants, spray with Karathane or Phaltan for control. Plants suffer most from this when they are kept in close, poorly aired corners.

Disbud, water, and fertilize dahlias. Spray with malathion or diazinon to control spider mites and leaf hoppers.

PACIFIC NORTHWEST

This is the driest period of the year: be ready with the hose and sprinklers when needed.

Follow recommendations given for the North as to vegetable crops.

If not done before, dig narcissus bulbs that need separating and replant. They make new roots earlier than do other spring-flowering bulbs.

At this time of year, recommendations for the Pacific Northwest and northern United States are much alike. Check July schedules.

AUGUST

Rich colors on the vellum cease to lay
When ev'ry lawn much nobler can display,
When on the dazzling poppy may be seen
A glowing red exceeding your carmine:
And for the blue that o'er the sea is born,
A brighter rises in our standing corn.

from "An Invitation to Daphnis"
Ann Finch, Countess of Winchilsea (1661–1720)

NORTH

Even though growth is at its lowest ebb in August, many important garden tasks should be scheduled this month. Many of these are in anticipation of improving next year's gardens, to be ignored by those who "take no thought of tomorrow."

LAWNS: In most years, mid-August is an ideal time to start new lawns and renovate old because fall rains usually begin then and nights begin to cool off. If, however, rains do not come, the gardener must go ahead as if they are certain to do so, falling back on the sprinkler as a temporary substitute.

The first week of this month is as late in the year as 2,4-D sprays can be used to control lawn weeds if any seeding is to be done this fall. Do not use Silvex or Dowpon this late, however, as their residual period is too long to permit reseeding bare spots.

Time for another feeding with lightweight turf fertilizers.

Keep a sharp outlook for turf diseases and insect damage: apply controls at once if discovered. At this time of year, chinch bugs and sod web worms are usually at their worst.

Just before reseeding is a good time to use one of the turf renovators that call for cutting thin slits into old turf. This will leave a fine seedbed. If soil compaction is responsible for poor root growth, rent a spring-loaded aerator to punch holes and loosen the soil to let air in before reseeding.

During cool, dry seasons, night dew will coat leaf blades with a film of moisture which is a perfect incubator for mildew. If left untreated, a serious infestation can kill bluegrass. Actidione, Karathane, and Panogen Turf spray are specific controls.

When a heavy infestation of crab grass must be killed before reseeding, Sodar (disodium monomethyl arsonate) is the safest chemical to use. It cannot hurt seed if applied a day or two before seeding is done. AMA or CMA have a longer residual period.

TREES AND SHRUBS: The most important needled-evergreen feeding of the year is the one applied after August 15. The same is true of broad-leaved evergreens and deciduous trees and shrubs. All are absorbing and storing the food which will feed their early growth next spring. Evergreens fertilized at this time are less likely to be injured by freezing. Organic fertilizers are too slow for this job: use only quick-acting chemicals.

As soon as this year's growth on evergreens is firm, they can be transplanted safely. The sooner this is done, the better, so new roots can form before freezing weather. Be sure the soil around the root ball is moist, but don't drown the plant with too much water.

Lilacs, pachysandra, euonymus and American bittersweet are attacked by a brown scale that resembles tiny brown oyster shells attached to the bark. These are the females—a tiny needle-thin gray male may also be present. Malathion or diazinon should kill them if not applied later than the first week in August.

Prune wisteria vines after they have flowered if they need trimming.

Remove suckers on all grafted plants. Pink and red dogwood, *Viburnum carlesii* and *V. carlcephalan,* as well as grafted lilacs, are likely to grow poorly if understocks on which they were grafted throw up suckers. Roses, too, need this treatment.

Tree web worms are active now: if possible cut off the branch with the web intact and burn it. Using a torch to destroy webs directly on the tree can damage or kill important branches.

FRUITS AND VEGETABLES: Plant turnips for fall use on August 1. Now is the important month for spraying vegetables for winter storage. Aphids that develop in storage are particularly annoying and destructive.

As soon as 10 percent of the onion tops in a row fall over, break down the rest of the row by hand to hasten ripening of the bulbs. Dig as soon as the tops are dead. Any undersized bulbs, 1 inch to 1½ inches in diameter, can be planted back in the row immediately: they will produce the earliest of green onions next spring.

Potatoes that die down in August are better off in the soil than they will be if dug. Dig them as needed for the table. Don't leave tubers in the soil after September 15, however; they may sprout.

If escarole is not of the self-blanching type, tops of heads should be closed and tied together when dry to shut out light. Florida Deep Heart is a widely distributed self-blanching variety.

Keep eggplant and peppers picked as soon as they ripen. Smaller fruits left on the plant may not fill out unless this is done.

If harvesting is delayed, cabbage heads may start cracking. To check growth, bend over the heads until you can hear the roots crack on one side. This reduces water uptake and prevents further expansion of the head.

Herbs for winter use should be dried now, before fall dampness hinders this operation. Tie in bundles of not more than ten stems and suspend upside down in a cool, dark, dry, airy place. If dried in light, both color and flavor will be poorer.

Examine rhubarb and asparagus beds to select plants that can be sacrificed for forcing next winter. Mark them now for digging in September.

In the cold frame, sow lettuce, Dutch or French horn carrots, radishes, and white mustard for early winter use.

Early apples and pears need very careful handling. They bruise easily. A polystyrene bucket or basket makes an excellent picking container.

As soon as raspberries and blackberries have finished fruiting, cut out the old, hard canes, leaving four or five strong canes of this year's growth for next year's crop.

Cut out all branches on gooseberries and currants three years old or older as soon as the fruit is harvested.

Bag grapes if bees or yellow jackets attack them.

FLOWERS: To fill spaces in the perennial border, move in chrysanthemum plants, even if in bud. Water well and they will go right on blooming. Finish planting bearded irises, Madonna lilies, mertensia, and Oriental poppies.

Its time to order bulbs for fall planting. Crown Imperial and the minor bulbs are particularly important to order early—they deteriorate rapidly if left out of the soil too long. They should be planted immediately on arrival, usually in late September or early October.

Peonies should be ordered for September delivery. Feed old clumps to increase size and quality of next year's bloom.

Pot up oxalis and freesia bulbs now and plunge in a cold frame until October 1. Then bring indoors for forcing. Hyacinths treated in Holland (the so-called prepared bulbs) should be potted, held in a frame to form roots until Thanksgiving, then brought in for forcing for Christmas bloom.

Doronicum and pyrethrum are semidormant in August and can be divided and reset at this time. If not divided every other year, they are short-lived.

Rock garden plants that were sheared back earlier should have strong new growth now, just right for making cuttings. Calendula, snapdragon, hardy phlox, carnations, sweet William, and marigolds can also be propagated in this way.

August weather is not always cool enough for good germination of pansies, English daisies, and forget-me-nots. Mix seed with damp sand and peat moss, then store in the crisper pan of the refrigerator for a week and sow. Mid-August is the latest these should be planted if good seedlings that will survive winter are to be produced. The Christmas rose, *Helleborus niger,* should be moved about mid-August so it can become established by the time freezing weather begins.

Keep up preventive sprays on ornamentals until September 1.

Make cuttings of English ivy, geraniums, heliotrope, fuchsia, and other tender bedding plants: these will make better stock plants for cuttings next spring than will older plants potted up from the garden.

Pots of herbs for the kitchen window should be planted now and kept plunged in soil until ready to bring in for the winter.

Plant bulbs of sternbergia, colchicum, autumn crocus, and hardy cyclamen if bulbs were not available earlier.

Dahlias should be kept sprayed and staked. Disbud if large exhibition flowers are wanted for cutting or for showing.

The bleeding heart, *Dicentra spectabilis,* is dormant now and can be moved safely.

Old hollyhock plants are best discarded after flowering: young plants started from seed in July or August will bloom better next year. If, however, certain outstanding colors are to be saved, cut back old tops and spray around the soil with Phaltan. The plant will then produce healthy foliage and survive the winter.

ODD JOBS: Any area of the garden not occupied by plants should be seeded down to winter rye as a green manure crop to be dug under next spring.

Prepare cold frames this month for winter use. They will be needed for storing half-hardy perennials of all kinds, as well as vegetables. Save some space for storing pots of bulbs for winter forcing.

If a walled-off section of the basement is to be used for winter storage, now is a good time to clean and repair it. A good coat of lime whitewash will do wonders in controlling fungus spores.

As weather and time permit, store soil, humus, sand, peat moss, and other potting necessities for winter use. If this is not done in August, it is often overlooked.

This is the most critical month of the year for woody plants. Late summer drought can dry out bark so that it cannot conduct water and food properly. This makes the plant more susceptible to winterkilling. Keep the hose going. If sprinkling is limited by municipal authorities, use the water on woody plants rather than the lawn: grasses can stand drought better than can trees and shrubs.

SOUTH AND WEST COAST

Plant Madonna lilies, Crown Imperial, sternbergia, colchicum, and autumn crocus if bulbs were not available earlier.

Feed, water, and disbud dahlias regularly.

The last of this month, give roses a good feeding and water freely to start new fall growth. Keep up a regular spray program to retain all possible foliage.

Mildew is a problem to plants in the shade and in moist, poorly aired spots. Karathane, Actidione, and sulfur are all effective. Sulfur, however, will burn foliage if applied when air temperatures are above eighty degrees.

Seeded now, the Pacific strain of calendula will bloom late in fall. In sheltered spots in warmer regions, they may continue flowering all winter.

Most hardy perennials can be sowed toward the end of the month in shaded cold frames. Spraying with cold water will aid germination. Seedlings large enough to set in permanent position this fall should flower next summer.

If northern stock is ordered for setting out in late September, peonies can be grown as far south as northern Alabama and Mississippi. In the South, single, Japanese, and anemone types will survive better than will the large-flowered double varieties. Avoid the use of manure around peonies because this harbors botrytis fungus spores which are far more damaging to the plants than they are farther north because the spores have a longer time to grow.

In sections where freezes are not common, sow seeds of annuals for late fall and early winter bloom.

VEGETABLES AND FRUITS: Plant Wando peas (a variety developed for the South by the USDA) for a late fall crop. Also sow snap beans, turnips, winter radishes, summer squash, and mustard. Lettuce seed germinates poorly in hot weather but can be pre-germinated in a refrigerator by mixing with damp peat and sand.

Chinese cabbage and escarole planted the first part of this month will provide salads for Thanksgiving Day.

TREES AND SHRUBS: The last week of this month, feed all woody plants, the most important feeding of the year. It will help increase winter hardiness of less-hardy species.

This is the critical month of the year for feeding and watering broad-leaved evergreens, such as rhododendron and holly. If they are allowed to get too dry, water-conducting passages will be unable to move food and moisture needed for next year's growth. Keep them moist and well mulched. Daily syringing or misting may be needed during unusually dry spells.

Hydrangeas that bear pink and blue flowers should have faded flower heads removed. Be careful not to cut away tips of branches as they usually carry the flower buds for next year's bloom. If blue flowers are wanted, feed with a mixture of iron sulfate and aluminum sulfate. Plants growing in tubs should be repotted now.

PACIFIC NORTHWEST

Soils in the Pacific Northwest are frequently deficient in both phosphorus and potash, elements important to winter resistance to cold. Now is a good a time to apply them to all plants, including lawns.

FLOWERS: Dahlias in particular need phosphorus and potash to form good tubers.

Most droughts in the Pacific Northwest occur in August; be ready with hose and sprinklers for use when needed. Shade-tolerant bedding plants, such as fuchsia and begonia, are particularly sensitive and may need daily misting or syringing.

Summer-flowering heaths, particularly *Erica vagans,* are at their best in August: make notes now for later selection of varieties.

Winds from the Pacific make staking a necessity in most gardens on the west slope.

Hardy cyclamen is dormant this month and can be planted, along with colchicum and autumn crocus. Now is the best time to move *Helleborus niger* (Christmas rose) and *Helleborus orientalis,* the Lenten rose.

Madonna lilies and *Lilium testaceum* are best moved at this time.

Transplant winter pansies into peat-fiber pots for easy transplanting later.

LAWNS: The beginning of August rains in the last part of August makes this the ideal time to reseed old lawns and to start new ones.

VEGETABLES: Sow seeds of broccoli (in milder sections) and Brussels sprouts. Set out plants of late cabbage and cauliflower. Radishes, lettuce, turnips, and endive can also be seeded now.

Removing some of the leaves of grapes will let in more sun to ripen the fruit.

Canes of raspberries and other cane fruits which bore berries this year can be cut away, leaving strong canes of this year's growth for next year's crop.

SEPTEMBER

Lift your boughs of Vervain blue,
Dipt in cold September dew;
And dash the moisture, chaste and clear,
O'er the ground and through the air.
Now the place is purged and pure.

William Mason (1724–1797)

NORTH

With first frosts only a month away in some sections, September is a month largely of preparation for next year. Except for chrysanthemums, the big floral displays are over for the year. Spring-flowering bulbs should be ordered for planting this month and later. Evergreen planting will be over for the year soon, and winter storage preparations must be completed.

LAWNS: A good rule to keep in mind in the northeast quarter of the United States is that October 1 is the deadline for safe sowing of grass seed. This is based on averages, of course, since not every year closes on schedule. However, the earlier in September that grass seed can be sown, the better.

Keep mowing as long as grass keeps growing. To send a lawn into winter under a mat of dead grass is to ask for trouble.

When a mixed ureaform feeding program is being followed, September is an ideal month to put on the major fertilizer application of the year. Apply four pounds of actual nitrogen per 1,000 square feet (i.e., twenty pounds of a 20-10-10). No more may be needed for an entire year, but if luxury turf is wanted, an application of half that amount in late June will work wonders.

Killing crab grass in September seems a waste of time since it will soon be killed by frost, but if it can be eliminated as competition, new seedlings will have a better chance. Sodar (disodium monomethyl arsonate) and Tupersan are two chemicals that will not injure new seedlings.

FLOWERS: Although tulips should be ordered this month, it is better to delay planting them until mid-October. Narcissus, however, should go in as early as possible, as they make roots early. This is also true of the minor bulbs and Crown Imperial.

Tulips wanted for forcing are an exception to the rule: the earlier they can be potted and plunged into a frame, the better. With bulbs for forcing, there is a problem of too-early shoot growth. Bulbs wanted for early forcing should be exposed to temperatures below fifty degrees as soon as possible. Those wanted for later forcing should be held at either below forty degrees or above fifty-five: in between these readings, they may even form roots in the bag.

In the North, Dutch, English, and Spanish bulbous irises will start growing the minute they are planted, producing above-ground shoots just as severe freezing weather begins. To prevent this, do not plant until late October or early November.

For an interesting house plant, grow the *Oxalis Pes-caprae,* Bermuda buttercup, in a hanging basket.

This month will be your last chance to dry flowers for winter bouquets. Suspend them in bundles of not more than ten stems in a dark, dry, airy place. If dried in the light, colors will be poor. Remove the lower leaves from the stems of bells of Ireland and strawflowers before suspending.

Pick ornamental gourds before they are touched by frost. Be careful not to snap off the stem and leave a wet scar: this is where rot usually starts. If stems break off accidentally, dip the scars in dusting sulfur.

Three popular annuals can be grown as biennials—bachelor's-buttons, annual poppies, and annual larkspur. Sown late in September, they will produce small seedlings that will often survive winter and flower right after the tulips the following spring.

"Peonies should be planted at nine in the morning on September 15" once said Mrs. Harding, a noted authority on this fine perennial. Timing is not that critical, although her dogmatic statement did serve to emphasize the need for mid-September planting.

Now is the time to begin making over old overgrown perennial borders and to set out new plants. Lily-of-the-valley beds that have grown too crowded should be dug up, the plants separated, and replanted immediately.

This is the high tide for dahlia bloom: continue feeding and watering the plants, but reduce nitrogen sharply while increasing phosphorus and potash.

Chrysanthemums can be moved in full bloom to any spot needing color. Try them as replacement for exhausted annuals in window boxes—the cushion type is perfect for this use.

To increase your stock of lilies, dig down along old stalks and harvest the small bulbils that form below ground but above the old bulb. Plant these in a light sandy loam at a depth of two inches so they can increase in size.

If they were not planted before the established bulbs bloomed, the hardy amaryllis, *Lycoris squamigera,* can be transplanted as soon as this fall's flower stalks die down.

Some annuals make excellent house plants and can be potted up now for moving indoors before frost. Browallia and coleus are particularly good. Try browallia in a hanging basket.

TREES AND SHRUBS: Don't rush the planting of woody plants before a good frost has removed all foliage. In an emergency, leaves can be cut off by hand, but not stripped: the stub of the old leaf is needed to form a seal when it cuts off the twig. Never plant a tree with its leaves intact unless it is first sprayed with an antidesiccant; otherwise the foliage will continue to give off water until the plant is dehydrated.

If the soil is fit for growing evergreens in the first place, about the only fertilizer they will need is superphosphate and potash added to the planting hole. They take up very little nitrogen until they have formed new hair roots. Do mulch them, though, soon after transplanting so that the freezing of the soil will be delayed, allowing roots more time to grow. Transplanting evergreens should stop with the first good frost.

Check Englemann and blue spruces for swollen tips, caused by hibernating aphids. If these are found, spray with diazinon or malathion.

In case of fall droughts, continue to water all woody plants, paying particular attention to all evergreens. If their bark dries out, food movement is checked and winter injury is almost certain to follow.

FRUITS AND VEGETABLES: If frost is predicted toward the end of the month, be ready to harvest squash, pumpkin, cucumbers, and melons and rush them into storage. Most melons are only fit for making pickles if immature—they will not ripen further after they are off the vine. Store squash and pumpkin at a temperature between fifty and sixty degrees.

Tomatoes will ripen further after picking only if the starch-to-sugar conversion (what we call ripening) has already begun in the fruit. They should have lost their grass-green coloring and show a tint of yellowing or blanching if this has begun.

Dig potatoes before the soil crusts over. Store at about forty-five degrees. If stored at a lower temperature, the starch will turn to sugar and the flavor will be poor.

Plan to store part of the parsnip crop indoors where it will be accessible during the winter, but leave the main crop in the soil to freeze over, which will improve flavor. Carrots and beets can survive light freezes, but should be stored when mature in a cool cellar as close to thirty-three degrees as temperatures can be held.

Just before freezing weather, dig clumps of rhubarb and asparagus and store in bushel baskets, covered with canvas or straw so they can freeze without drying out. Later, they can be brought into a cellar for forcing.

This is the last chance to pot up herb plants for winter flavor. Chives, sweet basil, and parsley are the easiest to grow.

Sort the onion crop, storing only those larger than 1½ inches in diameter. Replant the smaller onions at once to produce a spring crop of scallions. If these are not available, buy sets of Egyptian or potato multiplier onions to plant now.

Seed down any vacant spots in the vegetable garden to winter rye.

Allow apples and pears to remain on the tree as long as possible to develop full flavor. When picking, handle them gently. Wrap individual fruits in tissue paper. Winter pears should be firm-ripe when picked and should then be stored as close to thirty-three degrees as can be held, just above freezing. Bring in to a warm room to ripen for use.

ODD JOBS: Check all labels and tags on plants and see that they are attached firmly. If not legible, remake them.

Turn the compost heap at least twice this month. Heavy applications of organic matter to the pile need to come in contact with the older compost to become seeded with the bacteria that will break down plant wastes into usable humus.

Get ready for covering roses for the winter by borrowing soil from the vegetable garden and piling it between the rows to use later for hilling-up the plants. This soil, worked over by handling, can be returned to the vegetable garden in spring, combined with old rose mulch. For covering the tops, the new plastic cones made out of polystyrene plastic are much easier to use and often better protection.

Sheet plastic should never be used for winter protection: heat accumulates under it from the sun, yet heat is just as easily and quickly lost at night.

Never burn fallen leaves. The best place for them is on the compost pile. Light, fluffy leaves, such as those from honey locusts, oaks, and sycamores (but *not* cottonwoods or poplars that pack badly), make excellent mulching material for newly planted trees, shrubs, and evergreens. Many half-hardy plants, such as rhododendron in the Middle West, can be carried over the winter by surrounding them with a cage of chicken wire filled with dry leaves.

SOUTH AND WEST COAST

In warmer areas, even tender crops, such as bush beans, can be sown early in the month, with a fair chance that they will mature a crop. Toward the end of the month, cooler nights may make sowing of cool-weather crops a good gamble.

In cooler areas, plant narcissus bulbs as soon as received, but in warmer areas, wait until mid-October.

Late this month is a good time to start remaking perennial beds. Siberian, Japanese, and Asiatic irises can be moved now, as well as all fibrous-rooted Louisiana species. Don't, however, move bearded irises at this time.

In warmer sections, Wedgwood, Dutch, Spanish, and English irises can be planted for winter bloom, but their premature shoots can be badly frozen if planted in cooler areas. For English iris, wait until temperatures higher than forty degrees above zero no longer occur.

In warmer sections, such tender things as *Ornithogalum thyrsoides* (the Darling Chinkerichee) should be planted now, as well as all minor bulbs.

Roses should be fed well into October to force late bloom, which are usually the best flowers of the year. As temperatures drop, mildew becomes an ever-increasing pest. In cool weather, sulfur is an excellent control.

In warmer sections, sow seeds of cool-weather annuals for winter bloom.

FRUITS AND VEGETABLES: Fall is the preferred time for planting figs in warmer parts of the United States, but spring is a better time for planting in the cooler areas near the northern limits of fig culture.

Set new strawberry beds from runners of old plants.

LAWNS: Instead of the traditional Italian ryegrass, use Highland bent or other bent grass seeds to overseed Bermuda and zoysia lawns for winter color. Since they need an earlier start, they must be seeded now, but they are finer in texture and much less competitive. To prepare old turf for seeding, use a turf renovator that cuts slits in the old sod.

PACIFIC NORTHWEST

Much of the work to be done in cooler areas is like that of the northern sections of the United States, except that the rush to beat hard freezes is not a problem. Because of fall rains, September is a better month than August for starting lawns: long, fairly warm fall weather provides perfect conditions for growth.

Hardy cyclamen, *Cyclamen neapolitanum,* which does well only in the Pacific Northwest, is a gem for shaded areas.

Hardy lilies, almost a specialty of this region, should be transplanted as early as bulbs can be had. Try to get those with the old basal roots still attached and plump.

OCTOBER

Season of mists and mellow fruitfulness,
Close bosom-friend of the maturing sun;
Conspiring with him how to load and bless
With fruit the vines that round the thatch-eaves run;
To bend with apples the moss'd cottage-trees,
And fill all fruit with ripeness to the core;
To swell the gourd, and plump the hazel shells

With a sweet kernel; to set budding more,
And still more, later flowers for the bees
Until they think warm days will never cease,
For Summer has o'er-brimm'd their clammy cells.

John Keats (1795–1821)

NORTH

In October, the wise gardener prepares for anything and is ready to move whenever action is needed. This is perhaps the most difficult month of the year to schedule: killing frosts may occur in the northeastern quarter of the United States at any time from late September to Thanksgiving Day.

LAWNS: If night temperatures have fallen as low as thirty-five degrees several times, germination of seeds of two winter annual weeds—*Poa annua* and common chickweed—will have been stimulated. An application of calcium arsenate at this time will kill them when they are most vulnerable. This will also control crab grass next spring.

Keep mowing as long as grass keeps growing. A mat of dead grass or duff of dead leaves is a disease-breeder. Sweep and rake between each mowing.

Where snow mold was a problem last year, apply a good turf fungicide recommended for control of this pest. Some excellent summer fungicides have no effect on this problem.

FLOWERS: Protect dahlias against early frost with a covering of newspaper or other solid, opaque covering. Clear plastic is no good; heat goes right through it. Black plastic absorbs heat and radiates it, but is not as good as newspaper. Usually, the first frost is followed by a long period of fine weather during which dahlias can be enjoyed if this first frost can be outwitted.

Often, spraying frozen plants with a fine mist of water before the sun rises will save them. Chrysanthemums will sometimes bloom for a month after being saved in this way.

The sooner all bulbs can be planted, the better. The only exceptions are English, Dutch, and Spanish irises, which should only go in if soil temperatures will remain cooler than forty-five degrees.

Along the Ohio River and from Philadelphia south, fall sowing of sweet peas is good practice, but only if black-seeded varieties are used. Those with white seeds winterkill more readily.

Fall seeding of annuals is sound practice: the seeds will lie dormant all winter and then germinate very early in spring, long before the soil can be cultivated. Wait until just before freezing weather is expected, though, to sow so the seeds won't germinate this fall.

Even if frost or light freeze has not occurred by the end of the month, lift all summer-flowering bulbs. They are not improved by contact with cold soil. A sudden freeze can cause serious damage, particularly to tender plants, such as tuberous begonia. Dahlias are best left until their tops have been blackened by frost, but be ready for quick action if this does not happen until late October.

Newly planted perennials, shrubs, and trees should be mulched, but it is best to wait until the ground has a thin crust of frozen earth to apply this. Otherwise, mice might move in and set up winter quarters, causing irreparable damage to plants.

From October 1 to 15 all bulbs should be potted up for forcing. The only exceptions are paper-white Narcissus and hybrid amaryllis bulbs, both of which can be planted up to January 1.

For Christmas flowers, plant paper-white Narcissus in late October and store in the dark as close to thirty-three degrees as possible. Hold this temperature until about November 20, then bring in to a fifty-degree temperature to grow slowly. Specially prepared hyacinths can be purchased that will force for Christmas.

FRUITS AND VEGETABLES: Many salad vegetables can be held in the open garden until Thanksgiving time if they are protected with straw against severe cold. Chinese cabbage, curly endive, celery, and escarole can also be stored in cold frames if they are protected by mats over the glass, lasting often until Christmas time.

Both parsley and Swiss chard will survive winter if covered with a light fluffy mulch and will produce early crops next spring.

Wire guards, at least a foot taller than the deepest snow expected, should be placed around apple trees, pears, and other woody species attacked by rabbits. Less costly, but equally effective if it doesn't get torn, is aluminum foil.

Rake up windfalls to get rid of wormy apples that harbor the larvae of codling moths, which cause wormy apples. Scrape away loose and flaking bark on apple trees to destroy wintering-over pests which hibernate there.

TREES AND SHRUBS: Evergreen planting time is over, but the time for moving deciduous trees and shrubs is just beginning. Keep planting until the soil freezes hard.

Pruning can begin as soon as leaves have fallen and before wood freezes. Study naked branches with a view to shaping up specimens that are not in good form.

Keep watering evergreens, both needled and broad-leaved, as long as the soil remains unfrozen.

Except south of the Ohio River, fall and winter planting of roses is risky. Do, however, prepare the beds so that dormant roses can be planted as soon as possible in spring.

Protection should go on roses before air temperatures fall lower than twelve above zero. If soil is used as a mulch, it should be piled at least ten inches high around the canes.

If large specimen trees are to be moved, contact your nurseryman at once.

ODD JOBS: Move tools to the basement for attention during the winter. Often repairshops will welcome the chance to work on lawn mowers and other equipment during the winter when they are not rushed.

Although most plastic hose can withstand freezing, some plastics become quite brittle and will crack unless stored for the winter in a warm place.

Bird feeders should be kept filled constantly from now until natural food is available next spring. Once birds become accustomed to being fed, they are defenseless when the supply fails. An electrically heated water fountain to supply unfrozen water will be a big attraction.

Burn any diseased plant waste material—don't put it on the compost pile.

Cold frames should be covered with mats during sunny days to prevent too much of a heat build-up through the glass. The same mats will slow up the loss of heat when there is no sun.

Before the successes and failures of last summer are forgotten, make a record of them in a garden diary.

SOUTH AND WEST COAST

LAWNS: For overseeding lawns, use either Italian ryegrass or Highland bent grass. Highland bent grass will offer less competition for Bermuda or zoysia sod next summer.

FRUITS AND VEGETABLES: Sow spinach, turnips for greens, and onion sets. In warmer areas, broad Windsor beans can be sown for a winter crop. Also sow red Italian bottle onions, which will only bulb up during the short days of winter.

Plant herb seeds now—in the open in warmer regions; in cold frames in colder parts of the South to protect any seeds that germinate early.

FLOWERS: Sweet peas can be planted in warmer regions for winter flowering, or in colder areas, next month for spring bloom.

The following annuals can be sown now and will survive winter, even though some of the seeds will germinate this fall (as far north as the Tennessee–Alabama line and to about the center of northern California) alyssum, calendula, English daisy, *Centaurea cyanus,* annual chrysanthemum, candytuft, clarkia, cleome, cynoglossum, eschscholzia, gaillardia, gypsophila, hollyhock, larkspur, flowering flax, lupine, nigella, pansy, petunia, annual phlox, annual poppy, scabiosa, statice, stocks, sweet peas, and viola.

This should be the best month of the year for roses, but to do their best in sections where hard freezes are at least a month away, they will need both extra water and fertilizer.

Move house plants indoors before frosts occur.

Plant all bulbs at once, including bulbous irises. Wedgwood is a particularly desirable iris for warmer parts of the South and West.

Feed camellia, azalea, and rhododendron now to increase flower size.

PACIFIC NORTHWEST

The September schedule for the North pretty well fits the needs of the Pacific Northwest in October, except for upland areas where cold weather occurs early.

Now is a good time to move biennials into place for next summer's bloom.

In warmer sections, delaying tulip planting until November is a common practice, but if this is done, bulbs should be stored in a spot where temperatures are above fifty-five degrees but below seventy-five.

NOVEMBER

And when above this apple tree
The winter stars are quivering bright,
And winds go howling through the night,
Girls, whose young eyes o'erflow with mirth,
Shall peal its fruit by cottage hearth,
And guests in prouder homes shall see
Heaped with the grape of Cintra's vine
And golden orange of the line,
The fruit of the apple tree.

William Cullen Bryant (1794–1878)

NORTH

LAWNS: Don't use the lawn as a shortcut to the house just because it is frozen: as much damage is done by such use as is in growing weather. In fact, in summer such injury can heal over, but in winter, dormant grass does not grow.

If growing temperatures continue, keep mowing as long as grass keeps growing. Don't allow fallen leaves to stay on the grass; rake or sweep all clippings and dead leaves.

Apply snow mold controls at once if this was not done earlier.

A preemergence crab grass control containing calcium arsenate can still be applied, but it will not be quite as effective in controlling common chickweed and *Poa annua* as it would have been had it been applied in October.

FLOWERS: Tulip planting is still safe if sound bulbs can still be bought. At this late date, using a mulch after planting is advised.

Red hot poker plant (tritoma) is not hardy over much of the

North; digging the entire plant and storing it in a cold frame for the winter is recommended.

Even though hard freezing weather has not occurred, hill-up or cover roses—the risks in waiting longer are too great. Try the new rose cones made out of polystyrene—they offer excellent protection and are far easier to use than hilling-up with soil. One precaution—always spray the plants with a fungicide before covering with a cone. Fungus spores grow rapidly under such a covering when warm weather returns in spring.

The best winter protection for hardy chrysanthemums is lifting the entire clump with a spading fork, setting it on the surface of the ground, and then hilling-up around it more soil, covering the crown. In the spring, divide into single-stem divisions when growth begins.

Pansies, English daisies, and forget-me-nots in cold frames should be covered with loose, clean straw or excelsior and the sash put on and covered with matting. For ventilation, prop open the north side of the sash with a two-inch block, closing this opening if temperatures lower than five above zero are expected.

Winter protection for foxglove, hollyhock, primula, pinks, sweet William, and Shasta daisies should function as an umbrella rather than as an overcoat—light fluffy material such as fiber glass or excelsior is best. It should shade rather than smother. Where winter rains are heavy, lay a sheet of plastic over the mulching, but be sure enough rain reaches the soil to keep it moist, not wet.

FRUITS AND VEGETABLES: Clumps of rhubarb and asparagus can now be moved into a sixty-degree cellar for forcing if they are frozen through.

Forcing of French endive can begin.

Strawberry beds should be mulched with straw before air temperatures fall below twenty degrees above zero.

TREES AND SHRUBS: Trees and shrubs can be moved as long as the soil remains unfrozen. Wrap trunks of newly planted trees and mulch roots of both trees and shrubs.

Before last summer's growth on shrubs freezes, make hardwood cuttings and tie in bundles. Bury in sand or sawdust with the lower butts upward and the growing tip *down*.

Keep watering evergreens as long as the soil is unfrozen.

ODD JOBS: Float short sections of logs in lily pools and outdoor ponds to keep ice from cracking masonry or concrete walls. If the water over hardy lilies is deeper than eighteen inches, they are better off left in the water. Except for those who own greenhouses, tropical water lilies are best treated as annuals and discarded.

Keep feeding birds and providing them with unfrozen water.

SOUTH AND WEST COAST

There is still time to plant tulips where these can be grown. Deep planting in light, sandy loam makes it possible to grow them even along the Gulf of Mexico if they are dug and stored after flowering.

Set out pansies, violas, English daisies, and forget-me-nots for winter flowering.

Now is the time to order roses for December planting—the best month for this operation in both warm and cooler sections.

Move all broad-leaved evergreens.

In cooler sections, deciduous trees and shrubs can still be planted. In warmer parts of the West Coast and South, wait until December.

All the annuals listed for October can still be planted.

Stop feeding lawns—the two heavy feeders, zoysia and Bermuda, should be fully dormant by now and cannot use applied fertilizers. Overseeded ryegrasses or bents can get along very well with what is left in the soil.

Dig summer-flowering bulbs. In warmer sections where frost is infrequent, they can be left in, but should be dug and redivided before growth is active in the spring.

In cooler sections, hardy chrysanthemums are actually less hardy than they are farther north because of their tendency to make growth. For safety, store a clump of each variety in a cold frame to use as replacements if a yo-yo winter keeps bouncing temperatures up and down. Farther south, dividing them now and setting out as single-stem divisions should check growth enough to protect them.

PACIFIC NORTHWEST

The Pacific Northwest has about the most variable, unpredictable climate of any part of the United States. Watch out particularly for the sudden blasts of Alaskan air that can ruin tender plants.

LAWNS: Turf diseases, such as brown patch, thrive during the foggy days of November. Apply suitable fungicides to prevent serious damage.

It is too late for safe seeding of lawns; delay this operation until spring.

FLOWERS: Dig dahlias at the first hint of freezing weather: to delay is to court losing them. In milder sections, though, they can often be left in the ground over the winter if covered with a light mulch.

If black-seeded varieties are used, sweet peas can be sown now.

Sometimes lilies are not ready until now: preparation of the soil in advance of their arrival is good practice. There is still time to plant Dutch bulbs.

VEGETABLES AND FRUITS: Leave all cole crops—cabbage, Brussels sprouts, kale, and broccoli—in the garden as long as possible—they store badly indoors.

Root crops are best stored in sand in a cool cellar that keeps out frost.

Squashes and pumpkins keep best at fifty degrees: inspect them while they are in storage from time to time and discard any that rot. Handle them like eggs; they bruise easily.

Planting strawberries on heavy soils is a poor risk: if mulched they rot, and if not protected, they freeze out. Plan to set them on light, well-drained soil next year.

TREES AND SHRUBS: Deciduous trees are not always fully dormant by this time: moving nursery stock balled and burlapped is the best practice.

Cut back roses only enough to keep long canes from whipping in winter winds; wait until spring to do the final pruning.

ODD JOBS: Bring in potting soil, sand, peat moss, and other necessities for potting house plants and for starting seedlings indoors.

DECEMBER

And as, when summer trees are seen,
So bright and green,
The holly leaves their fadeless hues display,
Less bright than they;
But when the bare and wintry woods we see,
What then so cheerful as the holly tree.

Robert Southey (1774–1843)

NORTH

FLOWERS: Seeds of annuals to be started in January should be ordered now. If tuberous begonia seeds are sown now under fluorescent lights, they will produce mature flowering plants by late April.

Paper-white narcissus and prepared hyacinths for Christmas should show color ten days before December 25. If slow, bring them into a seventy-degree temperature, but if they are on time, they are better off kept at fifty-five to sixty degrees.

House plants should be given less water and fertilizer from now on to compensate for low light intensities.

Indoors, start calla lilies into growth by feeding and watering liberally; they make good house plants because they do not need high light intensities and will thrive in warm houses.

Amaryllis bulbs make excellent Christmas gifts, but select only those with a flower bud showing. They are erratic bloomers, and one without a bud may not bloom at all, or flower late. If the bulbs show leaf growth first, they will not bloom.

Geraniums for winter bloom need lots of light: supplement daylight with fluorescent tubes from 4:00 P.M. to 9:00 P.M. The old idea that they had to be grown dry in poor soil has been disproved. They will do better in fairly rich soil and when kept moist (but not wet).

FRUITS AND VEGETABLES: After every snowstorm, tramp down snow around the trunks of fruit trees to foil the mice who make runs under the snow.

Bring in roots of French endive, rhubarb, and asparagus at intervals during winter. Sow seeds of white mustard or curly cress thickly in small flats or bulb pans. Grow in a window and cut for sandwich fillings when the seedlings have made two or three leaves.

Prune grapevines at any time from now on when the wood is not frozen.

When snows are deep, spray trunks of fruit trees, as well as any branches rabbits can reach, with a suitable rabbit repellent, such as Arasan or Thiram.

Trees and Shrubs: After several weeks of freezing weather, branches of early-flowering shrubs, such as *Cornus mas,* forsythia, plum, and others, can be cut for forcing in the house. Spray with lukewarm water occasionally. A preliminary soaking overnight will speed the process.

When large trees must be cut down, wait until after a heavy snow has fallen to cushion the fall and protect the lawn.

Odd Jobs: A pleasant tradition worth following—in Sweden, a sheaf of wheat is tied to the rooftree for the birds' Christmas dinner. While few will want to climb to the roof to do this, such a sheaf tied to a tall pole would be just as welcome.

Get rid of any leftover seeds by feeding them to the birds.

The day after Christmas, begin a salvage operation on Christmas trees. See January notes for uses.

Write for seed catalogs, which are usually mailed out in January.

SOUTH AND WEST COAST

Trees and Shrubs: Make hardwood cuttings of crape myrtle, deutzia, weigela, forsythia, privet myrtle, mock orange, and others. These can be inserted directly in a sand bed for rooting.

Plant roses, trees, and shrubs this month. If dry, spray with an antidesiccant. Camellias should be moved before they come into flower. Grapes and deciduous fruits should be sprayed this month.

Pruning of holly, magnolia, nandina, and evergreen privet will provide greens for Christmas, but don't overdo it—sun scald on branches exposed by pruning can cause severe injury.

VEGETABLES AND FRUITS: In warm sections, plant lettuce, turnips, Chinese cabbage, broccoli, mustard, cabbage, and kale. Red Italian bottle onions sown earlier can be thinned and the thinnings transplanted.

This is a good time to set out a new strawberry bed from runners taken from an old planting. Avoid soil that was planted in grass recently.

FLOWERS: Sow seeds of sweet peas, California poppies, baby-blue-eyes, lupines, alyssum, candytuft, calendula, cornflower, larkspur, pansy, petunia, snapdragon, verbena, and stocks.

ODD JOBS: Even the warmest regions can suffer frosts; be ready to protect all tender plants when freezing temperatures are predicted. Clear plastic is a poor material for this purpose—it transmits heat as readily as it does light. Instead, try dampened newspapers.

This is a good time to clean up the garden for the year, when other activities are less demanding.

PACIFIC NORTHWEST

This is about the only area of the United States where having the so-called "living Christmas tree" is worth the bother. But do spray it with a wiltproofing compound and keep the ball moist but not sopping wet. After Christmas, treat again with an antidesiccant and plant out. A good idea is to prepare the hole in advance, filling in around the ball with some soil enriched with compost.

If the winter is open so holes can be dug, planting can continue through most of December.

Apply dormant sprays to fruit trees and ornamentals whenever a spell of weather above forty degrees can be relied upon for at least a day.

INDEX